Perspectives on Sino-Japanese Diplomatic Relations

JAPAN LIBRARY

Perspectives on Sino-Japanese Diplomatic Relations

The Yomiuri Shimbun
Political News Department

Translated by John Rossman

Japan Publishing Industry Foundation for Culture

Translation Note
The Hepburn system of romanization is used for Japanese words, including the names
of persons and places. All Japanese and Western names appearing in this book are given
in the English word order, with given name first, e.g., Shinzo Abe. Chinese words are
romanized using the pinyin system. The Japanese custom of placing the family name first
has been followed for the names of persons from other Asian countries.

Perspectives on Sino-Japanese Diplomatic Relations
by The Yomiuri Shimbun Political News Department. Translated by John Rossman.

Published by
Japan Publishing Industry Foundation for Culture (JPIC)
3-12-3 Kanda-Jinbocho, Chiyoda-ku, Tokyo 101-0051, Japan

First edition: March 2017

© 2014 by The Yomiuri Shimbun
English translation © 2017 by Japan Publishing Industry Foundation for Culture

This book is an English version that compiles sections from three Japanese publications.
Sections 1 to 4: Sections 1, 2, 4, and 5 of *Nitchukan gaiko senso* by SHINCHOSHA, 2014.
Sections 5 and 6: Sections 2 and 3 of *Abe kantei vs. Shu Kinpei* by SHINCHOSHA, 2015.
Section 7: Section 4 of *Ryodo soshitsu no akumu* by SHINCHOSHA, 2014.
Chronology of Key Events: Excerpt from the chronologies of *Nitchukan gaiko senso* by
SHINCHOSHA, 2014 and *Abe kantei vs. Shu Kinpei* by SHINCHOSHA, 2015.

Jacket and cover design by Hiroya Seno.

As this book is published primarily to be donated to overseas universities, research
institutions, public libraries and other organizations, commercial publication rights are
available. For all enquiries regarding those rights, the publisher of the English edition at
the following address: japanlibrary@jpic.or.jp

Printed in Japan
ISBN 978-4-916055-87-3
http://www.jpic.or.jp/japanlibrary/

CONTENTS

Preface to the English Edition

East Asia is at a crossroads – Will it maintain "the current state of free collaboration among countries centered on the United States" or shift to "a framework that excludes the United States in which China holds the economic and military upper hand?"

East Asia has become the center of global prosperity and growth since the Cold War ended. However, it is also a volatile region with the possibility of war due to fierce clashes of interests among countries. Many new Cold War-type situations have emerged over the past few years.

China is responsible for these developments in a majority of cases. China, as Asia's largest economic power, has strengthened its military capabilities to pressure nearby countries. China is trying to build a new international order that suits its interest via aggressive diplomatic and military intimidation. It is the most significant destabilizing element in East Asia along with North Korea that is developing nuclear weapons and missiles.

Japan's Shinzo Abe administration has been standing up to this aggressive stance by China. The Yomiuri Shimbun Political News Department has printed the "Front-line Politics" series, which draws from extensive contacts among senior officials of the Japanese government and representatives from the U.S., Chinese, and other related governments in order to provide in-depth coverage of Japan's diplomatic, economic, and security policies. It also published a book as a compilation of these articles.

This book is an English version that compiles sections from three Japanese publications written by The Yomiuri Shimbun Political News Department and published by Shinchosha Publishing – *Nitchukan gaiko senso* [Japan-China-Republic of Korea Diplomacy Battle], *Abe kantei vs. Shu Kinpei*

[Abe Administration vs. Xi Jinping], and *Ryodo soshitsu no akumu* [Nightmare of Territorial Loss]. It uses titles of officials and other information from the time when the books were originally written in order to provide a fresher perspective.

The book begins by looking at China's use of international propaganda and diplomacy ploys and military pressure against Japan.

Why is China targeting Japan?

The answer is fairly evident on if one looks at a map. The Japanese archipelago extends across a line that separates China and the Pacific Ocean. The U.S. military has bases in Japan under the Japan-U.S. alliance, and it works with Japan's Self-Defense Forces to constantly monitor and curtail activities by the Chines Navy and Air Force. Japan is a bedeviling presence that functions like a "plug on a bottle" that constrains China from pursuing its military ambitions.

China's offensive posture against Japan is focusing on the Senkaku Islands, which are an inherent part of Japan. China suddenly began claiming that "the Senkaku Islands are Chinese territory from ancient times" from the 1970s when it became evident that oil and other ocean floor resources exist around the Senkaku Islands.

The Japanese government bought the Senkaku Islands from the Japanese individual who owned them in September 2012. China pursued an opportunity presented by weakened relations between Japan and the United States at the time when Japan's Democratic Party held the government. It began a process of challenging Japan's sovereignty by sending warships and military planes to the area around the Senkaku Islands and having public ships of the China Coast Guard (including some refurbished warships) enter Japan's territorial waters.

The Senkaku Islands have very high military value with their position at the center of the East China Sea because of the close proximity to Okinawa's main island where the U.S. Air Force and U.S Marines operate important bases. If China somehow seized the Senkaku Islands, its military threat would extend more directly to Kadena Air Base and other U.S. military facilities on Okinawa's main island and substantially undermine their value as bases.

Okinawa is a vulnerable part of Japan, but it also has a unique culture that differs from mainland Japan. There is also strong sentiment against the U.S. military and a firmly entrenched anti-base movement. Okinawa experienced severe human losses during the invasion by U.S. forces near the end of the Second World War and continued to suffer under U.S. military rule for over 25 years thereafter. The Japanese government faces the difficult challenge of maintaining the deterrence that is vital to Japan's peace and security while also reducing the burden from the U.S. military bases that Okinawa shoulders.

China and Southeast Asian countries are vying for territorial rights over islands in the South China Sea. The situation in the South China Sea is worse than in the East China Sea because Southeast Asia is unable to stand up to China due to some countries being under Chinese influence.

China has been ignoring criticism by Southeast Asian countries with limited military resources and steadily building military bases through unilateral reclamation of shoals in the South China Sea. This is China's "Great Wall of Sand." China aims to establish military domination of the South China Sea, which is freely navigated by ships from countries throughout the world, as an "inland sea."

China responds to countries that criticize expansion of its sphere of influence ignoring international law with a tactic of rejecting diplomatic exchanges and propaganda maneuvers filled with exaggerations and fabrications.

In Japan's case, China rejected summit meetings and halted economic, cultural, and other interaction between the two countries for a period of three years. It also virulently spread mistaken views, such as "Japan stands for Nazism" and "Japan stole the Senkaku Islands from China," globally using all of its media avenues. "Autonomous" anti-Japan demonstrations in China piled more pressure on Japan.

The U.S. and European countries have similar experiences with China. China has shown its teeth when they have interacted closely with Taiwan or approved the activities of the Dalai Lama, the Tibetan spiritual leader who received the Nobel Peace Prize. Even Norway, which awarded the Nobel Peace Prize to Liu Xiaobo, a Chinese dissident writer, confronted fierce attacks from China.

Prime Minister Abe's approach might offer a reference for these countries in light of his persistent resistance despite being treated as a leading adversary by China and undergoing heavy pressure.

Mr. Abe is advocating diplomacy with a panoramic view of the world and has endeavored to build a majority that contains China. He has fostered global public opinion with the assertion that China "needs to accept peaceful solutions without using force and intimidation" through collaboration with obviously the United States and also Australia as well as Southeast Asian countries that fear the Chinese threat. This is not an "anti-China campaign." It aims to encourage a self-righteous China, which rejects discussions, to defend international laws and the global order and act as a major country with responsibilities to the world.

Mr. Abe has also revamped Japan's once overly restrictive peace and security policy. Japan has worked to enhance the quality of the Self-Defense Forces, despite budget constraints, in order to facilitate even closer collaboration with U.S. military forces and thereby maintain a certain level of deterrence against China.

While China's military emergence started a few decades ago, Japan has lacked a clear policy for many years. One reason for this outcome was the country's political instability in which the prime minister was changing year-to-year. Japan must have a stable government in order to bolster its national strength and resist China.

On the economic front too, Japan and the United States are engaged in a fierce conflict with China, which has become a massive presence.

The United States, Japan, Australia, and other countries targeted conclusion of the Trans-Pacific Partnership (TPP) Agreement that defines transparent trade and investment rules. China, meanwhile, pursued formation of the Asia Infrastructure Investment Bank (AIIB), a Chinese-version of the Asian Development Bank.

China's economic power is attracting many countries as the United States becomes inward-looking in its stance. China, which is run entirely by the Communist Party, operates its economy through the "rule of man" in a centralized system that lacks transparency. Spread of this system globally would distort markets and constrain free corporate activities. U.S. President Barack Obama emphasized that TPP's significance is "ensuring that China does not write global economic rules." The question is whether this message resonates in the Asia-Pacific region.

The book covers events through fall 2015, and we add some points here in regards to major changes since then.

The most obvious change has been the resumption of Japan-China summit meetings. Prime Minister Abe visited Beijing and met with Chinese President Xi Jinping in November 2014. China has finally softened its anti-Japan approach. China appears to have realized the "futility" of trying to exclude Japan amid deepening diplomatic ties between Japan and countries other than China. The Japan-China relationship, which moved out of the worst phase, remains tense, but has stabilized.

Additionally, Japan passed peace and security legislation that revised the legal framework that excessively restricted Self-Defense Force activities. Self-Defense Force ships were not even able to protect U.S. air carriers traveling in Japan's territorial waters because the previous framework prohibited all exercise of collective self-defense rights. The Self-Defense Forces had to stand by and watch even if another country attacked U.S. military planes flying near Japanese air space. This situation developed because opposition parties and others, who put less emphasis on the security perspective, argued that "it could be a constitutional violation if Self-Defense Forces protect the U.S. military."

If the Self-Defense Forces let the U.S. military suffer attacks, however, trust between Japan and the United States might suddenly collapse and it could even be difficult to sustain the alliance.

Japan enacted the new law in September 2015 that gives approval to limited exercise of collective self-defense rights. This step was necessary to support closer collaboration by the Self-Defense Forces with the U.S. military in response to China's heightened military threat. The United Nations Charter states that all countries hold the rights to individual and collective self-defense. Japan has finally become a "normal country."

The TPP signing ceremony was held in New Zealand in February 2016. Twelve Asia-Pacific countries, including Japan, the United States, and Australia, accounting for 40% of the global economy participated. Yet strong resistance to TPP in the United States is interfering with prospects of the agreement actually taking effect. The AIIB, meanwhile, was launched in December 2015, but it still lacks capabilities as a financial institution and is not wielding much influence at this point.

Japan, meanwhile, is struggling with the Okinawa problem because Takeshi Onaga, who is against U.S. military bases, became prefectural governor in December 2014. While the Japanese government prepared a proposal to transfer the U.S. Marine Corps Air Station Futenma, which is surrounded by a residential area and is considered the most dangerous base in the world, to an area on the eastern part of Okinawa with a smaller population, Mr. Onaga is fiercely resisting the move and taking on the government. The shift by Okinawan public opinion to an anti-base stance is likely to further broaden opposition to U.S. military bases and even weaken the Japan-U.S. alliance that underpins Japan's national security.

China holds an overwhelming presence in Asia and is strengthening its coercive diplomatic stance.

The decision by the Hague's Permanent Court of Arbitration in July 2016 harshly criticized China's heavy-handed actions in the South China Sea. Yet China ignored it. China is creating discord with the international community by placing more emphasis on its own interests than international law and the rule of law. It is not possible to "contain" China along the lines of the former Soviet Union during the Cold War period. How can Japan and the United States work things out with China? This is likely to consist of complicated maneuvering over a lengthy period. Yet the results will determine the future of Asia.

Hopefully, this book will be useful in understanding conditions in East Asia from Japan's perspective.

Takayuki Tanaka
Manager, Political News Department at Yomiuri Shimbun's
Tokyo Headquarters Office
Summer 2016

Chapter 1

Cold War between Japan and China

Driven by the conflict over the Senkaku Islands, Japan and China, the two major East Asian powers, have slipped into a state of permanent tension in which foreign policy, including summit meetings, no longer functions. The relationship with China, which takes the offensive by using historical issues as anti-Japan political propaganda to the fullest extent, has become what could be called a "Cold War." China's Xi Jinping administration is promoting the "Chinese Dream" slogan that signifies an effort to revive the Chinese Empire with regional hegemony of past years, and is strengthening coercive actions toward Japan and Southeast Asian countries in relation to the Senkaku Islands and the South China Sea. Although the United States has outlined a rebalance policy that places emphasis on the Asia-Pacific region and is striving to have a role in maintaining regional peace and stability, its sway as a superpower has suffered under the Obama administration and the power balance is fluid. What type of foreign policy and security strategy should Japan adopt? This chapter reviews the current state of the increasingly tense Japan-China relationship and the issues that it faces.

Promoting a concept of "Japan = Nazis" at international conferences

The World Economic Forum's Annual Meeting held in Switzerland's Davos resort area (the Davos Meeting) in January 2014 held a panel discussion on the topic of "Global Issues in 2014" on January 25, the final day, as a closing event of the general assembly. Panelist Jiang Jianqing, Chairman of the Industrial and Commercial Bank of China, aggressively stated that "Japan was Asia's Nazis in the Second World War. Whether armed conflict occurs or not depends solely on Japan."

The Davos Meeting is a global meeting that attracts 2,500 opinion makers from roughly 100 countries and has almost 300 events of various sizes. While the keynote presentation at the 2014 meeting by Prime Minister Shinzo Abe on the first day garnered interest as the first time a Japanese prime minister made this type of address, China sent more than twice as many chairs and panelists as Japan, totaling nearly 40 people.

Many of the Chinese attendees repeatedly criticized Japan. For example, China's Foreign Minister Wang Yi asserted that "Yasukuni Shrine is a symbol of Japan's militarism. The Prime Minister's visit to Yasukuni Shrine is an affront to international justice and order."

Aides close to Prime Minister Abe explain that "The government's acquisition of the ownership of the Senkaku Islands under the Noda administration served as a catalyst for worsening the relationship between Japan and China. China came under tough scrutiny from the United States and European countries for sending a wave of public vessels into the waters around the Senkaku Islands and setting up an air defense identification zone. Its focus on the Yasukuni issue is an effort to steer attention in a different direction." Yasuyuki Ishida, a researcher at the Japan Institute of International Affairs, has written that "China is reviving memories of past militarism and is trying to undermine trust in Japan from the United States, the United Kingdom, France, and Russia, the war victors, and Asian countries victimized in the war in order to foster a favorable environment for China."

However, China's one-sided attacks on Japan were not just accepted at face value by attendees from other countries. Laughs could be heard in the hall when Mr. Jiang Jianqing continued to say at the panel discussed where he equated "Japan with the Nazis" that "China is a country that loves peace. We have not invaded other countries nor have we threatened other countries."

Yet Japan cannot just passively accept this fierce "historical" propaganda because China's assertions might just be accepted without close scrutiny in some cases unless Japan firmly presents its counterarguments.

Fully responding to the public opinion battle initiated by China is a major foreign policy issue for Japan.

Anti-Japan public opinion battle intertwined with historical issues

Prime Minister Abe visited Yasukuni Shrine, which is located in the Kudankita area of Tokyo, on December 26, 2013. This was his first visit as prime minister, including the period covered by his first Cabinet, and the first time for a sitting prime minister to visit in seven years and four months since Prime Minister Junichiro Koizumi on August 15, 2006. Prime Minister Abe had expressed "great regret at not having visited Yasukuni Shrine at the time of the first Abe administration" in the Liberal Democratic Party (LDP) presidential election and the Lower House election in 2012 prior to becoming prime minister. After initially refraining from a visit after the launch of his second Cabinet to avoid a foreign policy flare-up, he decided to proceed with a visit one year after the launch of his administration amid an absence of improvements in the Japan-China and Japan-Republic of Korea (RoK) relationships.

After his visit in mourning attire, Prime Minister Abe commented to the press corps that "I selected this day to give an update on progress by the Abe administration one year after its launch and to make a pledge and express my resolve to create an era in which people do not have to suffer from the miseries of war ever again." He also noted that "I have absolutely no desire to hurt the feelings of Chinese and Korean people. Offering a prayer for the souls of dead soldiers to rest in peace is a common duty of leaders worldwide." He stated that his visit included the Chinreisha located on the grounds of Yasukuni Shrine that serves as a memorial for all war dead, including from other countries.

Ignoring this explanation by Prime Minister Abe, China exploited the Prime Minister's visit to Yasukuni Shrine to the fullest, and promoted anti-Japan propaganda worldwide. Chinese ambassadors and other representatives in 73 countries, regions, and international entities submitted articles to local media and conducted interviews over the monthlong period following the visit, engaging in persistent criticism of Japan.

Detailed analysis of the criticism finds some core themes.

The first is labeling Prime Minister Abe as a militarist and trying to spread a view of Japan as dangerous.

The submission to the Daily Telegraph, a newspaper in the United Kingdom, by Liu Xiaoming, the Chinese Ambassador to the United Kingdom, asserting that "Mr. Abe's behavior demonstrated that the spectre of militarism has returned in Japan. International society should take a vigilant stance" is a good example.

This claim sends a message that positioning Japan as a defeated country from the Second World War and China as a victorious country together with international society is still persistent today and thereby tries to foster a division between Japan and international society.

Zhu Haiquan, the Chinese Ambassador to the United States, criticized the visit in an article published in the Washington Post with the statement that "Fourteen class-A war criminals, including former Prime Minister Hideki Tojo, are enshrined at Yasukuni Shrine. The visit to Yasukuni Shrine is an affront to not only China, but the entire world." He also noted that the Yushukan, a military museum located alongside Yasukuni Shrine "details crimes committed by the United States during the Second World War."

The second theme is putting Japan in the same category as Nazi Germany, another defeated country from the Second World War. In many cases, the assertions claim that Japan continues to praise its war past and is still challenging the postwar order, in contrast to Germany's deep regret over the Nazi period, such as Gao Yanping's (Chinese Ambassador to Israel) comments that "Germany has directly confronted the history of Nazi Germany murdering 6 million Jewish people and sincerely apologized to the Jewish people and Israel. Meanwhile, Japan's Prime Minister visited Yasukuni Shrine that enshrines former Prime Minister Hideki Tojo, the "Asian Hitler," and other Class-A war criminals" and Zhai Jun's (Chinese Ambassador to France), appeal to "imagine placing flowers at Hitler's grave."

Fabricated media reports of "victorious China"

The Chinese media plays a major role in China's anti-Japan propaganda. Government authorities control China's media entities, and news media are almost always prepared to satisfy government aims.

"Japan walked out" amid applause for a victorious China

This was the headline of an article on a speech given by Shi Mingde, the Chinese ambassador to Germany, in Munich (Germany) in Wen Wei Po, a China-affiliated Hong Kong newspaper, on January 15, 2014, and the article reported that Akira Mizutani, Japan's Consul General in Munich, suddenly stood up and walked out amid unanimous applause by the German attendees.

China's state-run CCTV also reported on the speech with video coverage. The story explained that in the Q&A session after Shi Mingde's speech "Mr. Mizutani asked to make a comment and gave a far-fetched explanation that Prime Minister Abe visited Yasukuni Shrine to promote peace." It then asserted that Shi Mingde refuted this explanation with his comment that "Yasukuni Shrine is the psychological tool and symbol of the war of invasion and colonial control directed by Japanese militarism. Mr. Abe's visit is a severe affront. Japan must learn from Germany and deeply atone for its history."

The newscaster noted that "The audience agreed with Shi Mingde's rebuttal, and Japan's General Consul walked out before the event ended." The video shows Shi Mingde making his comments, applause from the audience, and Mr. Mizutani walking toward the exit shaking his head.

However, Japanese government sources explain that the Chinese media report distorts the truth and is "intentional anti-Japan propaganda."

Hiroshige Seko, Japan's Deputy Chief Cabinet Secretary, directly rejected the media coverage at his press conference on January 28, stating that "content reported by the Chinese media is completely different from the truth and aims to propagate China's own view."

The Japanese side gives the following explanation. In response to criticism of Prime Minister Abe's Yasukuni Shrine visit in Shi Mingde's speech based on an erroneous claim that he "praised Japan's actions prior to the war," Mr. Mizutani explained in the Q&A session the purpose of the visit and Japan's peace initiatives in the postwar period. He also asked Shi Mingde about the aim of China's reinforcement of military spending.

Shi Mingde did not answer the question and repeated one-sided criticism of the Yasukuni Shrine visit. However, Mr. Mizutani was not given an opportunity to respond because of the rule of "one question per person" for Q&A session comments. When asked next by a different person about the situation in the South China Sea, Shi Mingde raised criticism of Japan regarding to the Senkaku Islands, an unrelated matter, and Mr. Mizutani left early to express his dissatisfaction. He also thought it would be inappropriate to remain at the event too because of the formality of applause from the audience after the Q&A portion ends.

The Chinese media presented a picture of "applause by the entire audience" in reaction to Shi Mingde's rebuttal of General Consul Mizutani's question and the exit by a disheartened Mizutani. Mr. Seko countered that "the Chinese ambassador completely avoided the question and many people in the audience were laughing."

It can be seen in the CCTV news video that Shi Mingde is still speaking from the stage as Mr. Mizutani heads up to center aisle toward the exit. However, the article in the Hong Kong newspaper that "Mr. Mizutani suddenly stood up and walked out amid unanimous applause by the German attendees" clearly differs from the reality.

An official at the Ministry of Foreign Affairs notes that "Footage that edits what happens before and after an event is not reporting. Japanese media would be charged with fabrication if it did the same thing.

Japan's rebuttal - "the world fears China"

This type of anti-Japan propaganda tying in history from the Second World War is a common technique in China.

China's Foreign Ministry issued a critical statement when Prime Minister Junichiro Koizumi, who was aiming for Japan to become a permanent member country of the United Nations Security Council, visited Yasukuni Shrine in 2005, the 60th year since the war ended, that "Japan's ultra-right forces are going contrary to the times and distorting and rejecting the history of invasion at the 60-year commemoration of the world's victory in the war against fascism."

However, Japan's response this time differed significantly from its stance at the 60th anniversary of the postwar period in 2005.

The Japanese government did not engage in aggressive outward public relations in the first case on the basis that "it would not help in resolving the problem." Now, in contrast, it is making rebuttals each time as it finds various published assertions by the Chinese side.

This strategy reflects a strong resolve on the part of the Abe government. In comments to a meeting of the Lower House's budget committee on February 28, 2014, Prime Minister Abe criticized the Chinese stance as "engaging in an overseas campaign that aims to undermine Japan and promoting an image that totally differs from the real Japan as if it is true" and emphasized that "the Cabinet Office needs to strategically plan robust public relations efforts." Yoshihide Suga, Japan's Chief Cabinet Secretary, explained to officials that "the government did not actively make counter-arguments in the past due to taking an 'amicable' approach, but it must say what needs to be said."

The Ministry of Foreign Affairs also issued instructions to overseas consular offices that they should dispute claims from Chinese ambassadors and other representatives in articles and interviews in light of the Cabinet Office's views. While the Chinese side expressed its opinion in 73 countries, regions, and international entities, Japan's Ministry of Foreign Affairs responded through rebuttal articles by Japanese ambassadors and in other ways in almost all cases.

In its rebuttals, the Japanese side not only explained that the Prime Minister's visit to Yasukuni Shrine "reaffirmed a pledge to never start a war again" (Keiichi Hayashi, Japan's Ambassador to the United Kingdom), but also broadened its response from the past scope to 1) highlighting that Japan has consistently been a peaceful nation in the postwar period and 2) China is increasing its military spending and poses a threat to neighboring countries in the East China Sea and South China Sea.

A good example of the Japanese response is the rebuttal to an op-ed by Cui Tiankai, China's ambassador to the United States, by Kenichiro Sasae published in the Washington Post on January 17, 2014 quoted below.

"Ambassador Cui Tiankai's op-ed was wrong. It is not Japan that most of Asia and the international community worry about; it is China. Prime Minister Shinzo Abe visited Yasukuni Shrine to make a pledge for ever-lasting peace based on his deep remorse for the past. He did not go to pay homage to "Class A" war criminals nor to hurt the feelings of the Chinese or Korean people. What has become a serious, shared concern for the peace and security of the Asia-Pacific region is China's unparalleled military buildup and its use of military and mercantile coercion against neighboring states. China has escalated the intrusion of government vessels into the territorial sea around the Senkaku Islands and in waters claimed by the Philippines, Vietnam and other maritime states in the region. The path that postwar Japan is taking as a peaceful nation will never change. We fervently hope that China will cease its dogmatic anti-Japanese propaganda campaign and work with us toward a future-oriented relationship."

"Diplomacy that takes a panoramic perspective of the world map" while monitoring the situation with China

Top-level foreign policy activity aggressively promoted by Prime Minister Abe appears to be boosting trust in opinions presented by the Japanese side.

The Abe administration is pursuing "diplomacy that takes a panoramic perspective of the world map" with the Japan-U.S. relationship as the base and efforts to independently reinforce relationships with a broad range of countries while closely monitoring the relationship with China. Prime Minister Abe visited 31 countries in roughly one year and two months since the launch of the second Abe administration with focus on countries where China has been increasing its influence, including all 10 of the ASEAN countries and 11 countries in the Middle East and Africa.

Prime Minister Abe has held five summit meetings with President Vladimir Putin of Russia, which shares a national border with China, and Japan and Russia conducted a two-plus-two meeting with foreign ministers and defense ministers for the first time. Although some voices inside the U.S. government question Japan's strengthening of ties with Russia, there are also U.S. experts speaking highly about "Japan's own strategic diplomacy that takes into account China" to the Japanese government.

The Japanese government aims to utilize diplomacy that takes a panoramic perspective of the world map to broaden acceptance of the fundamental values of freedom, democracy, human rights, and rule of law and "apply pressure on China, which is attempting to change the status quo with force, through the international community" (Ministry of Foreign Affairs) in light of China's coercive actions toward the Senkaku Islands.

The UK-based Economist mentioned the following point in its January 25, 2014 issue.

"Passionate appeals by Mr. Abe, who has visited 10 ASEAN countries in his first year in office, have not been erased by anger surrounding the Yasukuni Shrine visit, and China is losing support in the ASEAN region."

Japan's careful rebuttals based on facts show something completely different from prewar Japan, and this might be a key factor in winning the global public opinion battle with China.

Anti-Japanese propaganda, permeating the U.S. capital

Nevertheless, the reality is that China's anti-Japanese propaganda is more organized and multifaceted, and Japan's strategy lags significantly behind. In particular, China has been targeting Washington D.C., the U.S. capital city. It aims to drive a wedge into the Japan-U.S. alliance that stands in the way of its ability to establish hegemony in the western Pacific region.

The Mansfield Foundation, a U.S.-based think tank, held a symposium entitled "Maritime and Territorial Disputes in the East Asian Waters" at a hotel in Washington on February 12, 2014. The roughly 50 participants listened to opinions presented by panelists from the U.S., China, and Japan, but then a representative from the Chinese Embassy in the United States asked to comment in the question portion and made the following assertions.

"China is always passive. It is just reacting to an unjustified invasion (of the Senkaku Islands by Japan)." "China is interested in a peaceful resolution of the issue through diplomacy."

The same person continued to promote this personal view at a meeting after the lunch, and the U.S. chair asked the person to curtail the comments.

While such simplistic propaganda might seem ineffective on the surface, the reality is that when it is repeated daily at meetings of think tanks that influence U.S. foreign policy "some people will start believing unusual claims that they would not accept from a single person if they hear it from 10 people" (official at the Japanese Embassy in the United States).

The growing nuances of Chinese propaganda also cannot be ignored. Veterans of the American Volunteer Group "Flying Tigers" that supported China in the Japan-China War sent a letter in early February 2014 to Cui Tiankai, the Chinese Ambassador to the United States, that protested the Yasukuni Shrine visit by Prime Minister Abe at the end of 2013 and criticized it as an action that "could only further open the wounds left by WWII." China's English-language media widely reported the letter and spread it on the Internet. China sought to enhance the propaganda effect by having US people argue its case.

China is dedicating much more effort than other countries into infiltrating Congress. The Washington Post carried an article entitled "Congressional staffers often travel on tabs of foreign governments" in its electronic version on February 18, 2013. It reported extensively on the reality of China's entertaining of US congressional staffers. The U.S.-China Policy Foundation and other organizations with close ties to China covered the full expense of visits to the Great Wall and Forbidden City, tours of Shanghai, and expensive dinners and accommodations at luxury hotels as "cultural exchanges" that receive an exemption from ethics rules that prohibit cost-free travel invitations.

Congressional staffers often make decisions on the content of bills and resolutions on behalf of Congress members and possess strong influence in congressional activities. Roughly 800 invitation trips to foreign countries for congressional staffers took place over the six years from 2006 through the end of 2011, and China was the undisputed destination leader with 219 trips, versus Japan at just 13 trips.

China also clamps down on uncomfortable assertions by U.S. media outlets and researchers using coercive means.

For example, it forced a journalist with the U.S.-based New York Times in Beijing to leave the country at the end of January 2014 because authorities did not approve a visa renewal. It is suspected that the Chinese government was unhappy with coverage by the New York Times on possible illicit financial assets held by former Prime Minister Wen Jiabao and his family, and the International China Journalists Association, which is comprised of foreign journalists residing in China, issued a statement of protest that "it can only be concluded that this is a sanction by Chinese authorities."

Even think tank specialists face the "threat" of rejection of visa requests if they make announcements that criticize China.

Professor Perry Link from the University of California at Riverside, who was rejected from entering China in 1996 because of contacts with human rights activities and his criticism of Chinese authorities, has expressed frustration with the current environment in which "almost all researchers curtail their actions and avoid criticism of the Chinese government's methods."

Spreading the message through state-run media

China seeks to propagate its claims globally through promotion of inroads by state-run media, such as Xinhua Press and CCTV, in countries around the world.

Japan's Minister of Foreign Affairs reports that Xinhua Press distributes its news inexpensively to media in Africa, Latin America, and other developing countries. In a certain Southeast Asian country, while well-known U.S. and European news firms charge $500-1,000 for monthly distribution fees, Xinhua distributes news for $100 a year. This reality distances local people from U.S. and European media and presents them with a flood of news from Xinhua. An official at the Ministry of Foreign Affairs notes that "China's strategic goal is obtaining a means to spread its own views. This is likely possible thanks to funding by the Chinese government." Xinhua has expanded its distribution to eight languages, including English, French, Spanish, and Arabic.

CCTV, which is also ramping up overseas initiatives, is hiring U.S. and European newscasters from UK-based BBC and other firms, and thereby trying to advance further by hiding the Chinese ties.

CCTV claims to hold a No.3 share in Los Angeles (U.S.) after CNN and FOX, and an official at the Ministry of Foreign Affairs worries that CCTV is "using a CNN style but embedding an anti-Japanese message in its media content."

While Japan has NHK World, this station "substantially trails qualitatively and quantitatively when compared to China's overseas broadcast and press firms" (according to an LDP member of the Special Mission Committee on Territory). The Japanese government launched a review of the current state of activities by Chinese media and started initiatives to strengthen news distribution from Japan in English in 2014.

Shifting blame to the Yasukuni visit

A contrived shift can be seen in the anti-Japanese propaganda that broke out globally after Prime Minister Abe's Yasukuni Shrine visit at the end of 2013. The op-ed by Cui Tiankai, China's ambassador to the United States, carried by the Washington Post on January 10, 2014 included the following point.

"Prime Minister Abe refrained from visiting the shrine during his first term as prime minister, which opened the door to improving Japan's historically strained relations with its neighbors. Unfortunately, his recent actions have closed the door to dialogue."

He indicates that the Prime Minister's visit to Yasukuni Shrine "closed the door to dialogue." Is that really true? It is worth remembering what Chinese officials were saying during the previous year.

"Japan must return Chinese territory (author's note = Okinawa Prefecture Senkaku Islands) that it stole" (Prime Minister Li Keqiang on May 26, 2013 in Potsdam, Germany).

"Japan claims that no conflict exists in the Senkaku matter. Talks are not possible unless a conflict exists. I think you can understand why talks cannot be conducted at this point. (Chinese Foreign Minister Wang Yi on September 20, 2013 at the Brookings Institute in Washington D.C.).

As these comments demonstrate, the Chinese side was already raising the Senkaku Islands issue and assumed a stance of only being willing to conduct a summit meeting if Japan acknowledges the existence of "a territorial issue between Japan and China."

In fact, although Prime Minster Abe made contact with Chinese President Xi Jinping at the Summit Meeting of the 20 major countries and regions (G20 Summit) in St. Petersburg (Russia) in September 2013, the last meeting among Japanese-Chinese leaders was a discussion, while standing, between Prime Minister Yoshihiko Noda and President Hu Jintao (positions at the time) on September 9, 2012 at the Asia-Pacific Economic Cooperation

(APEC) meeting in Vladivostok (Russia).

Hu Jintao pressed Prime Minister Noda to refrain from acquiring ownership of the Senkaku Islands at that time. However, Mr. Noda decided to proceed with the acquisition as planned on September 11, two days after the discussion with Hu Jintao, because of concern about the islands becoming the property of Tokyo under Shintaro Ishihara, who was the governor of Tokyo at the time, given Mr. Ishihara's tough attitude toward China since his proposal to purchase the Senkaku Islands in spring of the same year. China aggressively dispatched public vessels to the area around the Senkaku Islands thereafter. On December 13, a plane from the State Oceanic Administration violated Japan's air space around Uotsuri Island from the Senkaku Islands.

International public opinion criticized China's coercive actions. The US, in particular, clearly voiced through then-Secretary of State Hilary Clinton at the Japan-U.S. Foreign Ministers' Meeting held in Washington D.C. in January 2013 that it is "against any unilateral actions or behaviors that seek to undermine Japan's regional administrative rights."

Voices of criticism from Asian countries and the U.S. and European countries strengthened further after China declared an air defense identification zone (ADIZ) for air space above the East China Sea that included the Senkaku Islands in November 2013.

Chuck Hagel, the U.S. Secretary of Defense, issued a statement without missing a beat after China's declaration that "the U.S. reaffirms its longstanding policy that Article 5 of the Treaty of Mutual Cooperation and Security between Japan and the United States of America (Japan-U.S. Security Treaty), which defines the obligation of the U.S. to defend Japan applies to the Senkaku Islands." Experts in Japan and the U.S. indicated that this was probably the first time to specify application of Article 5 to the Senkaku Islands in an official document issued in the Secretary of Defense's name.

However, the focus of the U.S. and others regarding Japan-China issues shifted after Prime Minister Abe's visit to Yasukuni Shrine on December 26, 2013.

The U.S. government immediately issued an unusual statement after Prime Minister Abe's visit to Yasukuni Shrine that "it is disappointed in the

action by Japan's leader that aggravated tensions with neighboring countries." This was a very harsh response compared to the absence of public
criticism when Prime Minister Koizumi visited Yasukuni Shrine during the
Bush administration years on the basis that it was an internal matter. While
the U.S. Embassy in Tokyo released the statement, it obviously reflected the
White House view. U.S. government sources explain that Ben Rose, the White
House's Deputy National Security Advisor for Strategic Communications,
ultimately decided to add "disappointed" after a few hours of phone and
e-mail interaction between Tokyo and Washington.

U.S. and European media also negatively assessed Prime Minister Abe's
behavior. The Washington Post (electronic version) commented that "Prime
Minister Abe appears likely to behave in line with the view of conservatives
that believe Japan was unfairly criticized during the war." The UK-based
Guardian (electronic version) reported that "the visit on December 26 drew
the ire of China and Korea and is likely to further injure relations between
Japan and neighboring countries."

China undoubtedly switched from its aggressive offensive toward the
Senkaku Islands to just talking about Yasukuni because "it wanted to change
the topic by leveraging the Yasukuni visit to the fullest extent in order to
recover from its weak position in international public opinion" (according to
a Ministry of Foreign Affairs' official). Prime Minister Abe's visit to Yasukuni
Shrine and the subsequent U.S. reaction gave China an opportunity to take
the offensive.

Even some media sources in Japan carried articles based on the same
view as China.

One example is the "Tomorrow Yasukuni Shrine – Bond cut between
Japan and Korea" article that appeared in the Asahi Shimbun's morning
edition on January 28, 2014. This article highlighted the derailing of efforts
to improve relations with Korea and China by Prime Minister's Yasukuni
Shrine visit. Yet it did not make any mention of the issue surrounding the
government's acquisition of the ownership of the Senkaku Islands that
China used as a pretext to halt Japan-China summit meetings, including in
the chronology printed along with the article.

The reality of the Japan-Korea relationship was that the Korean side was
requesting various terms to resolve the comfort women issue in response to

Prime Minister Abe's appeal that "Japan's door to dialogue is always open." While "the Korean side needed to make changes in its approach to the comfort women issue if it was actually interested in improving relations," (according to officials close to the Prime Minister), there was no mention of this point in the article.

Prime Minister Abe's visit to Yasukuni Shrine clearly was not the trigger to "closing door of dialogue."

Nevertheless, the Prime Minister's visit to Yasukuni Shrine was a case in which Japan amplified a destabilizing diplomacy factor on its own and provided China with an opening at a time when Japan and the U.S. needed closer collaboration to deal with the Senkaku Islands issue. The Yomiuri Shimbun noted in its editorial on the day after the visit that "other countries are not in the position to question how the Prime Minister of a country pays respects to fallen soldiers," though offered criticism that asked "Why did the visit occur now and what readiness and preparation were made for the visit" and noted that "many questions have not been addressed." It also explained that the joint enshrinement of "Class A" war criminals, such as former Prime Minister Hideki Tojo executed as the verdict of the International Military Tribunal for the Far East (Tokyo Trials), "makes it difficult for the Emperor and foreign officials to visit Yasukuni Shrine" and suggested that "the government should review a policy that enables anyone to visit without concern based on the proposal to build a national memorial facility with no religious affiliation."

China's ADIZ exerts pressure on Japan

The above discussion reviewed China's anti-Japanese propaganda spurred by Prime Minster Abe's visit to Yasukuni Shrine, and the next topic is the background of China's coercive actions toward the Senkaku Islands.

China suddenly created an ADIZ.

China's Defense Ministry informed the officer in charge of defense matters at Japan's Embassy in Beijing on November 23, 2013 that China will be establishing an ADIZ in the East China Sea just 30 minutes before the official disclosure. While there is no treaty that provides the basis for an ADIZ in international law, it is normal practice to discuss the ADIZ ahead of time with nearby countries that might be affected.

The notification from China's Defense Ministry stated that aircraft flying in China's ADIZ "shall adhere to the instructions of the entity managing the ADIZ or organization given related authority (abbreviated) and China will take emergency defense actions with military force against aircraft that do not follow instructions." The Defense Ministry is the entity that manages the ADIZ.

Key issues of concern with China's ADIZ are 1) the inclusion of the Senkaku Islands that are far away from Chinese territory and under Japan's regional administration and 2) the declaration of an intention to take compulsory action against aircraft that do not follow instructions in the ADIZ unrelated to whether they pose a threat of violating territorial airspace.

Countries establish an ADIZ outside of their territorial airspace because it is likely to be too late, due to the ability to intrude through to national territory within a few minutes, if they wait to begin the response until a violation of territory or territorial airspace above territorial waters that extends about 22 kilometers off the coast line by bombers or other aircraft from another country given the high speeds of the aircraft. Based on their respective laws and rules, countries identify aircraft from other countries that have not given advance notification and execute an emergency launch of military planes (scramble) and issue warnings if there is danger of an entry into territorial air space.

The U.S. military established Japan's ADIZ after the war for its air defense and air traffic control activities. Japan's Defense Agency (at the time) retained the existing ADIZ through an order in 1969. The ADIZ encircles Hokkaido, Honshu, Shikoku, Kyushu, Okinotori Island, the Senkaku Islands, and Yonaguni Island. Yet it does not encompass the Northern Territories, the Ogasawara Islands, and Takeshima.

The ADIZ differs from territorial airspace given exclusive sovereign rights and does not support authority to make other countries adhere to one's own regulations. Japan's ADIZ management rules defined by the Ministry of Land, Infrastructure, Transportation and Tourism simply mentions "visual confirmation by an interceptor of aircraft that cannot be confirmed with a flight plan." The ADIZ established by China that mentions "defensive emergency measures" if the Ministry of Defense's instructions are not followed suggests the possibility in some cases of taking military measures, including destructive action. This qualitatively differs from ADIZ created by Japan and other countries.

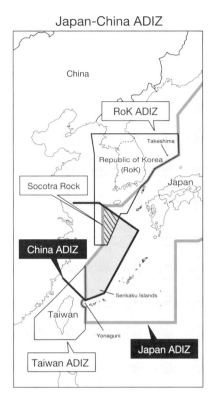

Japan-China ADIZ

Toshimichi Nagaiwa, the former commander of the Japan Air Self-Defense Force's Western Air Defense Force, commented on China's ADIZ that "it claims jurisdiction rights in contrast to the typical ADIZ concept and constitutes coercive targeting of Japan aimed at acquiring the Senkaku Island."

Mr. Nagaiwa, who was an F15 pilot, serves as director of the "Council on Political and Economic Affairs of China" comprised of former Self-Defense Force members and has extensively exchanged opinions with officials of the Chinese People's Liberation Army on annual visits to China. At the tripartite national security dialogue involving Japan, the United States, and China held in Hong Kong in January 2013, an expert from the Chinese side claimed that "Japan's ADIZ extends well beyond the intermediate line between Japan and China toward the Chinese side and is an intrusion on China's sovereignty." China's concept of linking the ADIZ and sovereignty came as a surprise.

Daniel Russel, Assistant Secretary of State for East Asian and Pacific Affairs ,agreed with Japan's reaction to the establishment of China's ADIZ as a coercive move aimed at taking the Senkaku Islands in his comments at a public hearing of the Asia-Pacific Sub-Committee of the House of Representatives' Foreign Policy Committee on February 5, 2014 that "Japan has regional administrative rights to the Senkaku Islands and unilateral attempts to changes the status quo do not strengthen China's assertion of territorial rights in any way."

The U.S. military flew two B52 strategic bombers capable of nuclear attacks through the ADIZ without giving advance notice to China on November 26, 2013 three days after China established the ADIZ. This action intentionally demonstrated that it does not accept China's ADIZ and will not adhere to it.

Divide between Japan and the U.S. regarding flight plans

However, a "divide" between Japan and the U.S. emerged early on.

Private airline firms started submitting flight plans to Chinese authorities and making other adjustments following the establishment of China's ADIZ. Even in Japan, Japan Airlines, All Nippon Airways (ANA), and other domestic airline firms agreed to submit flight plans on the basis that "they want to avoid not being allowed to pass through because of non-submission during a flight" (Japan Airlines) and "flight plans must be submitted in order to ensure safe travel" (All Nippon Airways). When it heard these responses, the Japanese government issued administrative guidance instructing domestic airlines not to submit flight plans on November 26.

Chief Cabinet Secretary Suga commented at his press conference on the same day that "The measures announced by the Chinese side have no validity whatsoever on Japan and Japan does not accept these measures that impose undue obligations on civil aircraft that fly through the zone. In light of this, the Government has notified the Chinese side that our policy will be to continue to operate according to the existing rules for civil aircraft that fly through the zone. Therefore, given the importance of the government and the private sector making a coordinated response to this matter, the Ministry of Land, Infrastructure, Transport and Tourism has once again issued a request for cooperation to respective airline companies, not to submit flight plans to the Chinese authorities."

The government convinced private-sector companies that their safety can be guaranteed after Vice Foreign Minister Akitaka Saiki called Cheng Yonghua, China's Ambassador to Japan, to the Foreign Ministry on November 25 and obtained a reply that "this measure does not hinder the freedom of flying, including private-sector airlines."

The Japanese government confirmed at the point when it issued administrative guidance on November 26 that 28 of the 33 private-sector airlines with routes that pass through China's ADIZ from other countries were not submitting flight plans. Only five companies submitted plans – four from Taiwan and one from Qatar. Furthermore, the Ministry of Foreign Affairs had assurance in unofficial contact with the U.S. Defense Department that "it thinks that U.S. private-sector companies also should not submit flight plans."

However, three days after the Japanese government issued administrative guidance on July 29, the U.S. State Department released a press secretary comment that "U.S. airlines with international routes operate in accordance with airline information from authorities in respective destination countries" and hence would not prevent them from complying with China's request for submission of flight plans. This position was a split between Japan and the United States.

The stance reflected strong requests from U.S. private-sector airlines. A Foreign Ministry official lamented that the background to the difference in public and private-sector responses in Japan and the U.S. fundamentally stems from "an attitude difference with Japan toward the Senkaku Islands in which the U.S. side actually views the islands as "just uninhabited rocks" and "China's tactic of targeting this point to elicit dissension between the U.S. and Japan worked well."

In light of this experience, Japan's foreign policy and defense authorities acknowledged "the importance of conducting sufficient coordination between the Japanese and U.S. governments."

Waiting for the day when Chinese planes scramble

The Chinese government announced after the ADIZ disclosure that its Su-30, J-11 fighter, and other main fighter planes scrambled to pursue foreign aircraft and implemented "oral warnings." However, Japanese and U.S. governments stated that "changes have not been seen since establishment of the ADIZ" (Admiral Samuel J. Locklear, Commander, U.S Pacific Command) by China, rejecting the notion that scrambles or unusual actions toward Japanese and U.S. aircraft by Chinese fighters are taking place. In fact, Japan's Air Self-Defense Force takes photos when it conducts a scramble against a Chinese plane and disclosures the photos as evidence in some cases. The Chinese side, however, not only is not disclosing photos, it does not even clarify the nationality of the subject plane.

A Self-Defense Force officials comments that "China's fighter planes are only flying in airspace near China even after establishment of the ADIZ, and China lacks the ability to conduct scrambles of its fighters in airspace close to Japan at this stage."

The earth's roundness prevents monitoring of airspace separated by over a certain distance from terrestrial radar sites. Much of China's ADIZ exists in the "blind spot" of its terrestrial radar. China thus needs to operate airborne early warning planes with monitoring capabilities from the air in order to monitor the entire ADIZ. Japanese and U.S. defense authorities agree that while China has the KJ-2000 Airborne Early Warning and Control system, it is not ready for permanent operation yet.

However, the Japan Coast Guard that protects the Senkaku Islands monitors airspace around the islands with helicopters launched from patrol ships and pilots feel the psychological pressure that "Chinese fighters might be coming."

China has increased the size of government vessels and otherwise built up its capabilities since it enacted the Territorial Waters Law that unilaterally claimed the Senkaku Islands as territory in 1992 and has repeatedly intruded into Japan's territorial waters around the Senkaku Islands since 2008.

A Defense Ministry official notes that "there will be a day in the future when China scrambles against Self-Defense Force planes."

Keeping U.S. air carriers away

The Chinese Navy implemented the Maneuver 5 large-scale military exercise in international waters of the western Pacific Ocean located about 700 kilometers to the south of the main Okinawa island in October 2013 roughly one month before it established the ADIZ in the South China Sea.

The Chinese Navy's three major fleets – North Sea Fleet (command in Tsingtao, Shandong), East Sea Fleet (command in Ningbo, Zhejiang), and South Sea Fleet (command in Zhanjiang, Guangdong) – all participated in the exercise and it was China's largest-ever exercise in the Pacific Ocean. The Chinese Navy praised the event as "clarification of the unwavering resolve and strong determination to pursue our national sovereignty and maritime rights" (Liao Shining, Chinese Navy Deputy Chief of Staff).

China is placing emphasis on a strategy of Anti-Access/Area-Denial (A2AD) that prevents the U.S. military from reaching the Chinese mainland. In the case of a military situation, China aims to 1) stop the U.S. military at the "second island chain" that extends from the Izu Islands to Guam (Anti-Access) and 2) prevent the U.S. military from entering the zone between the "first island chain" that extends from Kyushu to the Philippines and the Chinese mainland (Area Denial).

The catalyst for beginning efforts to realize the A2AD was the humiliation of the Taiwan Straits Crisis in 1996. The Chinese People's Liberation Army implemented missile exercises in waters close to Taiwan as a threat aimed at preventing the selection of Lee Teng-hui, who was viewed as an advocate of "independence" from China just before Taiwan's presidential election. China got cold feet and the situation settled down when the U.S. quickly deployed two aircraft carriers outfitted with fighter planes, Tomahawk cruise missiles, and other firepower to waters near Taiwan.

China's A2AD strategy hence seeks to keep U.S. aircraft carriers and other strong firepower away from the Chinese mainland and prevent direct attacks on Beijing.

Keiichi Kawanaka, a former associate professor at the National Defense Academy, explains that China's Maneuver 5 exercise adopted a scenario of employing electromagnetic disruption and long-distance anti-ship missiles based on the enemy possessing a firepower advantage versus China. He noted that "The ultimate aim of China's Maneuver 5 exercise is obtaining command of the sea in the northwest portion of the Pacific Ocean. The U.S. military's cruise missiles have a maximum distance of 3,000 kilometers, and the Maneuver 5 exercise area matches the anticipated waters for launching missiles against Beijing."

Protecting "Chinese seas" with missiles

China is proactively developing and deploying capabilities required to realize the A2AD strategy. While it is accelerating developments of the J20 and J31 next-generation stealth fighters and unmanned planes, China has been putting its strongest efforts into development of ballistic missiles that can make pinpointed attacks against U.S. military bases in Japan and aircraft carriers in the Pacific Ocean from mainland China.

RAND Corporation, a U.S.-based think tank with close ties to the U.S. Air Force, explained in a report entitled "Shaking the Heavens and Splitting the Earth: Chinese Air Force Employment Concepts in the 21st Century" issued in February 2011 that the Chinese People's Liberation Army has taken on a military doctrine of first-strike attacks on the runways and other facilities of enemy bases with advanced ballistic missiles.

The report, which was prepared from textbooks used at China's Defense Academy, speeches by Chinese senior military officials, and other sources by U.S. experts fluent in Chinese, explains that the Chinese Navy is placing primary emphasis in "surprise first-strike attacks" that damage runways and other facilities before enemy fighters take off as a way of securing command of the air above the conflict area. It concludes that "conventional missiles play an important role in this strategy." The "first-strike" theory is supported by advances in ballistic missile capabilities that allow for a scenario of pinpointed attacks on just airports without involving the general population, such as nearby homes and private-sector facilities.

It also notes that the targets for first strikes in a situation involving Taiwan are likely to be the U.S. Kadena Air Force Base, the U.S. Marine Corps Air Station Futenma, and the Air Self-Defense Force Naha Base in Okinawa.

The potential "game-changer" that could fundamentally alter a naval battle format between the U.S. and China is the much-lauded Dong-Feng-21 Anti-Ship Ballistic Missile (ASBM) capable of attacking an aircraft carrier in navigation. This missile has a maximum range of about 2,000 kilometers, and the U.S. Defense Department indicates that China has started initial deployment.

The concept envisions the ballistic missile flying in a parabola path with radar for guidance to the target at the final stage. This is very difficult technology, and some observers doubt whether it is possible to actually strike an aircraft carrier. Toshi Yoshihara, a professor at the United States Naval Academy, who specializes in China's maritime strategy, offers the following warning in regards to the psychological pressure of the existence of ASBMs in decisions by strategy personnel in the US government on whether to intervene in military conflicts between China and neighboring countries.

"China's A2AD places heavy emphasis on anti-ship ballistic missiles and other missiles targeting ships. A majority of the missiles will be launched from mainland China. The Chinese military can prevent interventions by third parties (such as the U.S. military) thanks to the A2AD umbrella from its mainland. China aims to encourage White House officials to weigh risks and costs associated with military intervention (particularly expansion of the conflict to involve mainland China)" (morning edition article in the Yomiuri Shimbun on March 19, 2014).

Fleets with a battle advantage owing to artillery protection from land are traditionally known as "fortified fleets." China is utilizing advances in science and technology to promote a "fortified fleet" strategy in the western Pacific and hopes to make the East China Sea a "Chinese sea."

Choke point for entry into the Pacific Ocean

Japan's Defense Ministry believes that China's A2AD strategy has already entered an operational phase. The Chinese military's H6 large bombers capable of carrying nuclear missiles crossed the first island chain for the first time on September 8, 2013. It is just a matter of time until China's first aircraft carrier "Liaoning" commissioned in 2012 embarks into the Pacific after further enhancements. China can also steal the U.S. military's freedom of action and obtain an option of attacking the U.S. mainland that greatly improves its position in negotiations with the United States once it can freely navigate nuclear-powered submarines in the Pacific.

Admiral Timothy Keating, who was commander of the United States Pacific Command at the time, offered an interesting comment on the Chinese military's ambitions in the Pacific at a Congressional public hearing in 2008. He noted that a senior Chinese Navy official proposed "split control of the

Pacific between China and the United States with Hawaii as the dividing line" in in the previous year.

Some observers view this comment as a "joke." However, Chinese President Xi Jinping similarly stated at the U.S.-China Summit Meeting on June 7, 2013 that "the vast Pacific Ocean has enough space to accommodate the two major powers of China and the United States."

Ou Jian-ping, president of the Institute of Force Building at China's National Defense University, made the following comment about the Chinese Navy's required capacity in an Internet program affiliated with the People's Daily, the Communist Party's newspaper, "It needs to extend far. The Chinese Navy must beyond the first island chain out into the Pacific."

However, the Chinese Navy has two major hurdles to overcome in order to operate freely in the western Pacific.

China first needs to establish air superiority so that Chinese ships cannot be attacked by fighter planes from the U.S. military or others. During the Maneuver 5 period, its Y8 airborne early warning planes and H6 bombers participated in the exercises each day by passing over international waters around Okinawa and Miyako Islands. Chinese military planes have been increasingly using this path to reach the Pacific Ocean since the summer of 2013.

The number of Chinese planes flying above waters close to Japan has sharply risen. Defense Ministry data on the number of scrambles for Chinese planes reported 31 times in fiscal 2008 and 38 times in fiscal 2009, but then increases to 96 times in fiscal 2010 when Chinese fishing boat collided with a Japan Coast Guard patrol ship around the Senkaku Islands and 156 times in fiscal 2011 and a further doubling to 306 times in fiscal 2012. Scrambles reached an all-time high of 415 times in fiscal 2013. Some observers think China's establishment of an ADIZ in the East China Sea is the first step toward securing air superiority and is linked to this activity.

The other hurdle is obtaining safe passage through the Nansei Shoto Islands, including the Senkaku Islands. The Nansei Shoto Islands are located on the route for the Chinese military to enter the Pacific Ocean.

Yoji Koda, a former commander in chief of a Self Defense Fleet of the Maritime Self Defense Force , delivered a speech at a symposium held by an organization affiliated with the United States Navy in the suburbs of

Washington D.C. on January 16, 2014 and emphasized that "The Nansei Shoto Islands are a choke point. Controlling this spot is an important role for Japan in standing up to China's A2AD."

China's military vessels cannot easily reach the Pacific Ocean as long as Japan firmly protects the Nansei Shoto Islands and always has the Self Defense Force ready for action. The Ground Self Defense Force conducted training to deploy 88-type anti-ship missiles from the mainland on Miyako Island in the Nansei Shoto Islands in November 2013 and demonstrated its capability to put Chinese military ships trying to move out to the Pacific Ocean in its firing range at any time.

The military reason is an important driver of China's earnest efforts to erode Japan's effective control of the Senkaku Islands.

Effort to take the Senkaku Islands started in 2008

China refers to national interests with absolutely no room for compromise as "core interests," and countries that violate these interests face unrelenting political and economic pressure. China has been utilizing such coercive measures without hesitation toward Japan's Senkaku Islands and the South China Sea since the global financial crisis in 2008 weakened the influence of the United States in the international community.

Edward Luttwak, a senior advisor at the Center for Strategic and International Studies (CSIS) who has been advising the U.S. Department of Defense and other agencies on external strategies for many years, offered the following analysis of changes in China's behavior after noting that the global financial crisis in 2008 was a "collapse of the Washington consensus (led by the United States) and the emergence of the Beijing consensus."

"The Chinese leadership elite gained significant confidence from around this period, and clear changes in China's behavior emerged from around 2009-10. Leanings and content of China's opinions suddenly changed, and Chinese leaders started expressing very strong opinions about a variety of issues ranging from currency policy to the Western democratic system. What stands out even more is that China almost simultaneously revived territorial issues with India, Japan, the Philippines, and Vietnam that had been largely ignored until then with an amplified voice" (page 27 of "The Rise of China vs. the Logic of Strategy" published by Fuyo Shobo).

It is true that China greatly altered its stance toward Japan's Senkaku Islands in 2008. Although China enacted the Territorial Waters Law that claim the Senkaku Islands as its own territory in 1992 and declared that it would conduct "patrol voyages to maintain its sovereignty" in the East China Sea in 2006, it did not take coercive actions that challenged Japan's regional administrative rights prior to 2008. In December 2008, however, a ship from the China Marine Surveillance Fleet operating under the State Oceanic Administration entered Japan's territorial waters around the Senkaku Islands for the first time in December 2008.

The Deputy Fleet Commander commented to a Chinese newspaper at the time that "It is not enough to just claim that these (Senkaku Islands) are ours. China needs to demonstrate that they are actually under our control. China Marine Surveillance ships confirm our presence."

China increased its patrols with government vessels around the Senkaku Islands after the incident in which a Chinese fishing ship collided with a Japan Coast Guard patrol boat in waters off the Senkaku Islands in September 2010. These vessels have been exhibiting demonstration-like behavior with responses to warnings from Coast Guard patrol boats that "Diaoyu Dao and affiliated islands (China's name for the Senkaku Islands) are Chinese territory. We are carrying out an appropriate mission." Since the Japanese government's acquisition of the ownership of the Senkaku Islands in September 2012, China escalated coercive actions aimed at taking the Senkaku Islands with constant dispatches of public vessels, repeated intrusions in territorial waters, violation of territorial airspace with the State Oceanic Administration's propeller plane (December 2012), target locking of fire control radar on a Maritime Self Defense Force ship by a Chinese naval vessel in the East China Sea (January 2013), and establishment of an ADIZ in the East China Sea (November 2013).

China recently has been asserting that "it is just reacting to prior efforts by Japan to change the status quo through the Japanese government's acquisition of the ownership of the Senkaku Islands," but the reality is that China started attempting unilateral changes of the status quo backed by force in 2008, four years prior to the Senkaku acquisition by the Japanese government.

Senkaku Islands as a core interest too

China almost entirely limited use of the term "core interests" to Taiwan, Tibet, and the Uyghur Region prior to 2008. Since around 2010, however, it broadened the scope of core interests to the Senkaku Islands and South China Sea. Hua Chunying, Deputy Director of China's Foreign Ministry Information Department, stated that the "Senkaku Islands are a core interest" at a regular press conference in April 2013. Additionally, Chang Wanquan surprised U.S. attendees at a joint press conference after a U.S.-China Defense Ministers' Meeting held in Washington D.C. on August 19, 2013 with his blunt comment after U.S. Defense Minister Chuck Hagel spoke about the importance of relationships of trust among military authorities, that "There should be no illusion that China will abandon its core interests. Do not underestimate our resolve in territorial, sovereignty, and maritime matters."

Few people in foreign diplomacy circles doubted that China viewed the Senkaku Islands as a core interest in 2014.

Jun Osawa, a senior research fellow at the Institute of International Policy Studies, sees "the change in China's long-term foreign policy stance by the former Hu Jintao administration" as the background to expansion of the country's core interests.

China's foreign policy had previously adhered to a strategy of "hiding one's talents and waiting for the right opportunity." This was the instruction of former top leader Deng Xiaoping that put priority on economic development and pursued a foreign policy path of avoiding conflict with other countries. However, then-President Hu Jintao presented a policy of "moving ahead with things that should be aggressively pursued" and dropped worries about conflicts with foreign countries in July 2009 at a meeting of foreign policy officials in the government and ambassadors stationed in foreign countries.

Mr. Osawa's research finds a sharp rise in use of the term "core interests" in the People's Daily, the Chinese Communist Party's newspaper, from around this time. While it was mentioned less than 100 times a year through 2008, usage climbed rapidly to 260 times in 2009 and 325 times in 2010. It remained at a high level during 2011-13 too at 284 times, 305 times, and 264 times respectively.

The same research found mention of core interests in reference to Diaoyu Dao and affiliated islands (China's name for the Senkaku Islands) in the single digits for 2006-09, but then 49 times in 2010 when the fishing boat collision incident occurred and a much higher 274 times in 2012.

Mr. Osawa explains that "I think China reached the mistaken conclusion that it could manipulate the U.S. too amid a decline in U.S. influence following the global financial crisis. While China's Foreign Ministry subsequently stated that it would maintain a peaceful path, the People's Liberation Army is persistently trying to come to the forefront."

Masayuki Masuda, a researcher at the Defense Ministry's National Institute for Defense Studies, noted that China changes its behavior depending on the counterpart.

"The psychological strategy of 'hiding one's talents and waiting for the right opportunity' still exists. This is particularly true in dealing with the United States. However, even with the United States, China has been changing its approach in foreign policy to vigorously pursuing its core interests based on a perception that the global financial crisis started a change in the power balance. China believes that the power balance has already flipped with Japan, and it does not hold back at all in dealings with counterparts for whom it thinks the power balance has changed."

Dream of restoring "Qing Dynasty" territory

The Xi Jinping administration has been continuing China's arrogant external strategy that started with the global financial crisis in 2008. In fact, President Xi advocates the "Chinese Dream" and appears to be strengthening an even harder-line position toward territorial and maritime rights issues than the previous administration.

The "Chinese Dream" was presented as an important statement by President Xi with the six other members of the Politburo Standing Committee of the Communist Party of China on a tour of the "Road to Revival" permanent exhibit at the National Museum of China, in November 2012 when the new administration took over. It has become the administration's slogan since then.

The People's Daily article on the statement reported that President Xi commented that "all party comrades must remember the lessons of history that falling behind results in weakness and strength comes through advancement" and then offered the following description of the Chinese Dream.

"Everyone has an ideal, something they are pursuing, and their own dream. Today people are talking about the Chinese Dream. I think realization of a grand revival of the Chinese people is the greatest dream of the Chinese people in the modern era. This dream brings together the ambition of multiple generations of Chinese people and reflects the interest of the Chinese people and all citizens of China. It is something desired by each Chinese person. History tells us that the future destiny of individuals closely correlates to the future destiny of their nation and people. Only if the nation is good and the people are good does every benefit. The grand revival of the Chinese people is an honorable and very difficult endeavor. One generation and then another generation of Chinese people must jointly pursue this goal."

The Road to Revival exhibit visited by President Xi "reviews the battle back by Chinese people from humiliation and hardship after the Opium War in 1840, various efforts aimed at realizing a revival of the people, particularly the Chinese Communist Party's guidance of the country's various peoples to self-determination, and the glorious path of liberation, enriching the nation, and winning happiness for the people" (People's Daily).

There is a view of the period from the 18th century through the mid-19th century prior to the Opium War as China's peak from the perspective of territory under its influence. In particular, China controlled Hong Kong, Taiwan, islands in the South China Sea, Mongolia, and other areas during the reign of the Qianlong Emperor (officially 1736-95).

Shin Kawashima, an associate professor at Tokyo University (specialist in Asian political and foreign policy history), explains the Chinese Dream in the following manner, "China strongly believes that "territory" it held in the Qing Dynasty years was taken. The East China Sea and South China Sea are part of the story of regaining lost possessions."

In other words, the Chinese Dream is the "dream of restoring territories from the Qing Dynasty."

The U.S. government, meanwhile, has not hidden its concerns about the

Xi administration's ambition to expand territory.

In December 2013, a senior U.S. official who attended a meeting between U.S. Vice President Joe Biden and President Xi commented after the event to a group of journalists that China's hardline stance regarding establishment of the ADIZ and other matters "is part of a long-term initiative to protect its sovereignty and territory and reflects very strong views of President Xi toward such core interests."

Unbridled expansion in the South China Sea

A dangerous incident took place on December 5, 2013 when the USS Cowpens, an Aegis cruiser in the U.S. Navy fleet, just barely avoided a collision with a Chinese Naval ship. The incident occurred in international waters that are open to free navigation by all countries, and the U.S. Defense Department explained that the Chinese ship approached the path being taken by the Cowpens and did not change its movement despite wireless radio warnings from the Cowpens to the ship that it was getting too close. The Cowpens conducted an emergency stop and narrowly prevented a collision. The distance between the two ships when they stopped was just 100 yards (about 91 meters).

This is China's third case of dangerous behavior toward U.S. military activity in the South China Sea following the collision between a U.S. Navy EP3 electronic surveillance plane and a Chinese F8 fighter in April 2001 and interference with the U.S. Navy's Impeccable surveillance ship by five Chinese Navy ships, including an intelligence gathering ship, in March 2009.

The Cowpens was monitoring movements by China's Liaoning air carrier that was engaged in exercises in nearby waters. The Chinese ship "tried to collide rather than just being about to collide" according to U.S. sources. U.S. Defense Secretary Hagel expressed strong concern at a press conference held on December 19 that this is "extremely provocative and could become a trigger or igniter of an unexpected situation."

China's dangerous behavior stems from its unique stance of "being against military actions in China's exclusive economic zone (EEZ) by any country without approval."

The EEZ refers to waters in which a country can claim economic sovereignty to search for and develop natural resources extending 200 nautical miles (about 370 kilometers) off a country's coast and is based on the United Nations Convention on the Law of the Sea (UNCLOS). While UNCLOS also has a provision stating that "reasonable consideration should be given to the coastal country," this concept differs from territorial waters deemed to be part of the coast country's sovereignty covering 12 nautical miles (about 22 kilometers). All countries are free to navigate ships, fly in airspace, and install underwater cables and pipelines in the EEZ. There are also naturally no regulations on military activities, such as intelligence gathering by military ships.

However, China refers to the EEZ as "maritime territory" and "waters with national jurisdiction" and views it as roughly the same as territorial waters. It engaged in obstructionist behavior toward the U.S. military from the perspective that "surveillance activities by the U.S. military in China's EEZ are a fundamental military security issue for maritime and airspace between China and the U.S."

The "maritime territory" concept shows up most prominently in the South China Sea. China, Vietnam, and Taiwan assert territorial claims to the Paracel Islands, and China, the Philippines, Malaysia, Vietnam, Brunei, and Taiwan lay claim to the Spratly Islands.

China has drawn nine lines on the map in the South China Sea extending in a U-shape from the north and claims sovereignty to the area within the nine-dash lines. It has aggressively utilized the People's Liberation Army to preserve this "territory" in recent years. The Territorial Waters Law enacted in February 1992 identified the Paracel Islands, Spratly Islands, and other islands as Chinese territory, and China announced the formation of Sansha City with jurisdiction over both islands groups and other islands in June 2012. The Hainan Province government adopted Fishing Law rules in January 2014 that make it obligatory for foreign fishing vessels operating inside of the nine-dash line zone to apply for a license.

China's sudden establishment of an ADIZ in the East China Sea, including the Senkaku Islands, and demand for all planes to follow instructions in this zone is similar to what it has done in the South China Sea in terms of being an arbitrary interpretation of international practices.

Growing friction with China in the South China Sea is not something that Japan can ignore. The Defense Ministry's National Institute of Defense Studies issued the following warning in the "NDIS China Security Report."

"China is pursuing defense of maritime rights, not only the security of its territorial land, waters, and airspace, as a historical mission of the People's Liberation Army. It is likely to strengthen collaboration between naval forces and the maritime law enforcement entity (comparable to Japan's Coast Guard).

The United States, Japan, and ASEAN countries are appealing to China to comply with international laws. However, Hirotaka Watanabe, the Director of the Institute of International Relations at the Tokyo University of Foreign Studies, notes that "it is difficult to reason with an overly confident major power." Other countries are unlikely to succeed in persuading China to abandon its maritime expansion strategy based on arbitrary interpretations.

Early signs of an anti-China alliance

Countries threatened by China's maritime activities are seeking military collaboration and cooperation in formats not seen in past years and starting to stand up to China.

Cam Ranh Bay, which is located on the South China Sea in southern Vietnam, is known as an excellent natural port. The Bay's opening is narrow at just about one kilometer, and this protects it from waves. It was a base for former Soviet Union troops in Asia during the Cold War years.

The Vietnam military has a base at Cam Ranh Bay now and monitors the Spratly Islands and other islands where it has conflicts regarding territorial rights with China.

Defense Minister Istunori Onodera visited Cam Ranh Bay on September 17, 2013 and was given a tour of Vietnam's newest frigate ship and other facilities. The visit came in response to an invitation by the Vietnam government and is the first visit by a member of the Japanese government. While Vietnam, with its communist government, and Japan did not have much of a cooperative relationship in security affairs in past years, Vietnam clearly wants to "curtail China's maritime advances through collaboration with Japan."

Mr. Onodera made the following comment showing interest in

arranging collaboration between the two countries after the tour.

"Vietnam and Japan are facing the same type of environment even though the East China Sea and South China Sea have different locations. There are many security response points that can be used as reference."

The stand-off between Vietnam and China in the South China Sea is difficult and dangerous with risk of developing into armed clashes. Chinese public ships fired on Vietnamese fishing boats in waters near the Paracel Islands in March 2013. Ships from the two countries repeatedly engaged in skirmishes in the same waters in May 2014. Naval forces from the two countries battled in waters around Johnson South Reef in the Spratly Islands, leaving many dead, in March 1988.

Truong Tan Sang, President of the Socialist Republic of Vietnam, who was visiting Japan as a State Guest met with Prime Minister Abe at the Prime Minister's Office on March 18, 2014, and the two leaders signed a joint statement that highlights the importance of resolving conflicts in accordance with the principles of international law in light of China's strengthening maritime initiatives. Prime Minister Abe communicated at the meeting that the Japanese government would soon dispatch a study group to Vietnam in order move forward with supply of patrol ships aimed at enhancing maritime monitoring capabilities of Vietnam's Marine Police Force.

Many countries besides Vietnam also feel a threat from China's maritime initiatives in the South China Sea.

China established effective control of the Scarborough Reef, where it has a conflict with the Philippines regarding territorial rights, in 2012. It sent Chinese fishing boats and encircled these boats for the purpose of protection with fishing patrol boats, maritime patrol boats, and military boats.

Navy General Zhang Zhaozhong, a professor at China's National Defense University, explained this technique in the following way in a program that aired on Beijing TV in May 2013, "We are using a 'cabbage strategy' whereby Philippine fishing boats or others trying to travel to the island must ask multiple layers of patrols (naval, maritime, and fishing) whether they can enter."

China's technique of building up multiple existing facts and ultimately taking rights is also sometimes called the "salami strategy." This term refers to acquiring thin slices of salami a little at a time and getting the entire salami by the time others become aware of what is happening.

The Philippines brought a case to the Arbitration Court in 2013 asserting that China's activities in Scarborough Reef are unlawful. China reacted angrily and took unprecedented action. It rejected the Philippine President's attendance at the China-ASEAN Expo held in China (opening ceremony on September 3, 2013) just before it started. China told the Philippines that "it wanted the Philippines to select a more appropriate time for the visit."

China and ASEAN countries signed a Declaration on Conduct of Parties that called for self-restraint from building new facilities on the islands in contention in the South China Sea in 2002. However, this was a non-binding agreement and China rejected protests from the Philippines. The ASEAN side requested formulation of a "Code of Conduct" that is more binding than the Declaration at a senior-level officials discussion between China and ASEAN held in China's Jiangsu Province from September 14, 2013, but China did not acquiesce to an in-depth debate.

Edward Luttwak, who was mentioned earlier, explained in an interview with the Yomiuri Shimbun that was published in the morning edition on March 14, 2013 that "China's behavior as a major power is generating significant reactions from outside the country, but the Chinese leadership takes an inward stance that addresses internal pressures and cannot heed messages from outside. This resulted in Myanmar, which had been close to China, distancing itself from China, and the Philippines, Japan, India, and other countries are exhibiting similar reactions."

Countries battling China's behavior in the South China Sea are interested in developments related to Japan's conflict with China in the dispute over the Senkaku Islands.

A Philippine official commented regarding the Senkaku Islands issue that "China is trying to change the status quo, but it appears to be acting more cautiously than in the South China Sea because of the strength of the Japan Coast Guard and Maritime Self Defense Force." ASEAN countries believe that resolution of the issue between Japan and China based on the law and justice, rather than force, could serve as a good precedent for settling the South China Sea dispute.

In this respect, the response taken by the Naoto Kan Cabinet (at the time) to the incident in which a Chinese fishing boat operating illegally in

China's claimed nine-dash line (▬) and main incidents of opposition

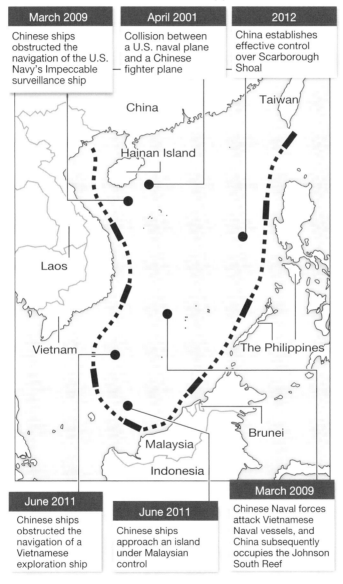

March 2009	April 2001	2012
Chinese ships obstructed the navigation of the U.S. Navy's Impeccable surveillance ship	Collision between a U.S. naval plane and a Chinese fighter plane	China establishes effective control over Scarborough Shoal

China

Taiwan

Hainan Island

Laos

Vietnam

The Philippines

Brunei

Malaysia

Indonesia

June 2011	June 2011	March 2009
Chinese ships obstructed the navigation of a Vietnamese exploration ship	Chinese ships approach an island under Malaysian control	Chinese Naval forces attack Vietnamese Naval vessels, and China subsequently occupies the Johnson South Reef

No location information has been released on the incident of the USS Cowpens, an Aegis cruiser in the U.S. Navy fleet, just barely avoiding a collision with a Chinese Naval ship.

Japan's territorial waters around the Senkaku Islands rammed a patrol boat of the Japan Coast Guard and attempted to flee on September 7, 2010 came as a major disappointment to Asian countries. While the Coast Guard arrested the Chinese boat captain on suspicion of interfering with performance of public duties, the Chinese government reacted with various retaliatory measures, such as banning rare earth exports. Then-Chief Cabinet Secretary Yoshito Sengoku worked behind the scenes to have Justice and Prosecutor authorities release the fishing boat captain, and the Naha District Public Prosecutors Office released him with action pending in light of "future Japan-China relations" on September 25. Observers saw the release of the fishing boat captain as a capitulation by the Japanese government to China's pressure.

The U.S.-based New York Times reported the incident as a "humiliating retreat" by Japan. The article noted that "the foreign policy stand-off between Japan and China that started two weeks ago finished with a compromise by Japan that appears to be a humiliating retreat in a test case for relations in the Pacific" and concluded that "this compromise demonstrates recent change in the power balance in Asia." Additionally, the Wall Street Journal reported that "China views the release of the fishing boat captain without pressing charges as a foreign policy victory" and voiced concern about adverse impact on the region by the Japanese government's decision that "stokes danger of even more boldness by China in territorial conflicts in Asia."

A foreign diplomat in Southeast Asia before an official at the Minister of Foreign Affairs wondered at the time "Why didn't Japan carry through with the rule of law?"

Rebalancing by the U.S. – Questions about the level of determination

Conflicts between China and Southeast Asian countries over islands in the South China Sea are closely related to the "power vacuum" created by the pullback of the U.S. military from the region.

The U.S. military left Vietnam under the Paris Peace Accords in 1973, the final phase of the Vietnam War. In the following year, China militarily invaded the Paracel Islands, defeating the South Vietnamese forces (at the time) and taking full control of the area.

Additionally, the campaign against U.S. military bases in the Philippines led to an exit of the U.S. forces from this country, and China three years later occupied Mischief Reef in the Spratly Islands that had been effectively controlled by the Philippines.

Security experts broadly share the view that China's moves filled a "power vacuum" created by the exit of U.S. forces.

The United States has outlined a "rebalancing" policy that places emphasis on deploying U.S. military power in the Asia-Pacific region and aims to raise deterrence capabilities against maritime initiatives by China backed by enhancement of its military capabilities. This strategy targets benefits of stability and prosperity by strengthening U.S. involvement in the region with growing economic importance but also rising military tensions.

The U.S. Defense Department released its Quadrennial Defense Review (QDR) on March 4, 2014, and presents specific rebalancing measures to confront China's maritime initiatives and A2AD strategy. The measures include 1) increasing Pacific deployment of U.S. Navy ships and other assets from an estimated roughly 50% now to 60% through 2020, 2) strengthening the U.S. military presence in Japan, 3) deploying cutting-edge littoral combat ships (LCS) and high-speed transport ships, 4) expanding deployments of naval and air forces and Marines to Guam, 5) bolstering fighter plane and intelligence, surveillance, and reconnaissance (ISR) capabilities, and 6) deploying Marines to Darwin (Australia).

The United States intends to continue making investments in fighters, including the most advanced F35 fighters as well as long-distance bombing, monitoring, submarine, and reconnaissance functions as counter measures to China's A2AD strategy.

However, some observers question the determination of the U.S. military's involvement in the Asia-Pacific region even with the Defense Department initiatives. Why is this?

"The decision in Syria had repercussions worldwide. Countries I have visited say that they can no longer rely on the United States."

Republican Senator John McCain offered this acknowledgement of a decline in U.S. prestige and criticized the Obama administration's response to the Syria situation in a session entitled "Future of U.S. Power" at the

The U.S. military's rebalancing in Asia (including planned actions)

Deployment of the most advanced F35 fighters

Ratio of naval ships in the Pacific Ocean and Atlantic Ocean changes from 5:5 to 6:4

Iwakuni

East China Sea

Pacific Ocean

Okinawa

Guam

Signing of a new military pact concerning the actual stationing of the U.S. Military

The Philippines

Rotation of the Marine Corps

South China Sea

Deployment of cutting-edge littoral combat ships (LCS)

Singapore

Indonesia

Free provision of F16 fighters

Australia

Davos Meeting in Switzerland on January 24, 2014.

President Barack Obama stated in the summer of 2013 that the United States intended to conduct military strikes if Syria's Assad government used chemical weapons in the country's civil war and asked for advance approval of an attack from Congress at the same time. While U.S. pressure worked to some extent, including an agreement by the Assad government to abandon chemical weapons prior to a decision in Congress, the United States allowed the Assad government to remain in power.

Senator McCain argued that "the U.S. should have bombed Syria" and the response of the Obama administration that had turned to Congress for a decision on military intervention undermined trust in the United States worldwide.

War weariness has been pronounced in the United States as an after-math of lengthy wars in Iraq and Afghanistan. President Obama was also originally against the Iraq War. Concerns spread in Japan too that "President Obama might not be prepared for war even if China acts recklessly."

Senkaku Islands buffeted by U.S.-China relations

Messages pointing to a different direction, than rebalancing, by key players in the Obama administration have been reinforcing concerns held by Japan and others.

"When it comes to China, we seek to operationalize a new model of major power relations. That means managing inevitable competition while forging deeper cooperation on issues where our interests converge."

This is what Susan Rice, the U.S. President's National Security Advisor, said in speech on Asian policy on November 20, 2013 prior to a visit by Vice President Biden to East Asia (December 2-7). It clearly gave an impression of U.S. acceptance of a "new major power relationship" between the U.S. and China proposed by China.

China established the ADIZ in the East China Sea, including airspace above the Senkaku Islands, and bolstering coercion against Japan on November 23 right after the speech. A source at the U.S. Embassy in Tokyo reflected on these developments with the comment that "China appears to have tested us."

While the Japanese government requested the inclusion of content critical of China's establishment of the ADIZ in the agreement document prepared for Vice President Biden's visit to Japan, the U.S. side rejected the proposal. An official at the Ministry of Foreign Affairs believes that "the U.S. State Department wanted to avoid getting entangled in a conflict between Japan and China over the ADIZ" ahead of the China visit. Vice President Biden emphasized in his comments at a joint press conference with Prime Minister Abe on December 3 during his visit to Japan that "The United States is very concerned about attempts to unilaterally change the status quo in the East China Sea and intends to take an unwavering stance toward its obligations that come from the alliance relationship," but the Japanese side was still dissatisfied.

The U.S.-China relationship had already affected the Obama administration's attitude toward the Senkaku Islands.

The Obama administration initially was more excited about strengthening pragmatic cooperation with China than its existing relationship with Japan and other allies. There was even talk among experts and in the media about a shift from the G8 Summit (Summit of the Major Industrialized Nations) to a two-country framework between the U.S. and China as the negotiating framework leading the world. In fact, President Obama commented in 2009 that the "U.S.-China relationship will shape the 21st century," clarifying his stance of viewing China as a partner in addressing global issues and thereby stoking concerns in Japan and Southeast Asia.

The Obama administration reacted passively to issues surrounding the Senkaku Islands around this time. The U.S. government had traditionally maintained a neutral stance toward the conflict over territorial rights in comments, such as "we do not take a position and hope for a resolution by the parties using peaceful means," but also shown that it would participate in the defense of the Senkaku Islands based on the logic that "the Japanese government has administrative control of the Senkaku Islands, Article 5 of the Japan-U.S. Security Treaty applies to territories under Japan's administrative control, and Article 5 therefore applies to the Senkaku Islands."

However, when a ship from the China Marine Surveillance Fleet entered Japan's territorial waters around the Senkaku Islands in December 2008 during the period of transition from the Bush administration to the

Obama administration, the U.S. State Department rejected Japan's request for a public reaffirmation of this opinion and simply stated that "the U.S will comply with international agreements that it has concluded." It appears to have provided this special consideration for China ahead of the Obama administration's launch, and President Obama continued the same type of response from January 2009 after becoming president. The U.S. State Department only reconfirmed the past official opinion to the Japanese government in early March 2009 after the Yomiuri Shimbun published an article on this topic. However, it did not state this official opinion in a press conference with cameras and took an unusual stance of responding later on by e-mail.

When five Chinese ships came abnormally close to the U.S. Navy's Impeccable surveillance ship navigating international waters 120 kilometers south of China's Hainan Island and obstructed its navigation in March 2009, White House officials expressed an opinion that this was an accidental event that ran contrary to the wishes of China's central government and sought to quell the issue.

In November 2009, President Obama visited China and released a joint statement that contained the sentence stating that "The two countries agreed that it is very important for steady advancement of the U.S.-China relationship that they mutually respect each other's core interests." While the U.S. appears to have interpreted core interests as limited mainly to Taiwan, some observers suggest that China might have misperceived this as a sign of a weak stance by the Obama administration toward the South China Sea and Senkaku Island issues.

"Pro-Chinese" officials, such as Jeffrey Bader, the National Security Council's (NSC) Senior Director for Asian Affairs, and James Steinberg, the Deputy Secretary of State (both at the time), reportedly spearheaded the Obama administration's China policy in 2009.

However, the U.S.-China relationship sharply changed in 2010. The starting point was President Obama's disappointment in China's uncooperative stance toward setting goals for reduction of greenhouse gases at the Fifteenth Session of the Conference of Parties to the United Nations Framework Convention on Climate Change (COP15) held in Copenhagen in December 2009. The G2 momentum rapidly dissipated after China criticized the U.S. provision of weapons to Taiwan in January 2010 and the meeting between President Obama and the 14th Dalai Lama, the spiritual leader of the Tibetan people, in February 2010 and froze military dialogue.

The path advocated by then-Secretary of State Hillary Clinton and then-Assistant Secretary of State Kurt Campbell of realizing the necessity of curtailing China came to the forefront with the change in the U.S.-China relationship. Secretary Clinton, who attended the ASEAN-related meetings held in late July 2010, sent a tough message toward China's coercive actions in the South China Sea that "Freedom of navigation in the South China Sea is a U.S. national interest, and it is against military threats" and began strengthening relationships with Southeast Asian countries.

Secretary Clinton told the Japanese side in a Japan-U.S. Foreign Ministers Meeting held on New York in regards to the collision incident involving a Chinese fishing boat in waters around the Senkaku Islands in September 2010 that "Article 5 of the Japan-U.S. Security Treaty clearly applies to the Senkaku Islands," becoming the first Secretary-class official to confirm its applicability, and in clearer language than in the past. Assistant Secretary of State Campbell, a right-hand man for Secretary Clinton and proponent of focusing on the Japan-U.S. alliance, led this effort. Mr. Campbell was the first U.S. senior government official to acknowledge that the Japan-U.S. Security Treaty applies to the Senkaku Islands in an interview with the Yomiuri Shimbun in 1996 when he was Deputy Assistant Secretary of Defense.

When then-President Hu Jintao visited the U.S. in January 2011, China requested inclusion of the sentence of "respect for mutual core interests," just as in 2009, the U.S. side was unwilling to compromise on its stance of keeping it out. It is generally thought that this change reflected the impact of replacement of the pro-Chinese Bader with Mr. Campbell, who placed emphasis on the Japan-U.S. alliance, as the person in charge of negotiations on the U.S. side.

However, the Secretary Clinton and Mr. Campbell, who delivered a tough message to China, left the administration in the second Obama government. Secretary of State John Kerry, the successor to Secretary Clinton, has shown stronger interest in achieving results in Middle East problems than Asia. Susan Rice, a close adviser to President Obama who gives advice on foreign policy, is "not well-versed in Asian affairs" (U.S. government source) and is viewed as seeking harmony with China as a permanent member of the U.N. Security Council following her experience as Ambassador to the U.N. This is the background to skepticism from Japan's Ministry of Foreign Affairs officials toward Rice's comment that "the U.S. is trying to leverage a new type of major power relationship."

Professor Yoshihara at the United States Naval Academy expressed the following dissatisfaction with the Obama administration's response to the Senkaku Islands in an interview with the Yomiuri Shimbun.

"Some people in the United States take the view regarding the Senkaku Islands issue that 'uninhabited rocks should be ignored.' However, this is a much larger issue of challenging the regional order because the United States returned regional administrative rights to the Senkaku Islands to Japan based on an agreement following the San Francisco Peace Treaty signed in 1951, and China is saying that it does not accept this return and 'is deciding what to maintain and what to change on its own.'

The U.S. government is currently explaining that 'it is not involved in the territorial rights, but the Senkaku Islands are being administered by Japan and come under the Japan-U.S. Security Treaty.' This phrasing is overly legalistic and is creating confusion and sending the wrong message to Beijing and Tokyo.

I am concerned that the day will come at some point when the number of ships that the China Coast Guard can send to the Senkaku Islands exceeds those from the Japan Coast Guard and China exercises regional administrative control. Will this end the U.S. obligation to protect Japan? That is not the case. The United States must clearly explain the importance of the Senkaku Islands. It needs to send a message that 'China cannot just unilaterally disregard regional orders that it does not like'" (morning edition of the Yomiuri Shimbun on March 19, 2014).

While it was thought that Vice President Biden had strong interest in the rebalance policy for Asia in the second Obama government, he mentioned a "new major power relationship" multiple times in various meetings with the Chinese leadership, including his comment to Chinese President Xi that "you are trying to advance a frank and constructive new relationship (with the United States)" on December 4, 2013 in his visit after establishment of the ADIZ. Vice President Biden directly communicated concern about the ADIZ to President Xi, but the UK-based Guardian reported in its online edition that "Mr. Biden praised President Xi's skill in harmonizing differences between the United States and China."

An official at Japan's Ministry of Foreign Affairs commented that "Having heard Rice's comments, China saw that the U.S. would not come out strongly against establishment of the ADIZ prior to the visit by Vice President Biden" and took the view that the Obama administration's ambiguous stance is giving China room to maneuver. A Southeast Asian foreign policy source in Tokyo noted that "this was a victory for China."

Toshihiro Nakayama, a professor at Keio University who specializes in U.S. politics and foreign policy, notes that "The United States does not have a concept of attaching itself to one side. It takes the approach of building positive relations with China while strengthening relations with allies to address risk," but also expresses dissatisfaction about "the lack of clarity about what is at the core of the Obama administration's message."

Kenichiro Sasae, the Japanese Ambassador to the United States, made an unusual request regarding the U.S. stance at a symposium in Washington D.C. on January 29, 2014.

"The United States should clarify who it deems to be a friend and who it thinks is a troublemaker."

Heavy wave of cutbacks in defense spending

Cutbacks in defense spending are casting a major shadow on security policy in the United States, and concerns have emerged in Japan and ASEAN countries about whether the U.S. government might be unable to sufficiently carry through with the rebalance policy.

Mandatory spending cutbacks, which force reductions of 1-2 trillion dollars during the 2013-2021 fiscal years if the U.S. Congress could not agree on fiscal restructuring measures, were triggered in March 2013. National defense spending cutbacks account for about 500 billion dollars of the total amount, or just over 40%.

Defense Secretary Hagel bluntly acknowledged at a press conference on February 24, 2014 that defense cutbacks would affect an air carrier that is symbolic of the U.S. military's deterrence capability in his comment that

"We can sustain 11 air carriers if the President's budget passes. However, we would need to retire the George Washington air carrier ahead of planned repairs if mandatory budget cutbacks continue through the 2016 fiscal year."

The QDR announced on March 4 also confirmed the possibility of the U.S. not having sufficient deterrence and fighting capabilities in the future with its comment that "Cutbacks on the scale of mandatory reductions would create serious risk for the Defense Department's ability to fully succeed in force deployment and conflicts. The Defense Department would have less deterrence and confront issues in rapid destruction of the enemy in major battles." It then notes that continuation of defense spending cutbacks "would leave the U.S. military too small and not modern enough to implement our defense strategy through 2021."

While the Defense Department naturally highlighted negative scenarios for the future in an effort to maintain the budget, it remains true that budget cutbacks reduce the frequency of equipment that can be purchased and training. Buck McKeon, a Republican who chaired the U.S. House Committee on Armed Services, explained that rebalancing in the Asia-Pacific region "simply means less reduction of defense spending than other areas and does not involve additional allocation of resources." Continuation of defense spending cutbacks is likely to have a serious impact on forward deployments of the U.S. military.

Meanwhile, China's 2014 defense budget (just the central government's portion) announced at the second meeting of the 2th National People's Congress of the People's Republic of China on March 5, the day after the QDR release, continued to increase spending at a double-digit pace with a 12.2% year-on-year increase to 808.230 billion yuan (roughly 13.4 trillion yen). China has expanded the budget by about fourfold over the past 10 years. While the total amount is about one-quarter of the U.S. defense budget, the U.S. Defense Department indicates that the actual size is about 1.3 to two times larger than the disclosed value because China does not include weapon procurement costs and other spending in its defense budget.

Prime Minister Li Keqiang commented in the report that "the budget strengthens preparations for peacetime conflicts and management and control of national borders, territorial waters, and airspace defense," presenting a policy of accelerating efforts to secure maritime and air superiority in the East China Sea, including the Senkaku Islands where it has a stand-off with Japan, and the South China Sea.

Air Sea Battle

Given these conditions, the power balance in the Asia-Pacific region is likely to increasingly change in China's favor over time. What strategy does the United States plan to take in order to win against an emerging China?

The first one presented was the Air Sea Battle concept. The Defense Department began Air Sea Battle research in 2009, and it became widely known through a report issued by the Center for Strategic and Budgetary Assessments (CSBA), a think tank that is close to the Defense Department, in May 2010. The CSBA report described air bombing of missile launch sites from outside of the A2AD zone to acquire access (arrival means) for the U.S. military as a strategy against China's development of an A2AD zone that consists of anti-ship ballistic missiles (ASBM) and other high-precision ballistic missiles and stealth bombers. It emphasized development of new long-range bombers and other long-range attack power.

Concerns surfaced in Japan, which is located within range of China's ballistic missiles, after the CSBA report's disclosure and amid acceleration of U.S. efforts to establish operational sites for U.S. military forces in Guam and Southeast Asia as part of the policy of rebalancing to the Asia-Pacific region that "The U.S. military appears to be envisioning initial removal of air carriers to outside the A2AD when an event occurs and return after it conducts long-range bombing."

However, subsequent reviews within the Defense Department transformed the Air Sea Battle concept. The first official document disclosed by the Defense Department in May 2013 removes direct mention of China with the assertion that "the operation plan and strategy do not envision a specific region or enemy," but calls for a broader response than the CSBA report on the basis that securing freedom of action in all fields (air, maritime, ground, space, and cyber) would improve the operational advantage in a scenario of an attack by the enemy without advance warning.

CSBA Vice President Jim Thomas offered the following explanation of the current state of the Air Sea Battle concept in an interview with the Yomiuri Shimbun.

U.S. Military strategy against China

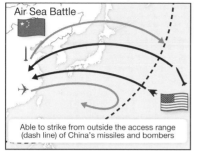

Able to strike from outside the access range (dash line) of China's missiles and bombers

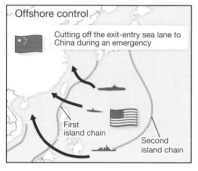

"The United States had a relatively easy time deploying force over the past few decades. It was able to send air carriers across the ocean to the coast of the other country or to use a nearby base to conduct operations. However, this might become tougher in the future because of the challenge from anti-ship missiles and advanced air defense systems.

In particular, China's People's Liberation Army has been modernizing its military power over the past 15 years with focus on a "strategy of preventing interventions" that makes it difficult for external forces to intervene in the western Pacific region and ensures heavy sacrifices.

My colleagues and I formulated a concept for use as the basis of discussion in 2010, and the Defense Department and allies have entered a stage of devising ways to carry out this concept.

The concept has six main aspects at this point – 1) ability to jointly conduct operations in the enemy's A2AD zone, 2) ability to handle duties at long distances outside of the A2AD zone, including reconnaissance, bombing, and space and cyberspace activities, 3) establishment of A2AD zones in allied countries that provide a safe area for the U.S. military to conduct operations, 4) ability to carry out operations in peripheral areas that can inflict losses on the enemy, 5) "deceptive operations" that incapacitate the enemy's command, control, communications, computing, information, monitoring, and reconnaissance capabilities, and 6) utilization of coast guards and other quasi-military capabilities to combat low-grade threats (besides high-grade threats with the latest weaponry). It is important to consider the balance and priority of these abilities." (Yomiuri Shimbun's morning edition on March 15, 2014).

Offshore control

The Air Sea Battle concept received criticism because it requires massive funds to develop new equipment, such as new long-range bombers, amid a trend of cutting defense costs and long-range bombing of the enemy could drive the enemy into expansion of the war.

The offshore control strategy of curtailing China with the threat of cutting off export and import routes for energy and industrial products with the cooperation of allies hence emerged as an alternative approach in 2012.

Thomas Hammes, a distinguished research fellow at the Center for Strategic Research of the Institute for National Strategic Studies, who proposed this strategy, gave the following explanation of offshore control in an interview with the Yomiuri Shimbun.

"Offshore control does not contain China. Countries worldwide, including Japan and the United States, want to trade with China. The strategy sends a message to China that we will engage in trade as long as China upholds international law and does not threaten friends. However, the deterrence comes in demonstrating that damage can be inflicted in the Chinese economy if necessary.

Restraining an enemy requires the ability to stop breathing in area of value to the enemy. This means shutting down sea lanes in China's case. A blockade at the first island chain that connects Kyushu, Okinawa, Taiwan, and the Philippines could strike at a weakness in the Chinese economy. China must pass through the first island chain in order to conduct trade, and we have a major geographical advantage.

China's Communist Party uses economic growth to justify its control. It would lose this economic growth if exports are halted. Would China try to take the Senkaku Islands even if it faced the possibility of an economic blockade?

While China is rapidly strengthening its military power, the United States and Japan are capable of blocking the first island chain even today with their existing military power. In contrast to the Air Sea Battle concept, offshore control does not require high-priced investments in bombers and other equipment and is not affected by fiscal conditions." (Yomiuri Shimbun's morning edition on March 16, 2014).

However, there is criticism of the offshore control strategy too, including the difficulty of building an international containment network around massive China and the prospect of China finding openings as well as abandonment of hegemonic stability from maintaining military supremacy because it does not incorporate an attack on mainland China. Offshore control also has not gained much traction in the U.S. military because it is not adopted by the Defense Department.

In any case, even the United States lacks a clear answer to the A2AD strategy adopted by China, which is steadily expanding its military. This reality is contributing as well to worries in Japan and Southeast Asia.

Chinese Communist Party's intentions are unclear

A fishing boat carrying Chinese activists collides with a Japan Coast Guard ship in waters around the Senkaku Islands, and the activists get onto the Senkaku Islands.

This was a simulation for the response by the U.S. government in a Senkaku crisis conducted by the Washington D.C.-based Center for Strategic and International Studies (CSIS) in November 2013.

"A missile base in mainland China sets its target in the direction of the Senkaku Islands and the press secretary for the People's Liberation Army announces that 'we have designated the 12 nautical miles around the Diaoyu Islands as exclusionary waters and demand that ships from other countries leave.'"

"It is necessary to let China know that this behavior goes beyond the acceptable range. The U.S. absolutely cannot accept establishment of a zone of 12 nautical miles."

"Let's dispatch the Nimitz-class air carrier heading from San Diego to the Middle East."

"Is the Middle East theater fine?"

"The problem right now is the Senkaku Islands. This is a matter related to U.S. national interests. It is necessary to act now."

Richard Armitage, a former Deputy Secretary of State, and other former senior government officials played Defense Secretary, State Secretary, and other officials in a tense exchange for over one and a half hours.

After it finished, the participants commented that "we must devise our response in a position of not knowing the intentions of Chinese leaders" and "official dialogue channels with the Chinese side are very limited." They agreed that the lack of understanding of the aims of China's core officials is a major problem.

It is normal to gauge the true aim of foreign policy authorities in other countries when a crisis occurs by making contact with foreign policy officials in the counterpart country to find out whether it was an accident or an organized action approved by the government's core leaders. This method might not work in China's case.

While China has a Foreign Ministry that is comparable to the U.S. State Department and Japan's Ministry of Foreign Affairs, "it is simply an entity for carrying out policy decided by the Chinese Communist Party" (Ministry of Foreign Affairs official). Foreign Minister Wang Yi is just one member on the Community Party's Central Committee with 205 members and is not even a member of the 25 people in the Politburo that constitutes the party leadership.

In fact, the Japanese Embassy in Beijing contacted the Chinese Foreign Ministry on November 23, 2013 when China's Defense Ministry announced the establishment of the ADIZ in the East China Sea, but it provided little help and the Foreign Ministry representative just responded that "we do not know because this is not our jurisdiction."

Who decides China's foreign policy? The Party's Central Foreign Affairs Leading Group makes important decisions on foreign policy, and the Party's Central Military Affairs Committee handles military decisions. President Xi chairs the Central Foreign Affairs Leading Group, Prime Minister Li is the deputy chairman, and State Councilor Yang Jiechi is the head secretary, as of February 2014. Members include the Foreign Minister, the Public Security Minister, the Defense Minister, and the Deputy Chief of the General Staff. The Central Military Affairs Committee is also chaired by President Xi, a military person serves as the deputy chair, and members includes the Defense Minister, the Chief of the General Staff, and Navy and Air Force Commanders. These are party entities, and it is difficult for U.S. and Japanese foreign policy and defense authorities to contact these organizations in emergency situations. Discussions in these bodies are completely obscured from the outside.

Utilization of individual foreign policy situations as part of power struggles within the Communist Party also complicates foreign policy with China. Former Prime Minister Yasuhiro Nakasone disclosed in his book "Tenchi Yujo [Mercy in the Heaven and on Earth]" (published by Bungeishunju) that he decided to stop visiting Yasukuni Shrine after his 1985 visit because "there was danger that Communist Party General Secretary Hu Yaobang (who was favorable to Japan) might be purged due to my Yasukuni Shrine visit."

The threat of a harmonious stance toward Japan being used as material for attacks from political adversaries continues today. A European diplomat in Tokyo familiar with Chinese politics sees the position of President Xi in the following way.

"President Xi faces risk of being attacked by rivals if he meets with Prime Minister Abe. He probably thinks that it is better to aggravate the relationship."

Little progress toward creating a mechanism for crisis management

There has been talk about the need to create a "crisis management mechanism" that sets up communication methods and other rules ahead of time in order to prevent an accidental incident from escalating into a military conflict amid China's increasingly threatening behavior related to the Senkaku Islands.

"My father often said that 'There is only one thing worse than a planned clash. That is an unplanned clash.' This is because of the much higher possibility of misinterpretations and mistakes in the latter."

Vice President Biden made this comment at a joint press conference with Prime Minister Abe on December 3, 2013 when he was visiting Japan and indicated that he would encourage Chinese leaders to establish a crisis management mechanism, or channel for necessary dialogue, between Japan and China at his next destination in China.

However, establishment of a crisis management mechanism is easier said than done.

Prime Minister Abe and then-Prime Minister Wen Jiabao agreed to create a "contact mechanism" between Chinese and Japanese defense authorities to prevent an unexpected maritime event in April 2007 during the first Abe Cabinet, but detailed discussion did not advance.

Even in the U.S. case, while it signed the Military Maritime Consultative Agreement (MMCA) with China in January 1998, the mechanism was not effective at the time of the collision between a U.S. naval plane and a Chinese fighter plane in the South China Sea in April 2001 and obstruction of a U.S. Navy surveillance ship in the South China Sea in March 2009.

Michelle Fournoy, the Under Secretary of Defense for Policy who handled senior official defense negotiations with China for the U.S. side in the first Obama administration, criticized the Chinese response, "We tried to use the MMCA, but the Chinese side was not enthusiastic. There is a mechanism, though China has almost no interest in following it." (morning edition of the Yomiuri Shimbun on February 4, 2014).

New defense guidelines targeting the Senkaku Islands

MierCn, a well-known Chinese military affairs site, proposed measures for the Chinese government against Japan in the ongoing conflict over the Senkaku Islands on December 6, 2013.

- Shoot down planes or sink ships that enter the waters or airspace around the Diaoyu Islands without approval from the Chinese government
- Encourage high-volume travel by Chinese people to the Diaoyu Islands
- Plan a missile exercise in the waters around the Diaoyu Islands within a few days and give notification to international community
- Indefinitely suspend all negotiations with Japan related to the Diaoyu Islands and declare the Okinawa Trough as the division line between China and Japan
- Prepare for mid-range missile attacks on mainland Japan

While the author is unclear, the content resembles steps proposed for the Senkaku Islands and South China Sea in 2012 by Rear Admiral Luo Yuan, who is the Vice Secretary of China Association of Military Science. Luo Yuan is a spokesman-like presence for the military who was previously Assistant Director of the Global Military Affairs Research Division at the

People's Liberation Army's Academy of Military Science, a military think tank. It was thought that authorities were using Luo Yuan's comments to gauge domestic and overseas reactions. Japanese defense experts focused on the proposals as "indicating one of China's policy options."

The United States also thinks that the possibility of China taking the Senkaku Islands has materialized. Captain James Fanell, the Assistant Chief of Staff of the U.S. Pacific Fleet's Information and Intelligence Operations, discussed China's training for a scenario of invading the Senkaku Islands in fall 2013 at a meeting organized by a naval-related organization held in California on February 13, 2014 and stressed that "We concluded that the People's Liberation Army was given a duty of conducting a quick battle to destroy the Self-Defense Forces in the East China Sea and take the Senkaku Islands."

"We need to make changes so that the Self-Defense Forces can defend the Senkaku Islands by itself without relying on the United States."

This is the instruction that Prime Minister Abe delivered to Defense Ministry officials in June 2013 for formulation of new defense plan guidelines (Defense Guidelines) and the five-year Medium Term Defense Program starting from fiscal 2014.

The Defense Ministry implemented a highly confidential assessment of Self-Defense Force capabilities for multiple emergency situations, such as an invasion of the Senkaku Islands by the Chinese military, an event involving Taiwan, and a missile attack by North Korea, in its formulation of the new Defense Guidelines. It assigned scores to equipment and capabilities of the Self-Defense Forces and counterpart countries, and conducted a computer analysis assuming no assistance from the U.S. military.

The results were "terrible" (Defense Ministry official). For the Senkaku Islands, they showed significant shortages in the Self-Defense Force fighting power and transport capabilities and indicated that it would be difficult to take back the islands. This exercise demonstrated that Japan would be unable to withstand a Chinese invasion with its own resources. Defense Minister Onodera was speechless and clearly shocked upon seeing the results.

The Defense Ministry listed the following issues that require strengthening in order to defend the Senkaku Islands and other distant islands in its "interim report on a review of the format of defense capabilities" prepared

on July 26 in light of the outcome.
- Airplane quality
- Fighting and patrolling capability in the air
- Anti-submarine patrolling capability
- Anti-ship missiles
- Transport capability
- Supply site development
- Amphibious troops

Japan's defense budget, however, is limited, and Minister Onodera lamented that "many areas still need to be addressed."

The Medium Term Defense Program completed at the year-end stated that "Japan needs to give priority to building defense capabilities that reliably support maritime and air supremacy vital to realizing deterrence and responding to various situations, including the reinforcement of defense capabilities in the southwestern area."

Change to an emphasis on "protecting the South"

Japan's defense plans focused for many years on "protecting the North" by having Ground Self-Defense Force tank regiments halt a landing operation in Japan by the former Soviet Union. The latest Defense Guidelines hence signified a major shift to emphasis on "protecting the South" by defending islands against the Chinese threat.

This major shift has shown up in budget ratios for key equipment (contract basis; excluding personnel costs and other fixed expenses) for the three Self-Defense Forces (Ground, Maritime, and Air).

In the fiscal 2014 initial budget, the Maritime Self-Defense Force retained a top position at 43.0% (379.8 billion yen), while the Ground Self-Defense Force dropped to 25.6% (226.2 billion yen) as its downward trend accelerates. The latter has been confronting budget curtailment since the Cold War ended and slipped to the lowest percentage among the three Self-Defense Forces as the Air Self-Defense, which had been in the lowest position for about 25 years, moved ahead at 31.4% (277.5 billion yen).

A key driver of the steep increase in the Air Self-Defense Force budget was the shock of the territorial air intrusion in airspace above the Senkaku

Islands by a propeller plane from China's State Oceanic Administration in December 2012. Airspace for the Senkaku Islands is located in a blind spot of terrestrial radar, and the Air Self-Defense Force allowed the violation of territorial air without detecting the Chinese plane ahead of time. Japan thus decided to allocate budget resources mainly to strengthening its warning and monitoring capabilities, such as permanent operation of an airborne early warning E2C with radar capabilities.

For warning and monitoring, the U.S. military plans to deploy the Global Hawk unmanned reconnaissance plane operating from a base in Guam to the U.S. military base in Misawa (Aomori Prefecture) from 2014. The Global Hawk has excellent capabilities for monitoring over a broad area from a high altitude of over 18,000 meters. It can operate for more than 32 hours at a time, a much longer period than manned planes. It photographed images of damage at the time of the Great East Japan Earthquake by flying from Guam to Japan's airspace without taking off from or landing at bases in Japan.

The Ground Self-Defense Force, which has been facing budget cutbacks, decided to proceed with a rollout of the MV22 Osprey, a new transport vehicle. While it lacked enthusiasm because of "likely cutbacks to budgets for tanks and other existing equipment" (according to an official), the Defense Ministry's non-uniformed leaders (Internal Bureau) promoted the rollout in line with the Prime Minister's Office interest in adding an important tool for island defense.

However, the government has not substantially increased the defense budget. The fiscal 2014 defense budget only rose by 0.8% (about 40 billion yen) excluding increases in personnel costs and other obligatory spending, and defense officials are highly concerned.

"The military balance between Japan and China will collapse unless Japan enhances its facilities in line with China's military expansion. A war is likely to occur if Japan gives China the impression that it can 'win'."

This is the concern expressed by Tomohide Murai, a professor at the National Defense Academy who covers international affairs.

Lacks the power to "retake outlying islands"

Roughly 10 rubber boats headed toward the shore off the coast of San Diego in the Pacific on a night in late January 2014 and eight men from each boat entered the cold ocean without making noise and quickly moved onto land.

This was the Iron Fist joint field-training exercise conducted by Japan and the U.S. at the Coronado Naval base in California. It was a training exercise for a secret landing on an outlying island occupied by an enemy.

The training lasted through February 24, and around 270 people from the Western Army Infantry Regiment (Light) (based in Sasebo, Nagasaki), who are likely to have the role of "retaking remote islands" from the Group Self-Defense Force, and other forces participated along with U.S. Marines.

Lieutenant Colonel Kenji Hamamatsu, a company leader for the Western Army Infantry Regiment, spoke positively about the exercise, "We confirmed technical movements and troop flow and learned from the knowhow of U.S. Marines with an understanding of real battles."

While neither country (Japan/U.S.) will offer official acknowledgement, this exercise envisions an occupation of the Senkaku Islands in Okinawa Prefecture by China. The rubber boat landing is an essential activity for dispatching a forward team to conduct reconnaissance, such as intelligence gathering prior to issuance of a public safety operation order (Self-Defense Forces Act Article 79, Point 2).

Japan decided to create the Amphibious Rapid Deployment Brigade, similar to the U.S. Marines, in the new Defense Guidelines and Medium Term Defense Program formulated at the end of 2013. It also plans to deploy 52 amphibious vehicles that can accommodate 3,000 troops. The brigade is a key component in defining the Senkaku Islands and will mainly consist of 700 troops from the Western Army Infantry Regiment.

Defense Minister Onodera toured a landing exercise by the Western Army Infantry Regiment at the Ground Self-Defense Forces' Camp Ainoura in Sasebo (Nagasaki Prefecture) on March 2, 2014.

Troops jumped from the Ground Self-Defense Forces' CH47 transport helicopters flying low just above the water surface into 12-degree water, swam to the shore, and conducted a landing operation while securing the site's safety. Mr. Onodera, who watched with a sense of satisfaction, emphasized to the press corps that "Japan has many outlying islands and island areas. These islands are the foundation of Japan's exclusionary economic zone that is the sixth largest in the world, and it is important to continue defending these outlying islands. We have newly created the Amphibious Rapid Deployment Brigade, and this exercise confirmed that the Western Army Infantry Regiment will have a central role."

Reception by military experts, however, has been more realistic: "The capabilities of Ground Self-Defense Forces in operations to retake remote islands is not even close to those of the U.S. Marines."

Amphibious operations that involve landing from the sea to take back land are likely to result in major losses unless safety is ensured at the landing point. This requires assistance in removing enemies with firepower from planes and ships.

The U.S. Marines have their own air regiment and also operate jointly with the Navy in peacetime. The III Marine Expeditionary Force (3MEF) stationed in Okinawa carries out operations together with the fighter plane regiment at the Iwakuni Base and Navy ships, such as Sasebo's amphibious assault ship and Yokosuka's nuclear-powered air carrier.

The Self-Defense Forces, meanwhile, intend to separately manage the Amphibious Rapid Deployment Brigade under the Ground Self-Defense Force, fighter planes under the Air Self-Defense Force, and transport ships and destroyers under the Maritime Self-Defense Force. Weapon procurement and training are handled autonomously too. The Defense Guidelines presented an image of "integrated rapid deployment defense capabilities" that jointly operates the three Self-Defense Forces, but this is likely to take some time.

For example, when Self-Defense Forces headed to the Philippines to provide assistance after heavy damage from a typhoon in November 2013, it needed two days to dissemble Ground Self-Defense Force helicopters for loading on a Maritime Self-Defense Force transport ship and then another two days for assembly at the destination. Rotors on Ground Self-Defense Force helicopters cannot be folded, and it is necessary to remove the rotor for loading and then reattach it at the destination. This does not work well for island defense. The U.S. Marine Osprey can fold rotors with the flip of a switch.

Image of retaking remote islands

Fighter planes

Landing by the transport aircraft Osprey

Air strikes

Air strikes
(attack helicopters)

Enemy

Landing by helicopter

Naval bombardment

Military transport vessel

Escort vessel

Landing by amphibious vehicle

Landing by boat

When the Self-Defense Forces were dispatched to Izu Oshima (Oshima-cho, Tokyo) affected by heavy rains from Typhoon No.26 in October 2013, they unloaded goods from an LCAC hover-craft air cushion boat also used in operations to retake outlying islands because the port was not accessible, but Ground Self-Defense Force could not utilize the planned beach site from pre-typhoon research, and the operation took longer than expected.

Japan does not have field exercise sites for full-fledged training of an island retrieval operation jointly utilizing ground, maritime, and air forces. In January 2014, the Self-Defense Forces conducted an island retrieval exercise by treating the Ground Self-Defense Force's Narashino training site (Chiba Prefecture) as the island. The exercise used a scenario of the Ground Self-Defense Force's 1st Airborne Brigade in wetsuits parachuting into the area deemed to be the ocean and type-10 tanks, which cannot be transported to outlying islands, overpowering the enemy troops.

While the Defense Ministry wants to conduct exercises comparable to actual battles at the field exercise site in Guam that is being built as part of the transfer of U.S. Marines to Guam, it must wait at least a few years until the site is ready.

An official at the Defense Ministry acknowledged that "We do not have adequate equipment or training even for joint exercises with the U.S. Marines. This is the reality faced from not having envisioned integrated operation and actual battles in past years."

The Self-Defense Force has just begun the process of "conversion to a marine-type force," but reality might not wait.

Grey zone of outlying island defense

Japan's legal framework is also not ready for outlying island defense.

One hundred and six Chinese fishing boats filled Arakawa fishing port on the Goto Islands (Nagasaki Prefecture) located on the East China Sea at one point in July 2012. While they came to the port to seek refuge from a typhoon, fishing boats flying Chinese flags converged on the same inlet. Minoru Kubo, the director of the mayor's office of Goto city, recalled that it was "an unusual sight."

Even though the outward reason was "refuge," Tetsuo Kotani, a senior fellow at the Japan Institute of International Affairs, suggests that "This was a practice exercise for an invasion of the Senkaku Islands by China. Some fishing boats carry militia and armored vehicles. They tested a scenario of landing militia and armored vehicles using an opening that Japan could not halt."

Japan cannot activate self-defense rights through defense actions unless there is an "organized and planned exercise of armed force" (armed attack) against Japan. It is widely held that Japan would have difficulty issuing a defense action order to combat an "armed attack" if China utilized fishing boats in this manner to land on the Senkaku Islands. While the government can utilize the Self-Defense Force for safety action if policing force is not enough (Article 78 of the Self-Defense Forces Act), police-style weapon use, such as legitimate self-defense, is the principle. Weapon use is allowed "within the range deemed reasonably necessary to handle the situation" as an exception to deal with groups armed with semi-automatic rifles, machine guns, rapid-fire weapons, chemical weapons, biological weapons, or other means (Article 90 of the Self-Defense Forces Act). Yet it is generally thought that this is not enough for remote island defense. Some government officials note that "a safety action cannot be ordered because outlying islands lack public safety that needs protection."

The government refers to incidents in which it cannot order a defense action because of the inability to immediately determine that an armed attack has taken place as "grey-zone situations." The Advisory Panel on Reconstruction of the Legal Basis for Security, a panel of experts chaired by former Ambassador to the United States Shunji Yanai, cited the need for redefining the legal basis in a report submitted to the Prime Minister on May 15, 2014. Legal framework changes are a pressing issue because of growing intimidation toward the Senkaku Islands.

Additionally, the U.S. military might not immediately come to Japan's assistance in a grey-zone situation because its obligation to defend Japan under Article 5 of the Japan-U.S. Security Treaty only applies to issuance of a defense action order by Japan. Guidelines for Japan-U.S. defense cooperation that detail burden-sharing by the Self-Defense Forces and U.S. military do not contain clear provisions on the type of assistance the U.S. military will provide in grey-zone situations and simply mention "obtaining suitable assistance from the U.S. military depending on the situation." In other words, there is leeway for the Chinese side to think that "it might be possible to take the Senkaku Islands in a way so that the U.S. military cannot intervene."

Satoshi Morimoto, a research professor at Takushoku University who served as Defense Minister during the Democratic Party of Japan's administration period, commented on BS Nippon TV's "Japan In-depth" program on February 4, 2014 in light of a discussion of the difference in capabilities between the U.S. Marines and Self-Defense Forces that "We cannot rule out the possibility of China trying to take effective control of the Senkaku Islands by landing in a manner that finds an opening in Japanese laws and avoids military intervention by the U.S. military."

COLD WAR BETWEEN JAPAN AND CHINA

Guideline revisions taking into account the Senkaku Islands

Revisions to the guidelines for Japan-U.S. defense cooperation will be a key point for how the Japanese and U.S. governments respond to this type of "worst-case situation."

The Japanese and U.S. governments agreed to revise the guidelines by the end of 2014 in a meeting of the Japan- United States Security Consultative Committee (2+2), which is comprised of foreign affairs and defense minis-ters, in October 2013. The Japanese side wanted the revisions to clarify the content of assistance by the U.S. military in the case that China tried to take the Senkaku Islands and "send a strong message to curtail adventurism by China" (Self-Defense Forces source).

The current guidelines were revised in 1997, and renewed revisions are a major initiative for the first time in 17 years.

The guidelines were initially formulated in 1978. The main aim at that time during the Cold War between the United States and the Soviet Union was combating an invasion of Japan by the former Soviet Union and thereby defending Japan. The 1997 revisions added a model of Japan-U.S. cooperation for peripheral events, in addition to an attack on Japan, in light of the former Soviet Union's collapse in 1991 and the Korean Peninsula crisis related to North Korea's development of nuclear weapons in 1994.

It appears that the guidelines need to be updated about once every 20 years in accordance with security conditions in Japan at the respective times. The latest revisions are likely to focus on dealing with China as it rapidly expands military strength and pursues maritime activities and bolstering the Japan-U.S. alliance in new areas such as outer space and cyberspace.

However, discussions between Japan and the U.S. based on the 2-plus-2 agreement did not move forward as anticipated because of major delays in planned efforts by the Japanese side to update constitutional interpretations and the legal framework regarding the exercise of collective self-defense and grey-zone situations.

The outlook at the timing of the 2-plus-2 meeting envisioned issuance of a report on new constitutional interpretations by the Advisory Panel on Reconstruction of the Legal Basis for Security during 2013 and statements by the government on the new interpretations and legal framework by the end of the year. However, the Advisory Panel needed until May 2014 to finalize the report, and this delayed the government's schedule for updating its constitutional interpretation by a half year from the initial plan.

The Self-Defense Force's operation for retaking the Senkaku Islands from the enemy cannot be decided until the government makes decisions on the new constitutional interpretation and legal framework. This obviously delayed decisions on the content of assistance from the U.S. military.

The Japanese government has maintained a constitutional interpretation regarding collective self-defense, which defines the right of using force to stop an attack on a country closely related to the home country, even if there is no direct attack on the home country, that it "possesses the right but cannot exercise it." Japan's Self-Defense Forces therefore cannot help a U.S. military ship being attacked in international waters around the Senkaku Islands even if a Self-Defense Force ship is located in the vicinity. This constraint could lead to undermining of the Japan-U.S. alliance that is at the core of Japan's national security framework.

The U.S. side was expecting an expansion of the Japanese role-sharing that contributes to reduction of defense costs through the revisions. Specifically, it anticipated a significant expansion of Self-Defense Force assistance during an event on the Korean Peninsula. This required revision of Japan's constitutional interpretation to allow for exercise of a collective self-defense right. The U.S. lacked incentive to aggressively advance revisions to the guidelines unless Japan can exercise the collective self-defense right and broaden assistance to the U.S. military and responsibility for regional security.

In fact, the U.S. side unofficially told Japan in administrative-level discussions regarding revisions to the guidelines that "we would like to wait on guideline revisions until this process finishes because of the importance of updates to Japan's constitutional interpretation."

The guideline revisions entail lengthy reviews with face-to-face meetings by the U.S. military and Self-Defense Forces that consist of repeated map exercises for various anticipated situations, identification of problem points, and development of new responses. Delay in the Cabinet decision on updates to the constitutional interpretation would naturally postpone completion of guideline revisions slated to be ready by the end of 2014. China is the only nation who would be pleased by this outcome. Seiichiro Takagi, a senior adjunct fellow at the Japan Institute of International Affairs with expertise in U.S.-China relations, notes that "Japan must shoulder a larger role than in the past in order to maintain the deterrence of the Japan-U.S. alliance amid cutbacks in defense costs by the United States and should make the revisions as scheduled."

How should it address the Cold War between Japan and China across the East China Sea? Japan does not have the leeway to stand idle.

Changes to the guidelines for Japan-U.S. Defense Cooperation, and points for revision

Formulated in 1978, for combating an invasion of Japan by the former Soviet Union.

Revised in 1997, to address the Korean Peninsula crisis related to North Korea's development of nuclear weapons.

Revised by the end of 2014, to address China's military expansion and increasing maritime activities.

Bolstering cooperation during unforeseen emergencies in which an armed attack is not immediately possible, such as the landing of armed Chinese fishermen on the Senkaku Islands and other actions.
- Clarifying the division of roles assuming that Japan exercises its right of collective self-defense.
- Addressing new strategic areas such as space and cyberspace
- Expanding cooperation in global fields of terrorism, anti-piracy measures, disaster support, etc.
- Promoting security cooperation with regional partners other than Japan and the U.S.

(Follow-up: The two sides reached an agreement on new guidelines in April 2015. Japan can protect US naval vessels using force even in grey-zone situations, and the US military bolstered its assistance for Self-Defense Forces. Furthermore, passage of security-related legislation in September 2015 provided limited approval of collective self-defense rights.)

Chapter 2
Senkaku Turbulence

The Senkaku Islands located in the East China Sea belong to Ishigaki City in Okinawa Prefecture. They consist of five islands (Uotsuri Island at 3.6 square kilometers, Kita Kojima at 0.26 square kilometers, Minami Kojima at 0.32 square kilometers, Kuba Island at 0.87 square kilometers, and Taisho Island at 0.04 square kilometers) and three rocks (Okinokita, Okinominami, and Tobise). Their total surface area is roughly the same size as Kawaguchi Lake in Yamanashi Prefecture.

The world's third and second largest economies (Japan and China) are clashing fiercely over these tiny islands. Territorial and maritime issues are intertwined with foreign policy, security, and a global power game as explained in the previous chapter. In this chapter, we will look more closely at developments and the background related to the Senkaku Islands.

Islands located in rough waves

The Senkaku Islands are isolated islands in distant seas. Black currents that travel from Taiwan's eastern shore change to a northeasterly direction around the islands and collide with the mainland shelf's coastal flow. While the dark green waters are rough, this is an excellent fishing area with bonito, tuna, marlin, and other fish, and fishing boats from Japan, China, and Taiwan operate in the area.

Uotsuri Island, the largest island in the Senkaku Islands, is about 170 kilometers from Ishigaki Island and roughly 410 kilometers from Okinawa's main island. It is also positioned about 330 kilometers from mainland China and 170 kilometers from Taiwan.

It has two peaks with heights of 363 meters and 327 meters, and the southern edge is a steep cliff. The island is covered in breadfruit trees, banyan trees, and other greenery and has rich springs of water suitable for drinking despite the limited amount of flat land. It was a lively spot with dried bonito processing facilities and other structures built by Japanese people during the Meiji to Taisho periods. It is still possible to see remains of the buildings from that time.

Uotsuri Island also has a sad history.

A passenger ship carrying about 180 residents of Ishigaki Island headed for Taiwan was attacked by U.S. military planes in July 1945 in the closing phase of the Second World War and drifted ashore on Uotsuri. The people faced excruciating hunger after depleting their food supply, and older and injured people steadily died. While survivors initially dug holes on the beach as graves for victims, they later resorted to just putting tree leaves on top of their bodies.

They managed to fix wreckage from a ship that drifted to the island and a group headed for Ishigaki Island. It was almost 50 days from drifting ashore until the rescue boat arrived. Roughly 120 people reportedly survived. One of the survivors explained that "the island seemed to be rejecting the presence of humans."

A memorial for the victims was built on Uotsuri after the war. However, the Japanese government, which manages the island, stopped allowing families of the victims to visit the island after China and Taiwan claimed territorial rights in order to avoid trouble. The Senkaku Islands face not only rough waves from the East China Sea, but also rough waves of international politics.

Next, we look back at developments related to Japan's possession of the Senkaku Islands.

The starting point was a survey of the Senkaku Islands conducted in 1884 by Tatsushiro Koga, who was originally from Fukuoka Prefecture and engaged in a wide range of businesses from an operation based in Naha. He confirmed that many short-tailed albatrosses, a source of feathers, lived on the islands and that the islands were also suited to obtaining fish and shellfish.

Based on the survey results, Okinawa Prefecture submitted a request to place a national marker to show that the Senkaku Islands were Japanese territory to Home Minister Aritomo Yamagata.

It took roughly 10 years thereafter, until January 1895, for the Japanese government to arrange a Cabinet decision on establishing a national marker and approve inclusion of the Senkaku Islands as part of Okinawa Prefecture. While Home Minister Yamagata, an elder statesman of the Meiji Restoration and key member of the Meiji government, wanted to approve establishment of national marker, Foreign Minister Kaoru Inoue's concern about possible trouble with China (Qing Dynasty at that time) led to the cautious response.

In light of these conditions, the Ministry of Foreign Affairs gives the following explanation in its "Basic view of territorial rights to the Senkaku Islands."

"The government conducted multiple on-site surveys of the Senkaku Islands since 1885 through authorities in Okinawa Prefecture and other methods and carefully confirmed that not only were the islands uninhabited but they did not have remains of being controlled by the Qing Dynasty. Based on this outcome, Japan passed a Cabinet decision to place a national marker on the islands and officially make them part of Japanese territory on January 14, 1895."

International law approves occupation of uninhabited land that does not belong to any other country as one's own territory if the country takes control prior to other countries. The Foreign Ministry asserted that Japan acquired the islands through occupation after confirming that they were not under the Qing Dynasty's control.

The government decided in the following year to lease four islands (Uotsuri, Kita Kojima, Minami Kojima, and Kuba) to Tatsushiro Koga at no charge for a period of 30 years in light of the Cabinet decision from January 1895.

Mr. Koga subsequently launched a variety of businesses on the islands, including albatross feather gathering, dried bonito production, and coral collection. A village was formed for the Senkaku Islands, and records indicate that 248 people lived on Uotsuri Island at the peak.

In 1932, the Japanese government sold the four islands, which had been leased, in response to a request from Zenji Koga, the son of Tatsushiro

Koga. However, all of the island's population left around 1940 ahead of the war because of dwindling supplies of ship fuel oil and other goods, and the Senkaku Islands returned to being uninhabited.

After the war ended, Japan abandoned territorial rights to Taiwan and other holdings based on the San Francisco Peace Treaty that took effect in 1952. However, the Senkaku Islands were included as part of the Nansei Islands, which are Japan's territory, and placed under U.S. administrative control along with the main Okinawa Island. The U.S. military concluded a lease contract in 1958 with Zenji Koga, who owned Kuba Island, and paid leasing fees so that it could use Kuba Island and Taisho Island as bombing training sites. The Japanese government continued to lease Kuba Island and made it available to the U.S. military along with Taisho Island, which was national land, after the return of Okinawa to the Japanese government from the U.S. in 1972.

While Zenji Koga subsequently transferred the four islands that he owned (Uotsuri, Kita Kojima, Minami Kojima, and Kuba) to an industrialist family in Saitama Prefecture from 1974 to 1988, the Japanese government leased Uotsuri, Kita Kojima, and Minami Kojima islands from the land-owner and bolstered its control over the islands in 2002 amid rising tensions between Japan and China regarding the Senkaku Islands. This arrangement put all five of the main Senkaku Islands under the national government's control and enabled the government to restrict landings by third parties and place some limits on resale of the islands.

China's unreasonable claims

"Japan must return Chinese land that it stole."

This was the coarse expression used by Chinese Prime Minister Li Keqiang on May 26, 2013 at a speech delivered on his visit to Potsdam, the old capital city in northern Germany, to call on Japan to "return" the Senkaku Islands. Why did Prime Minister Li claim that "Japan stole" the islands and what was the reason for making the claim in distant Germany?

Below, we summarize China's logic in calling for a "return" of the Senkaku Islands.

Japan stole the Senkaku Islands from China (Qing).

Japan was required to return land that it had taken as the defeated party in the Second World War.

Japan hence does not have territorial rights to the Senkaku Islands.

Potsdam was the place where the Allied Nations prepared the Postdam Declaration that called for an unconditional surrender by Japan in 1945 in the final phase of the Second World War. This declaration also called for implementation of the Cairo Declaration (1943) that clearly stated that "all areas stolen by Japan from the Qing government" should be returned to China. Potsdam was an ideal location to highlight the "unfairness" of Japan's territorial possession of the Senkaku Islands to the international community from China's perspective.

It is true that the Sino-Japanese War was taking place in January 1895 when the Japanese government added the Senkaku Islands to the country's territory. The Sino-Japanese War started in the summer of 1894, and Japan was on track to a victory by this point. However, the peace treaty, which is known as the Shimonoseki Treaty, concluded in April 1895 between Japan and the Qing Dynasty clearly states in Article 2 that the Qing Dynasty cedes Taiwan and the islands appertaining to it and the Pescadores Islands but does not include the Senkaku Islands (Ministry of Foreign Affairs, "Basic view of territorial rights to the Senkaku Islands"). Japan obtained the Senkaku Islands through occupation approved in international law and unrelated to the Sino-Japanese War. It did not "steal" the islands from China.

China only started claiming territorial rights to the Senkaku Islands in 1971, or 76 years after Japan's Cabinet decision on territorial rights. Japan concluded the San Francisco Peace Treaty with the United States and other Allied Nations in 1951 and ended the war state and regained independence in 1952. While the United States exercised administrative control of the Senkaku Islands along with Okinawa on the basis that these islands are part of Japan, China did not protest at that time.

"It is similar to a party B who walked past the home of party A suddenly claiming that it is "party B's home.""

This is how the late Akira Kotera, a professor at The University of Tokyo with expertise in international law, explained the unreasonableness of China's claims regarding territorial rights to the Senkaku Islands.

China suddenly started arguing that it had territorial rights in 1971 once the possibility of oil reserves at the bottom of the East China Sea, including the Senkaku Islands, emerged.

The United Nations Economic Commission for Asia and the Far East noted in a report issued in 1969 that "the shallow seabed extending between Taiwan and Japan might become a global oil production site in the future." China's Foreign Ministry then issued a statement in December 1971 that "Diaoyu Dao (China's name for Uotsuri Island) and affiliated islands have long been Chinese territory. The Ming Dynasty already included these islands in China's maritime defense zone, and they were part of islands belonging to Taiwan rather than the Ryukyus (current-day Okinawa)." Taiwan similarly issued a Foreign Ministry statement in June 1971 claiming the Senkaku Islands as territory.

However, many materials exist on the Chinese side that acknowledge the Senkaku Islands being part of Japan. The People's Daily, the Chinese Communist Party's newspaper, wrote on January 8, 1953 that "The Ryukyu Islands are located in the sea extending from the northeastern part of Taiwan (China) to the southwestern part of Kyushu and consist of the seven island chains of the Senkaku Islands, Sakishima Islands, Daito Islands, Okinawa Islands, Oshima Islands, Tokara Islands, and Osumi Islands. In 1920, the Republic of China's Nagasaki Consular-General sent a letter of gratitude to Japanese people who helped Chinese fishing boat that drifted ashore to Uotsuri Island in the Senkaku Islands that specified "the Imperial Japan's Senkaku Islands in Yaeyama, Okinawa."

The San Francisco Peace Treaty with the United States and other Allied Nations finalized Japanese territory after the Second World War. The Cairo Declaration and Potsdam Declaration, meanwhile, are just unilateral political documents issued by the Allied Nations during the war and do not ultimately determine Japan's land as a result of the war. The Japanese government indicated that "Taiwan and the Pescadores Islands" to which it abandoned territorial rights in Article 2 (b) of the San Francisco Peace Treaty does not include the Senkaku Islands. In fact, Japan's possession of the Senkaku Islands was not a problem in the treaty negotiations process.

The Japanese government uses this fact as the basis for its assertion that the Senkaku Islands are clearly part of Japan and it does not have territorial issues with foreign countries. The government's explanation text from May

18, 2012 contains the following statement.

"There are no doubts historically and in international law that the Senkaku Islands are an inherent part of Japan, and Japan currently exercises effective control of the islands. This means that no territorial rights problem needing resolution exists for the Senkaku Islands."

However, some Japanese people have expressed understanding for China's claim. Yukio Hatoyama, a former Prime Minister, is an example.

Mr. Hatoyama visited China in January 2013 after resigning the Prime Minister's post, and held a meeting with Jia Qinglin, the Chairman of the People's Political Consultative Conference, at the Great Hall of the People in Beijing. At the meeting, Mr. Hatoyama commented that the Senkaku Islands are "contested land" and thereby acknowledged the existence of a territorial issue related to the Senkaku Islands between Japan and China, the complete opposite of the Japanese government's opinion.

Mr. Hatoyama continued to make statements that flummoxed the Japanese government. He participated in a TV program in Hong Kong in June 2013 and commented that "it is not surprising that the Chinese side thinks that they (Senkaku Islands) were stolen (by Japan)."

He applies the same basis as China. Mr. Hatoyama told reporters who congregated in front of his home in Denenchofu (Tokyo) on the night that the program was broadcast that "It is written in the Potsdam Declaration. Hokkaido, Honshu, Shikoku, and Kyushu are Japan's territory. Japan lost the war, and these areas were defined as its inherent territories."

Disagreement regarding the behind-the-scenes "postponement" concept

China's Foreign Minister Wang Yi is known as someone who is friendly with Japan in light of his excellent Japanese and experience as the Chinese Ambassador to Japan. Wang Yi has been a steady proponent of the "post-ponement" concept regarding the Senkaku Islands issues at international meetings.

He proposed the following approach in a speech to a think tank in Washington D.C. on September 20, 2013, "Chinese and Japanese leadership reached a very important agreement when they normalized the diplomatic

Japan's counterarguments against China's claims

China	Japan
The documents of the Ming and Qing Dynasty stated the area up to Kumejima Island is a part of the Ryukyus, and the Senkaku Islands west of there are included in China's maritime defense zone, and are Chinese territory.	There is no mention of the Senkaku Islands west of Kumejima Island belonging to China as it claims is evidenced in documents of the Ming and Qing Dynasty. These are utterly insufficient grounds for territorial rights.
Japan stole the Senkaku Islands from China in the First Sino-Japanese War.	From 1885, prior to the Sino-Japanese War, the Japanese government conducted numerous on-site surveys over 10 years and confirmed the Senkaku Islands were uninhabited and not under the control of the Qing Dynasty. Only after this did Japan include the Senkaku Islands into its territory.
The Potsdam Declaration (1945) and the Cairo Declaration (1943) clearly stated that "all areas stolen by Japan from the Qing government" should be returned to China. As Japan accepted these Declarations, the Senkaku Islands along with Taiwan were returned to China.	Under the the San Francisco Peace Treaty, Japan relinquished its territorial rights over Taiwan and other areas; however, this did not include the Senkaku Islands, which were under the administrative control of the United States. When Okinawa was returned to Japan in 1972, the Senkaku Islands were also returned to Japan as a part of Okinawa.
Japan refused to go public about the victory of the global antifascism war, and challenged the post-war international order.	China suddenly started arguing that it had territorial rights in 1971 once the possibility of oil reserves at the bottom of the East China Sea, including the Senkaku Islands, emerged. The actions of China protesting against the treatment of this territory, as stipulated in the San Francisco Peace Treaty, is itself a serious challenge to the post-war international order.

relationship 41 years ago. Namely, they decided to put aside this issue (Senkaku Islands) and deal with it and find a solution later on."

What is the "postponement" concept that Wang Yi references?

Japan and China established diplomatic relations in 1972, and this theory asserts that the two countries agreed to "postpone" efforts to reach a decision related to the conflict on territorial rights to the Senkaku Islands in the negotiations. Japan broke this agreement when the Japanese government acquired ownership of the Senkaku Islands in 2012, and this is the basis for the criticism that "Japan is responsible for disrupting the relationship between the two countries."

Deng Xiaoping, China's supreme leader in past years, spoke about "postponement" too. He gave the following comments at a press conference held at the Japan National Press Club in October 1978 during his visit to exchange instruments of ratification for the Treaty of Peace and Friendship Between Japan and the People's Republic of China.

"We refer to the Senkaku Islands as the Diaoyu Islands. The names used by the two sides are different. We promised in normalization of diplomatic relations between Japan and China that the two sides would not raise this problem. We agreed again this time in negotiations for the Treaty of Peace and Friendship Between Japan not to get into this issue."

"This issue can be temporarily put aside. Leaving it alone for 10 years is not a problem. People of our generation do not have enough knowledge. The next generation should be smarter. We should be able to discover a good format that everyone can accept at that time."

These comments by Deng Xiaoping can be read as calling for "postponing conflicts" for the sake of friendship between the two countries. However, the "postponement" concept proposed by China assumes that "territorial rights to the Senkaku Islands" are unconfirmed. Acceptance of the postponement concept "means that territorial rights with China must be negotiated and is likely to result in talk of joint management of the Senkaku Islands" (University of Tokyo Professor Akira Kotera).

China's behavior raises questions about its assertion of the existence of "an agreement to postpone the Senkaku Islands issue," particularly the Territorial Waters Act from February 1992 that designates the Senkaku Islands as China's "territory" and the surrounding area as "territorial waters." The

Act also states that "all necessary measures will be taken" toward violations of the territorial waters. China's dispatching of government ships to the area around the Senkaku Islands as patrols and repeated violations of Japan's territorial waters are measures based on this Act. While China asserts that there is an agreement to postpone the issue of territorial rights, it also passed a law that runs contrary to this stance and contributes to a change of the status quo.

However, the Japanese government's response is not without blame. While Japan protested when China enacted the Territorial Waters Act, it did not raise major diplomatic concerns following China's explanation that "This is not an attempt to take new measures, and China has not altered its existing (postponement) stance."

Japan is also paying a price of not having clearly rejected the "postponement" concept. Takakazu Kuriyama, a former Japanese Ambassador to the United States involved in negotiations to normalize diplomatic relations as the Treaty Director at the Ministry of Foreign Affairs, expressed his opinion that Japan "tacitly agreed" by not rebutting China's "postponement" approach in an article printed in Asia Jiho (December 2012 issue). Yet he also wrote that to claim the existence of a clear agreement between Japan and China related to China's "postponement" approach is overly one-sided.

The Japanese government currently states that there was no "promise to avoid the Senkaku Islands issue" as explained by Deng Xiaoping in negotiations to normalize diplomatic relations or to conclude the Peace and Friendship Treaty (government's official opinion on October 26, 2010).

However, some voices in Japan accept the "postponement" approach asserted by China as "true" and this creates complications.

A Japanese person appeared on a program aired by China's national central TV station on September 23, 2012. It was Magosaki Ukeru, a former Director General of the Ministry of Foreign Affairs' International Information Bureau and a former professor at the National Defense Academy.

Mr. Magosaki commented on Xinwen Lianbo, a news program broadcast nationwide in China, that "there was an agreement to postpone the Senkaku Islands issue (between Japan and China)." He also asserted that the Japanese government must have some aim in not admitting the agreement's existence at this stage.

What is Mr. Magosaki's basis for saying that a postponement agreement existed? In his book "Japan's Border Problems – Senkaku Islands, Takeshima, and the Northern Territories" (Chikuma Shinsho), he introduced the following transcript of a meeting between Japanese Prime Minister Kakuei Tanaka and China Prime Minister Zhou Enlai in September 1972.

(Zhou Enlai) Japan and China should overcome smaller differences by pursuing major agreements.

(Tanaka) I generally understand your point and agree with the view of removing minor obstacles and focusing on broader consensus in dealing with specific issues.

(Tanaka) What are your thoughts on the Senkaku Islands? I'm hearing various things.

(Zhou Enlai) I would rather not discuss the Senkaku Islands issue at this point. Now is not a good time for this discussion. It has become an issue because of the presence of oil. Neither Taiwan nor the United States would care without the oil."

Mr. Magosaki proceeds to write the following.

"The term postponement was not used, but the Chinese side effectively proposed a postponement and it was accepted by the Japanese side."

It would appear as if Prime Minister Tanaka accepted the postponement approach in acquiescing to the concept of "removing minor differences and focusing on major agreements" as concluded by Mr. Magosaki if this was the exchange. However, confirmation in the Japanese Politics and International Relations Database, which contains published meeting transcripts, compiled by the University of Tokyo's Institute for Advanced Studies on Asia shows that Mr. Magosaki's quotation method leads to misinterpretation.

The Tanaka-Zhou meetings took place four times over four days, and the "Japan and China should pursue major agreements…" comment by Zhou Enlai came in the first meeting on September 25, 1972, while the "agree" comment by Kakuei Tanaka emerged in the second meeting on September 26 and both comments were in discussions unrelated to the Senkaku Islands.

Kakuei Tanaka's question regarding China's thoughts about the Senkaku Islands and Zhou Enlai's "do not want to discuss" reply reflects an exchange from the third meeting on September 27. Mr. Magosaki cut and pasted portions from the transcripts of the Tanaka-Zhou meetings.

Mr. Magosaki also wrote in the same book that "The most in-depth discussion of the Senkaku Islands issue between Japan and China occurred in the meeting between Deng Xiaoping and Foreign Minister Sonoda in the Treaty of Peace and Friendship Between Japan and China negotiations. The two countries signed the treaty on August 12, 1978, and Foreign Minister Sunao Sonoda handled negotiations for the Japanese side.

Mr. Sonoda explained the following points from his meetings with Deng Xiaoping at a Lower House Foreign Affairs Committee meeting on May 30, 1979, "The Chinese side has its own opinion regarding territorial rights to the Senkaku Islands," and "He suggested that keeping things in the current state should be beneficial for Japan's own interests."

However, Mr. Sonoda stated clearly in the Lower House plenary session on the next day (May 31) that "The Senkaku Islands issue is not a condition, nor a topic, for the Treaty of Peace and Friendship Between Japan and China. We are not discussing a territorial issue."

The Ministry of Foreign Affairs (official) rejects Mr. Magosaki's assertions on the basis that "an agreement to postpone the Senkaku Islands issue between Mr. Sonoda and Mr. Deng is unlikely to have been recorded on paper."

Japan's Ministry of Foreign Affairs disclosed transcripts from the Tanaka-Zhou meetings held during September 25-28, 1972 in 2011 (though noted that they are not originals and were typed in September 1988).

The Chinese government, meanwhile, has not disclosed meeting transcripts. Yet the People's Daily reported in an article on October 12, 2012 that a record of the following exchange regarding the Senkaku Islands not disclosed by Japan's Ministry of Foreign Affairs exists.

Zhou Enlai: "Other problems are not that big. The primary issue at this point is normalization of relations between our countries. We can discuss other issues after seeing how things go."

Tanaka: "I believe other problems can be resolved once diplomatic relations are normalized."

Japan's Ministry of Foreign Affairs (official) rejected this media report stating that "this type of exchange does not exist in the Japanese records."

Some observers think that China is making a three-pronged effort to pressure Japan on the Senkaku Islands issue. It uses "public opinion tactics" by controlling opinions in China through provision of favorable information, "legislative tactics" by creating advantageous rules, and "psychological tactics" of information manipulation and intimidation that undermine the will of the counterpart. China's actions in trying to propagate the "postpone-ment" concept offer an excellent example of "public opinion tactics."

Main exchanges in a series of meetings between Japanese Prime Minister Kakuei Tanaka and Chinese Prime Minister Zhou Enlai in September 1972

Meeting 1 (September 25)

Zhou Enlai

I think it is bothersome for Japan to address the issue of bringing an end to the state of war; however, we cannot fully consent to the proposal of Foreign Minister Ōhira. If there has been no state of war since the San Francisco Peace Treaty until the present day, then although China is the concerned party here, we cannot be included in such a proposal. Japan and China should overcome smaller differences by pursuing major agreements; furthermore, the common ground between us should be incorporated into a communique.

Meeting 2 (September 26)

If the Japan-China Peace Treaty and San Francisco Peace Treaty are included in the issue of establishing diplomatic relations between both countries, it will no longer be resolvable. Recognizing this confirms Chiang Kai-shek's legitimacy and our unlawfulness.
Therefore, we have considered not seeking reparations for the sake of fostering friendly relations between the citizens of Japan and China. Although we cannot accept the stance of accepting the renunciation by Chiang Kai-shek.

Tanaka

I generally understand what Prime Minister Zhou Enlai is saying. There are numerous real issues that need to be addressed in order to normalize diplomatic relations between Japan and China.
I am extremely grateful to hear that China is not seeking reparations. I was deeply impressed by the position taken by China, which goes beyond love and hate. While I appreciate the attitude adopted by China, I should state that Japan's Diet and ruling party have some issues with it.
Nonetheless, I agree with Prime Minister Zhou Enlai's view of removing minor obstacles and focusing on a broader consensus in dealing with specific issues.

Meeting 3 (September 27)

What are your thoughts on the Senkaku Islands? I'm hearing various things.

I would rather not discuss the Senkaku Islands issue at this point. Now is not a good time for this discussion. It has become an issue because of the presence of oil. Neither Taiwan nor the United States would care without the oil."

Clashes between Japan and China begin

Just after 9am on September 7, 2010, the Japan Coast Guard's Yonakuni patrol ship discovered a Chinese fishing boat operating illegally in Japan's territorial waters around Kuba Island in the Senkaku Island chain. The fishing boat ignored orders to stop the boat and caused an unprecedented incident by ramming into the Yonakuni and the Mizuki, another patrol boat located nearby.

The patrol boats tried to stop the fishing boat by spraying water, but it did not follow the orders and a patrol boat needed to bump the fishing boat with the front portion of the boat covered with a rubber cushioning material to get it to stop.

Damage included two broken deck supports on the Yonakuni and a crack in the starboard outer panel of about three meters in length and one meter in width and a number of broken starboard supports on the Mizuki. The Japan Coast Guard detained the 41-year old Chinese captain on suspicion of interfering with the administration of public duties.

The Prime Minister's Office received a report on the incident's events right away.

The Democratic Party's Naoto Kan was Prime Minister and Yoshito Sengoku was Chief Cabinet Secretary at the time. Prime Minister Kan was engaged in a fierce election battle with former Party Secretary General Ichiro Ozawa to beg representative of the Democratic Party one week later and let Mr. Sengoku primarily deal with the incident.

The first thing the government needed to decide was how to handle the captain of the Chinese ship who was detained. Its choices were arresting the captain and taking him to trial or allowing him to return home out of consideration for the Japan-China relationship. While Japan could exhibit a strict stance domestically and outwardly if it arrested the captain, China would definitely react negatively. Opting for a political decision, meanwhile, would be criticized as a sign of "weakness" and send the wrong message to China that had been repeatedly engaging in provocative behavior.

Dealing with Chinese nationals who committed illegal behavior by the Senkaku Islands was already a troublesome issue for the Japanese government. In March 2004, when seven Chinese nationals illegally landed on Uotsuri Island and were arrested in the act by Okinawan Prefectural Police on a violation of the Immigration Control and Refugee Recognition Act (illegal entry into the country), the Junichiro Koizumi administration at the time did not prosecute the seven people and decided instead on a mandatory return based on a special case in Article 65 of the Immigration Control and Refugee Recognition Act. There was also suspicion of damages to a commemorative momentum built by a Japanese political organization on Uotsuri Island. The government reached a political decision to not look into this matter. The Democratic Party was skeptical of the Koizumi government's response and stated that they planned to pursue the matter in National Diet discussions.

What would the government do this time? Mr. Sengoku discussed a response with Minister of Land, Infrastructure, Transport and Tourism Seiji Maehara and Foreign Minister Katsuya Okada. While it could have quickly defused the situation through mandatory return of the Chinese fishing boat captain utilizing the special case in Article 65 of the Immigration Control and Refugee Recognition Act, similar to the Koizumi government, Article 65 stated in the preface that it is only applicable in the absence of other suspicions besides the Immigration Control and Refugee Recognition Act. Media sources had already reported heavy damages to patrol boats due to the incident, and the Japan Coast Guard possessed a video covering a portion of it. The Chinese boat captain's actions clearly fit under criminal obstruction of public duty implementation, and it was difficult to resolve the situation just with mandatory return.

The government finally decided to arrest the Chinese fishing boat captain in the early hours of September 8 after struggling to reach a decision. This was the first time to arrest a Chinese person for obstructing implementation of public duty related to the Senkaku Islands.

Chief Cabinet Secretary Sengoku announced the arrest of the boat captain on the morning of September 8 and emphasized "strict action based on Japanese laws." When asked by the press corps whether the decision "involved any diplomatic consideration," Chief Cabinet Secretary Sengoku decisively answered that there was none.

Although the arrested Chinese boat captain faced a strong likelihood of a trial, he protested his innocence and thereby created the need for a careful investigation. The Naha District Court approved detention of the Chinese boat captain for 10 days on September 10 and then another 10 days on September 19. The Chinese government's reactions steadily escalated as time went on.

China's State Councilor Dai Bingguo called Uichiro Niwa, Japan's Ambassador to China, for a meeting on September 12 and requested an early release of the boat captain. This was the fifth call since the incident and broke with diplomatic courtesy, as it came after midnight.

The Chinese government cancelled negotiations regarding development of oil fields in the East China Sea with the Japanese government and did not accept a Japan-China Summit Meeting that had been under review at the timing of the United Nations General Assembly in New York. Chinese Prime Minister Wen Jiaboa provided opening remarks at a meeting of Chinese people living in the United States held in New York on the night of September 21 that included remarks critical of the Japanese government saying that "the Diaoyu Islands are sacred Chinese territory and detention of the boat captain is an entirely illegal action." He also warned that "China will take further action if Japan presses ahead with behavior on its own (such as judicial proceedings for the boat captain). Japan must take all responsibility for resulting serious outcomes."

As promised, the Japanese government confronted a series of surprising news, such as suspension of new contracts for rare earths and orders to halt loading procedures.

Akihiro Oohata, the Minister of Economy Trade & Industry, clarified that China is suspending exports of rare earths to Japan at a press conference on September 24. Rare earths are precious metals that improve durability and heat resistance when mixed into metal materials and are vital to hybrid cars, LCD TVs, and other high-tech products. Chinese products accounted for a majority of rare earths traded in the market thanks to their inexpensive collection and refining costs. Slowdown in the supply might have interfered with operations at Japanese manufacturing firms.

State-run Xinhua News Agency reported an unsettling story for Japan the previous day. The Ministry of State Security officials in Shijiazhuang (Hebei) reported an investigation of four Japanese people videoing a military control zone. The four people were employees of Fujita, a construction firm, and had gone missing after sending e-mails to related people asking for "help" a few days earlier. The Japanese government adopted a calm stance on the surface staying that "it is going too far to link this case" with the fishing boat's ramming incident (Chief Cabinet Secretary Sengoku), but tensions were running high because of the possibility of a death penalty if they were deemed to be spies.

This was an example of China's escalating harassment toward Japan. Demonstrators carrying aggressive banners with comments, such as "Damn Japan," repeatedly filled the streets in China, and these conditions resulted in cancellation of many private-sector interaction events. Some reports suggested that China considered dispatching a guided missile destroyer to near the intermediate line between Japan and China in the East China Sea.

The U.S. government acted too on concerns about the growing crisis. U.S. Secretary of State Clinton clearly stated that "Article 5 of the Japan-U.S. Security Treaty applies to the Senkaku Islands" at a Japan-U.S. Foreign Ministers' Meeting held at a hotel in New York on September 23. Article 5 in the treaty is the clause that defines obligation of the United States to defend Japan. Clinton's statement meant that Japan and the United States would jointly protect the Senkaku Islands and called upon China to refrain from military activity. The Japanese government welcomed Clinton's statement. While a lack of progress on issues related to moving the U.S. Air Station Futenma had been disrupting Japan-U.S. relations, the Senkaku Islands situation ended up "providing a catalyst that reconfirmed the importance of the Japan-U.S. Security Treaty and necessity of remote island defense to many Japanese people" (Minister for National Policy Kenichiro Genba).

Prime Minister Kan, meanwhile, was increasingly frustrated at the inability to find measures to improve relations between Japan and China. He beat former Party Secretary General Ichiro Ozawa in the Democratic Party's representative election on September 14 and launched a reshuffled Cabinet. However, the administration faced risk of losing momentum if it mis-stepped in its response to the Senkaku Islands issue that was attracting strong public-opinion interest. Japan was also hosting the Asia-Pacific Economic Cooperation (APEC) Summit Meeting in Yokohama in November and would have been embarrassed as the host country if China stayed away. Prime Minister Kan angrily asked advisers whether extra-legal measures could be applied and strongly pressed Chief Cabinet Secretary Sengoku for a quick solution to the incident.

Unusual finish

The incident in which a single fishing boat significantly shook both Japan and China had a very unusual finish.

Tooru Suzuki, the Deputy Chief Prosecutor at the Naha District Prosecutor's Office, held a press conference in the afternoon of September 24 to announce the release of the detained Chinese boat captain with procedures pending.

He explained that "We decided that it does not make sense beyond this point to continue the investigation while still detaining the accused in light of the impact on the Japanese people and implications for Japan-China relations if the investigation continued with the accused still in custody."

This was an unusual expression of a policy of halting the investigation in light of Japan-China relations. Deputy Chief Prosecutor Suzuki read from a prepared paper.

At his press conference on the same evening, Chief Cabinet Secretary Sengoku explained that, "The government accepted the report on the prosecutor's conclusion at this point that it should release the detained person with procedures pending after conducting the investigation." He emphasized that it was the prosecutor's decision to release the boat captain. The boat captain was released with procedures pending in the early hours of September 25, gave a victory sign as he boarded a charter plane dispatched by the Chinese government to Ishigaki Airport, and returned to China.

The Supreme Public Prosecutor's Office in Tokyo received more than 100 complaints and protests that "it is not appropriate for the prosecutor's office to make political decisions" and "Japan is buckling to Chinese pressure." While the Chief Cabinet Secretary, a core component of the administration, had stated that Japan would "take a strict approach," the Prosecutor's Office, which is only a judicial entity, and just a regional branch (Naha district) used a highly unusual tactic aimed at ending the incident because of implications for Japan-China relations.

After some time, it became apparent that the closure was a political decision that hid behind a "prosecutor's assessment." Chief Cabinet Secretary Sengoku, who consistently explained that it was the "prosecutor's assessment," acknowledged in an interview with the media that he had been working behind the scenes with top Justice Ministry officials to secure the release of the boat captain.

A meeting took place at the Royal Palace in Brussels on the afternoon of October 4, 2010. Prime Minister Kan who attended the Asia-Europe Meeting (ASEM), met with Chinese Prime Minister Wen Jiabao for roughly 25 minutes on a seat in the hall outside of the main forum after the evening dinner reception. It was arranged as a joint request of both leaders (Japanese government official), and the leaders agreed that the current state of the Japan-China relationship was not healthy. While it was just a short meeting using English translation on both sides, it halted dissension between Japan and China for the time being.

However, the two leaders simply stuck to repeating their own principled views that the Senkaku Islands are part of their home country territory. The political decision brought the incident under control and led to a summit meeting, but the sources of conflict still remained.

Decision to "acquire ownership of the Senkaku Islands" and repercussions

There was a person who was fuming at these interactions by the Japanese and Chinese governments – Shintaro Ishihara, the Governor of Tokyo known for his hawkish stance toward China.

"I'm going to stir things up some."

This is what Mr. Ishihara stated in a speech to the Heritage Foundation, a conservative think tank, on April 16, 2012 during a visit to the United States, and then he presented his idea of having Tokyo purchase the Senkaku Islands.

"(China) claims that it has rights to the Senkaku Islands. That's ridiculous. Tokyo will buy the Senkaku Islands. While the Japanese government should be buying the islands, the Ministry of Foreign Affairs is afraid of angering China."

Mr. Ishihara explained after the speech to journalists who gathered around him to confirm the facts that Tokyo is already in talks with the landowners to purchase the islands. He also commented that, "The owner expressed willingness to sell if the buyer is Tokyo, and I decided to make the purchase. The agreement has already been reached and I think lawyers on both sides are currently handling related procedures."

At this stage, Japan owned Taisho Island, the industrialist living in Saitama Prefecture held Uotsuri Island, Kita Kojima Island, and Minami Kojima Island, and the latter's sister owned Kuba Island out of the five major Senkaku Islands. The government was leasing four islands from the landowners and managing them, but Mr. Ishihara secretly contacted the landowners about buying the islands and was on the verge of an agreement.

When Mr. Ishihara returned to Japan, he immediately moved ahead with preparations for the purchase, created a dedicated team at the Tokyo city headquarters for buying the Senkaku Islands at the end of April, and began donation collections to cover purchase expenses. Mr. Ishihara's idea elicited a large reaction, and donations exceeded 300 million yen in just over 10 days. Some people donated a few hundreds of thousand yen at a time.

The government was surprised by this development. There was no doubt that a purchase of the Senkaku Islands by Tokyo under the auspices of Mr. Ishihara with a hawkish stance toward China, would agitate the Chinese government. Then-Prime Minister Yoshihiko Noda instructed Deputy Chief Cabinet Secretary Hiroyuki Nagahama and others to gather information, and the administration began a review of acquiring ownership of the islands by having the national government purchase the islands from the landowner before Tokyo.

The Chinese government reacted swiftly. Tang Jiaxuan, chairman of the China-Japan Friendship Association and former member of the State Council, visited Japan on April 26 and met with Prime Minister Noda at the Prime Minister's Office. Mr. Tang explained to journalists after the meeting finished that they did not discuss the Senkaku Islands, but also noted that, "I hope that problems in one portion do not harm the relationship between our two countries," reflecting his anticipation that the government could rein in Mr. Ishihara. He used harsh language aimed at tempering Mr. Ishihara's moves at a symposium in Shanghai during June (perhaps realizing that his thoughts were not getting across) that "he is manipulating public opinion among both peoples to profit for himself" and "this could even be called a coup."

A Japanese government source explained that Vice-Minister for Foreign

Affairs Kenichiro Sasae and the Cabinet Office's Assistant Chief Cabinet Secretary Chikao Kawai discussed remedial strategies mainly with China's State Councilor Dai Bingguo and Vice Foreign Minister Zhang Zhijun and "convinced the Chinese side that it would be better to acquire ownership of the islands than be manipulated by Governor Ishihara." They noted the possibility of a harbor, light tower, and other facilities being built if Tokyo purchased the islands, inciting the Chinese government, and promised not to build facilities if the islands are acquired. They requested China's understanding of the government's acquisition of ownership of the Senkaku Islands given this context.

The source said that Japan felt that China "realized acquisition of ownership was unavoidable" through contacts with Mr. Dai and others. However, it did not obtain understanding from uppermost officials in the Chinese government.

This was a sensitive time of shifting power from the Hu Jintao government to the Xi Jinping government in China. The above-mentioned government source states that "it was unclear whether Dai Bingguo was rejected when he reported to upper officials or he simply abandoned efforts to win them over."

The Japanese government was unable to effectively read the reaction by the Chinese government to its acquisition of ownership of the Senkaku Islands, and the situation quickly escalated. A protest ship dispatched by the Action Committee for Defending the Diaoyu Islands, an anti-Japanese private group based in Hong Kong, approached rocks on the western side of Uotsuri Islands and seven activists from Hong Kong climbed onto the island on August 15, 2012. The protest ship displayed a banner with the phrase "we cannot give up even a tiny amount of land." The activists resisted efforts by the Japan Coast Guard's patrol ship to stop them from reaching land by throwing brick chunks at the ship, and the seven individuals who reached shore waved Chinese and Taiwanese flags on land.

The Okinawa Prefectural Police and Japan Coast guard arrested the 14 people, including those on the protest ship, but the Japanese government adhered to the precedent set by the Koizumi administration by deciding a compulsory return of the 14 people without holding a trial based on Article 65 of the Immigration Control and Refugee Recognition Act on August 17.

The Action Committee for Defending the Diaoyu Islands was established in 1996 and managed to get members onto the Senkaku Islands during that year. However, it tried landings on the Senkaku Islands at least seven times since then, but was held back by Hong Kong authorities out of consideration for Japan-China relations and did not realize its goal. The decision by Hong Kong authorities not to stop the boat headed for the Senkaku Islands this time clearly reflected the attitude of the Chinese government angered by the attempt to convert the Senkaku Islands into "city land."

The landowners started changing their minds too. The male landowner who lives in Saitama Prefecture gradually leaned toward selling the islands to the national government, rather than Tokyo, during multiple interactions with Deputy Chief Cabinet Secretary Nagahama. A government source noted that the proposal of a large purchase price worked well.

The problem was Mr. Ishihara. At a press conference on August 17, he strongly criticized the Japanese government's response in allowing Chinese people land on Uotsuri Island as "weak foreign policy and a pathetic effort to curry favor with China." However, Mr. Ishihara suggested that he ultimately intended to transfer the Senkaku Islands to the national government, even if Tokyo acquired them initially, and did not appear to be adamantly against a purchase of the islands by the government.

Prime Minister Noda invited Mr. Ishihara to the Prime Minister's residence through Hiroyuki Sonoda, a Lower House member for Sunrise Party of Japan (at the time) that was close to Mr. Ishihara, and held a top-secret meeting on August 19. Mr. Noda explained the government's review of acquisition of ownership and requested Mr. Ishihara's consent. Mr. Ishihara asked for construction of a harbor that could accommodate temporary refuge (refuge harbor) by fishing boats during rough weather conditions and wireless facilities as a condition for letting the national government purchase the Senkaku Islands.

The government prepared plans A-H for utilizing the Senkaku Islands after the meeting.

Plan A maintained the status quo with no changes to the islands, plan B implemented environmental conservation measures, plan C repaired the lighthouse, plan D built the harbor requested by Mr. Ishihara, and plan E called for surveys to identify maritime resources. Content in these plans incrementally increased the likely ferocity of negative reaction by China and Taiwan. Plan H, the most aggressive, provided for a permanent Self-Defense Force base. This plan included a footnote that it could elicit unprecedented reactions by China and Taiwan.

On August 30, a very small number of core administration leaders, including Prime Minister Noda and Chief Cabinet Secretary Osamu Fujimura, held a meeting to discuss final plans for acquisition of the ownership of the Senkaku Islands based on plans A-H. Foreign Minister Koichiro Genba, who wanted to minimize China's reaction, advocated "plan A for doing nothing." Mr. Noda, however, disagreed with this view on the basis that "we must do something," taking into account Mr. Ishihara's request and expressed interest in plans B and C.

Mr. Genba continued to work on convincing Mr. Noda with Deputy Prime Minister Katsuya Okada who also wanted to avoid agitating China. Mr. Noda held his ground that the government could at least change the source of the light tower on Uotsuri Island to LEDs, but ultimately accepted the exhortations of Mr. Genba and others and agreed to plan A.

The government approved the purchase of three Senkaku Islands (Uotsuri, Kita Kojima, and Minami Kojima) for 2.05 billion yen from the male landowner living in Saitama and acquisition of ownership of these islands on September 11. Tokyo had raised 1.46 billion yen in donations nationwide, but the government purchased the three islands for a substantially larger amount. The government continued to lease Kuba Island because the man's sister, who owns this island, refused to sell.

Chief Cabinet Secretary Fujimura explained at a press conference held in the morning on September 11 that the acquisition of ownership aimed for "peaceful and stable upkeep and management over the long term." He also requested a calm response from China with his explanation that "Japan is not at all interested in affecting the overall relationship between Japan and China."

However, other countries had difficulty understanding the basis for the national government buying the islands ahead of Tokyo and acquiring ownership of them.

Leon Panetta, then-U.S. Secretary of Defense, who visited Japan six days after the Japanese government's acquisition of ownership, peppered

Defense Ministry officials with questions at a welcome lunch.

"Why did the owner suddenly decide to sell the islands?"

"Why was the Tokyo Governor involved?"

He pressed then-Defense Minister Satoshi Morimoto at the Japan-U.S. Defense Ministers' Meeting held before the luncheon with the following comment: "We are concerned about China's provocative behavior developing into a major incident. However, we need the Japanese government to take a constructive approach."

The United States has a "complex relationship that mixes competition and cooperation" with China (Vice President Biden) in light of its enhanced economic and military powers. The U.S. government puts priority on the Japan-U.S. alliance and presented an official stance that the Japan-U.S. Security Treaty coverage includes the Senkaku Islands, but wants to avoid getting caught up in a battle between Japan and China over the Senkaku Islands.

Anti-Japanese demonstrations spread

On September 9, 2012, just before the Japanese government's official decision on the acquisition of ownership, the APEC meeting in Russia's Far East city of Vladivostok involving leaders from 21 Pan-Pacific countries and regions and held over two days was about to finish after a working lunch.

Prime Minister Noda walked over to Chinese President Hu Jintao who arrived late in the waiting room for country leaders. He wanted to express condolences regarding the massive earthquake that struck China's Yunnan Province and had many casualties two days earlier.

However, Mr. Hu responded to Mr. Noda's offer to "feel free to ask if there is anything that Japan can do to help" with criticism of the policy of acquiring ownership of the Senkaku Islands in an angry tone.

"Buying the islands is illegal and invalid no matter what format is used, and China is firmly against this action."

Tension filled the air between the two leaders. Mr. Noda responded that "there are no issues in terms of international law or historically" and indicated his desire to address current relations between Japan and China from a comprehensive perspective." Yet Mr. Hu's expression remained rigid. The two leaders went back and forth in their comments with interpreters for a period of about 15 minutes.

The Japanese government proceeded with a Cabinet decision to acquire ownership of the Senkaku Islands two days later. China's Defense Ministry issued a statement protesting the acquisition of ownership on September 11 and suggested it would take countermeasures with the mention of "retaining the right to take corresponding actions." The People's Daily similarly called for undermining "Japan's plot to invade and occupy the Diaoyu Islands."

China "places very heavy emphasis on honor" (Ministry of Foreign Affairs official). The intensity of the Chinese government's reaction against acquisition of ownership of the Senkaku Islands might have been affected by Japan's decision to approve acquisition of ownership just two days after the contact between Prime Minister Noda and President Hu in Vladivostok. Tang Jiaxuan, chairman of the China-Japan Friendship Association, who invited Yohei Kono, former Speaker of the House of Representatives, and representatives of seven Japan-China Friendship groups visited Beijing for the 40th anniversary of normalization of diplomatic ties between Japan and China on September 27 commented with disapproval that this "damaged China's honor."

A wave of harsh anti-Japanese demonstrations that went beyond past levels broke out in China.

"Destroy little Japan!" "Boycott Japanese products!"

A group of about 100 demonstrators carrying portraits of Mao Zedung gathered in front of the Japanese Embassy in Beijing on the morning of September 15, the first weekend after the Japanese government's decision to acquire ownership the Senkaku Islands and loudly repeated these chants.

This group was following by second and third groups of 100 demonstrators shouting chants. The demonstrators started pelting the Embassy with eggs, PET bottles, tomatoes, rocks, and other items as the three lanes on the Embassy side of the street filled up. Security guards providing security for the Embassy simply instructed demonstrators not to stop. Demonstrators steadily increased their violence and started jeering that "some of you are Japanese reporters" and throwing rocks and other things at the press corps covering the developments.

The crowd of demonstrators expanded to 10,000 people just before noon. Fully armed police guarded the front entrance of the Embassy with 3-4 rows and pushed back demonstrators when they started kicking the Embassy fence and tried to enter.

Anti-Japanese demonstrators in regional cities were even more violent than in Beijing. People just passing by joined demonstrators in the Changan area of Dongguan city (Guangdong Province), which is close to Hong Kong, and the crowded quickly expanded to 3,000 people on the same day. Order in the rows of demonstrators collapsed as the number of people increased, and violence erupted with people breaking the windows of offices that appeared to be occupied by Japanese companies and overturning parked Japanese cars. Demonstrators broke the glass door to a conveyor-belt sushi restaurant in the city and a few dozens of them thoroughly destroyed the store.

Demonstrators rushed into 10 plants affiliated with Japanese companies, including an electronic parts plant operated by Panasonic Group, in Tsingtau (Shandong Province), which faces the East China Sea, during the afternoon of September 15 and set fires and destroyed production lines. They also attacked the Japan-affiliated JUSCO supermarket and looted it.

Images of smoke coming out of burned plants were reported globally. China's Foreign Ministry assembled journalists in Beijing from other countries on the day before the demonstrations and provided a warning that "It is unclear what will happen tomorrow so be careful of your safety."

Anti-Japanese demonstrations that broke out across China largely appeared to be "government-led activities" organized by Chinese authorities. Buses steadily arrived at demonstration sites, and people came off the buses holding Chinese flags to join the demonstrators.

The Japanese government, meanwhile, sought to avoid agitating China amid these intense anti-Japanese demonstrations.

The Japanese and U.S. governments had planned to use Irisuna Island, an uninhabited island in Tonaki village (Okinawa) located about 60 kilometers northwest of Naha, which the U.S. military utilized as a shooting and bombing range, for island retaking exercises in November 2012. The plan envisioned a scenario of Ground Self-Defense Forces and U.S. Marines based in Okinawa retaking an outlying island occupied by an enemy with air assistance, and this was going to be the first full-fledged island retaking exercise conducted in

Japan by the Self-Defense Forces.

However, the Japanese government cancelled the exercise at the last minute because of concern about agitating China by implementing this type of exercise close to the Senkaku Islands. Japan dispatched a senior government official to the United States to explain the decision after dissatisfaction with the last-minute cancellation voiced by the U.S. government, according to a related person.

Additionally, the government instructed Maritime Self-Defense Forces monitoring Chinese Navy ships in the East China Sea to stay at a distance out of the sight range of the Chinese ships. The visual observation distance for ships on the seas is roughly 30 kilometers, and Maritime Self-Defense Forces remained at least this far away and switched to monitoring with radar. The Maritime Self-Defense Force ships pulled back and retained the distance when Chinese ships moved closer. While this measure reflected concern about possible contact between the Maritime Self-Defense Forces and Chinese Navy resulting in heightened tensions, it might have sent a "mistaken message" to China that Japan was retreating. These measures continued up until the departure of the Noda administration.

Sharp erosion of Japan-China relations related to the Senkaku Islands overlapped with the years of the Democratic Party government (September 2009 to December 2012). The Japan-U.S. alliance, the bedrock of Japan's national security, faltered and responses to China vacillated between "resolute" and "appeasement" during this period. Former Vice-Minister for Foreign Affairs Shotaro Yachi reflected on the Japan-China relationship under the Democratic Party administration in an interview with the Yomiuri Shimbun after the Democratic Party lost control of the government and the launch of the second Shinzo Abe administration by the Liberal Democratic Party and Komeito Party in December 2012.

"China has moved past Japan in gross domestic product (GDP) and become the world's No.2 economic power. It has gained confidence and is strengthening its opinions. This is the background to China's hawkish stance toward Japan related to the Senkaku Islands in Okinawa Prefecture and on other matters. Also, the Democratic Party government, and particularly the Hatoyama administration, weakened the Japan-U.S. relationship. The international community has seen a waning of Japan's power and is now observing issues in national management. China probably thought that the U.S. might not back up Japan. Japan has let its vulnerabilities be revealed." (Morning edition article in the Yomiuri Shimbun on December 25).

Japan amplified the problems it faced surrounding the Senkaku Islands with its meandering foreign policy and failure in crisis management. It will not be easy to repair the damage even under a new administration as China takes increasingly provocative actions.

Escalating conflict

"This is a highly unusual move, and a single misstep could lead to very dangerous conditions. Japan is aware of this difficulty."

Defense Minister Itsunori Onodera disclosed on the night of February 5, 2013 at the Defense Ministry in Ichigaya (Tokyo) that an escort ship and helicopter from the Maritime Self-Defense Forces had been separately targeted by fire control system radar from Chinese Navy ships.

Fire control system radar is used to pinpoint a cannon or missile target when attacking an enemy's ship or plane. The missile or other projectile moves into a lock-on state, and firing preparations are ready.

The Defense Ministry explained that the radar targeting occurred in international waters well over one hundred kilometers north of the Senkaku Islands. At about 10am on January 30, the Chinese Navy's Jiangwei-2 class frigate targeted radar at the Maritime Self-Defense Force's Yudachi escort ship while it was navigating from a location about three kilometers away. It lasted for a few minutes, and Yudachi made course changes and took other evasive actions.

At around 5pm on January 19, the Chinese Navy's Jiangkai-1 class frigate targeted radar at an SH60 helicopter from the Oonami escort ship while it was flying a warning mission.

It is generally possible to fire a missile or other projectile in a few seconds after targeting by fire control system radar. These were truly dangerous actions that constitute threats using military power (Defense Minister Onodera). The U.S. military is permitted to counterattack on the basis that being targeted by the counterpart's radar is equivalent to an attack.

A Defense Ministry official explained that escort ships monitors radar waves by converting each frequency to a sound. Standard radar has a fixed interval between sounds, but targeting by fire control system radar is immediately identified because of a continuous alarm sound. However, the Defense Ministry sent the recorded data to Tokyo for analysis just to be sure and disclosed the events after confirming that it was definitely radar targeting by the Chinese military.

The Japanese government sought to analyze the background of the incidents in terms of whether radar targeting took place as the independent judgment of the ship commander or was a planned action by the Chinese government.

There is fear of an accidental clash evolving into a war even if the incident was an "excess by a rural naval captain unfamiliar with the rules of the seas" (Self-Defense Force official). Japan and China do not have a system to prevent unexpected clashes between front-line troops from evolving into a full-fledged battle via contacts between upper-level commanders. Although the two countries agreed to begin a review of the establishment of a hotline at a meeting of senior defense officials in 2011, discussions were suspended after the Japanese government's acquisition of ownership of the Senkaku Islands.

The problem is even more serious if the Chinese government approved the radar targeting.

Sankei Shimbun reported in a morning edition article on January 9, 2013 just before the series of radar targeting incidents took place that, "The government has started a review of reinforcing countermeasures by the Self-Defense Forces, such as firing warning shots" in response to provocative actions by the Chinese military with a headline of "Chinese military coming close to territorial airspace daily, government reviews warning shots." The article described specific response as "firing warning shots with tracer ammunition if a plane violating territorial airspace does not follow wireless warnings or deploying Maritime Self-Defense Force ships within a certain range if Chinese Navy vessels advance close to Japan's territorial waters."

The Chinese Embassy in Tokyo carefully monitors movements by the Prime Minister reported in newspapers and closely analyzes friendly contacts and other interactions. Prime Minister Abe held a dinner meeting on the night of January 8, the day before the article, with Chairman Takehiko

Kiyohara, President Takamitsu Kumasaka, and others from Sankei Shimbun at the ANA Intercontinental Hotel Tokyo in Akasaka (Tokyo). "The Chinese side felt that Prime Minister Abe encouraged the Sankei Shimbun to write the article" (government source).

Two J-10 fighters and one reconnaissance plane from the Chinese military entered Japan's ADIZ in the East China Sea and this triggered a scramble of Air Self-Defense Force F15 fights on January 10, the day after the article. While the Chinese planes did not enter Japanese airspace, the possibility of an accidental clash dramatically increases when fighter planes traveling at high speeds come face-to-face. The Chinese government clearly ordered the approach by these fighters, and the first incident of targeting by fire control system radar occurred nine days later.

Sea of unending tension

P3C patrol planes affiliated with the Maritime Self-Defense Force's Fleet Air Wing 5 (Naha) patrol territorial waters around the Senkaku Islands. They closely monitor China's public vessels and military ships as well as fishing boat groups.

The P3C lowers its altitude to 150-170 meters in order to conduct visual observation when its radar finds ships navigating in the East China Sea. It flies parallel to the forward direction of the ship on the right side, and a crew member photographs the ship with a single-lens reflex camera.

On July 25, 2013, a P3C identified five Chinese military ships, including a destroyer, in waters about 100 kilometers northeast of Miyako Island. It appeared that these ships navigated to the Pacific through the La Perouse (Soya) Strait after a live-shell firing exercise with the Russian military in waters around Vladivostok in the Sea of Japan. This was the first time to confirm Chinese military ships traveling a full circle around the Japanese islands.

Chinese Y8 Airborne Early Warning planes flew between the main Okinawan island and Miyako Island on the previous day. This was also the first time for Chinese military planes to fly past the Nansei Islands out to the Pacific. Defense Minister Onodera, who was touring a Maritime Self-Defense Force's Kanoya Air Base in Kagoshima Prefecture at the same time disclosed this information to the press corps and expressed concern that "China will be increasingly heading out to the Pacific."

It is thought that the Y8 planes implemented some type of joint training with the five ships on the Pacific. It takes some proficiency for airplanes and ships to move collaboratively on the Pacific far away from the Chinese mainland. This event confirmed a substantial improvement in the Chinese military's unit operational capabilities in a maritime environment.

Japan's Self-Defense Forces monitor movements by the Chinese military with a terrestrial radar network too. However, it was unable to detect an airplane from China' State Oceanic Administration that violated territorial airspace around the Senkaku Islands on December 13, 2012. The Chinese plane had already flown away by the time that the Air Self-Defense Force's scrambled F15 fighters arrived on the scene after receiving notification from a Japan Coast Guard patrol vessel that observed the plane.

The Defense Ministry bolstered its warning and monitoring capabilities from the air via airplanes after this incident. It dispatched the Air Self-Defense Force's Airborne Early Warning Group's (Hamamatsu) AWACS to the East China Sea and moved some E2C Airborne Early Warning planes to Okinawa. While the government also intends to deploy Global Hawk unmanned reconnaissance planes and strengthen the terrestrial radar network, it must continue manned warning and monitoring flights for the time being. Masataka Tsuda, who commands the Airborne Early Warning Group, noted that, "Equipment and human resources are limited. Our issue is how to manage capabilities as effectively and efficiently as possible."

The Self-Defense Forces are not the only ones confronting China under difficult conditions.

"Front-line operations cannot last in the current state. We need to devise a plan to strengthen capabilities."

Takashi Kitamura, Commander of the Japan Coast Guard (at the time), issued this instruction at a meeting of roughly 10 officials in his office in later September 2012. The 11th Regional Coast Guard Headquarters (Naha), which has jurisdiction for waters around the Senkaku Islands, has seven large (100-ton or more) patrol boats, but this is not enough to respond to the Chinese government's public ships that are repeating provocative actions in Japan's territorial waters. It had been somehow getting by with assistance from patrol ships from Coast Guard Headquarters from other regions nationwide.

The proposal prepared through a review that lasted about two months under Commander Kitamura called for establishment of a "dedicated unit for the Senkaku Islands" based at the Ishigaki Coast Guard Office (Ishigaki, Okinawa) with 12 large patrol ships and 600 people to address China's activities by the end of fiscal 2015. (Editor's note: Establishment of a "dedicated unit for the Senkaku Islands" under the 11th Regional Coast Guard Headquarters finished, and full-fledged operations began in April 2016.) The initiative approved lengthening of the retirement age for Coast Guard officers in order to secure personnel, and eighty-six people participated in fiscal 2012.

China is bolstering its maritime policing capabilities too as a response to Japan.

A large sign measuring about two meters with the "China Coast Guard" name was installed on a building in central Beijing on July 22, 2013.

China's maritime policing had previously been split among five entities that acted separately – the State Oceanic Administration's Marine Surveillance, the Ministry of Agriculture's Fisheries Law Enforcement Command, the Ministry of Public Security's Coast Guard, the Ministry of Customers and Trade, and the Ministry of Transport's Maritime Safety Administration. The Chinese government recognized its issues and formed a powerful China Coast Guard combining four of these entities (besides the Ministry of Transport's Maritime Safety Administration).

China's reinforcement of the maritime policing capabilities aims to pressure Japan in relation to the Senkaku Islands issue. The Chinese government's national maritime strategy meeting held in Beijing in January 2013 set the following activity policies. <Bolster maritime law enforcement capabilities and cooperate in a united manner>

<Carry out patrols to maintain sovereignty and support permanent law enforcement in the waters around the Diaoyu Islands>

The China Coast Guard is almost permanently stationed in waters by the Senkaku Islands. Many Chinese fishing boats that also carry armed private militia (Defense Ministry official) operate and China's military vessels often appear in waters behind this area.

The Defense Ministry's China Security Report compiled in 2012 indicates that China has roughly 40 ships that could be sent to the Senkaku Islands. The Japan Coast Guard has also obtained information that China intends to build 50 new public ships.

It is unclear when the face-off between Japan and China might end. Some government officials think it could continue for 10 years.

No summit meetings, unable to find solutions

Chinese President Xi Jinping's face suddenly froze.

Prime Minister Abe quickly approached Mr. Xi when he saw him at Constantine Palace in St. Petersburg (Russia) where the meeting of leaders from 20 major countries and regions (G20) was being held on the night of September 5, 2013 and beckoned "Mr. Xi Jinping."

Mr. Xi, albeit with some uncertainty, shook Mr. Abe's extended hand. He initially muttered something to himself and then stated the official opinion on the Senkaku Islands that is regularly heard from China's Foreign Ministry spokesperson" (according to an official working with the Prime Minister). While it was just 4-5 minutes, these were the first words spoken between the leaders of Japan and China, which are bickering fiercely over the Senkaku Islands, since acquisition of ownership of the Senkaku Islands in September 2012.

The Japanese and Chinese government had not arranged a summit meeting in St. Petersburg, but Mr. Abe wanted to speak with Mr. Xi if there was a chance. He asked senior government officials about the Chinese reading of Xi Jinping's name and generally exhibited strong interest on the government plane headed for Russia.

However, the back-and-forth exchanges between Japanese and Chinese Coast Guard authorities around the Senkaku Islands continued. Four ships from the China Coast Guard ignored warnings from the Japan Coast Guard and intruded into Japan's territorial waters on the night of September 6 right after the handshake between the two leaders.

The Straits Times, an influential newspaper in Singapore, selected Mr. Abe and Mr. Xi as the "Asian of the Year" with the most influence in

Asia during the year at the end of 2013. Mr. Abe revitalized the Japanese economy and earnestly promoted international cooperation, while Mr. Xi led China in a rapid expansion of economic and military power. These two men, who are the faces of Asia and also top global leaders, have been unable to hold an official meeting. Mr. Abe has repeatedly stated that "the door to dialogue is open," but the Chinese side has reacted coolly that "we cannot hold a summit meeting without an outlook for results." China intensified its rejection of a summit meeting after Mr. Abe's visit to Yasukuni Shrine in December 2013 with comments that "He is not welcome with the Chinese people, and Chinese leaders also will not meet with him" (Qing Gang, Director of Foreign Ministry Information Department).

Diplomatic authorities in Japan and China worked behind the scenes to find a compromise proposal through diplomatic negotiations to avoid conflict.

Large-scale anti-Japanese demonstrations were not seen in September 2013, which marked one year since acquisition of ownership of the Senkaku Islands by the Japanese government. If arson, plundering, and other anti-Japanese demonstrations went too far, they could disrupt society itself and a minor spark might shift focus to criticism of the Chinese government controlled solely by the Communist Party. The Chinese government clearly did not approve anti-Japanese demonstrations. Xiong Bo, Deputy Director-General, Department of Asia of China's Foreign Ministry, who handles issues with Japan, visited over a few days in late September and secretly held discussions with Japan's Ministry of Foreign Affairs officials.

The foreign ministries of the two countries were leading discussions of a compromise proposal for the Senkaku Islands issue during this period, according to a government source.

The proposal called for both countries to recognize the existence of a problem regarding the Senkaku Islands with Japan viewing the problem as a "diplomatic issue" and China seeing it as a "territorial matter." While it might appear to be a word game, this was an attempt to find a compromise by using ambiguity in order to save face for the Japanese government with its assertion that a territorial problem does not exist for the Senkaku Islands and the Chinese government claiming territorial rights. They even looked at the possibility of exchanging an agreement document.

The Prime Minister's Office, however, did not accept the proposed compromise. While it was willing to recognize a diplomatic issue, acceptance of a territorial problem would give the Chinese government's public ships a justification for intruding into Japan's territorial waters. A senior government official reflected that "This was a line that could not be yielded."

The Chinese leadership also could not accept the compromise proposal. The Xi Jinping government formed in November 2012 was continuing to solidify its power base in China through the trial of Bo Xilai, a former member of the Central Politburo and Secretary of the Communist Party's Chongqing Committee and corruption arrests related to Zhou Yongkang, a former member of the Politburo Standing Committee (former Secretary of the Political and Legislative Affairs Committee of the Party's Central Committee). Mr. Xi was still in the process of gaining control of the military and would have been undermined by rival factions if he appeared to be compromising with Japan in relation to the Senkaku Islands problem at a sensitive time for internal politics.

Conflict on a global stage

"China's assertion regarding the Diaoyu Islands is reasonable." This is what a column in the New York Times, a leading U.S. newspaper, reported in paper's December 5, 2013 issue. Well-known columnist Nicholas Kristof was the author. While the Japanese government immediately protested to the New York Times and Mr. Kristof, this type of opinion has been increasingly appearing in overseas newspapers.

The Ministry of Foreign Affairs faced a shocking development in fall 2012. Advertisements criticizing Japan surfaced in newspapers worldwide. The scope also went beyond just leading newspapers, such as the Washington Post and New York Times. It included Pacific island countries, African countries, and other "unexpected countries" (Foreign Ministry official). Chinese diplomats frequently appeared on television programs in many countries, broadening criticism of Japan.

The Japanese government's public relations strategy, meanwhile, focuses on encouraging people with influence on the formation of public opinion in the international community to understand Japan's position. It believes that this approach is more effective in shaping public opinion than comments by the Japanese government as a one of the parties involved.

The government invited Jim Frederick, a U.S. journalist who previously worked as the Tokyo Bureau Chief of US-based Time magazine, to Japan and arranged a tour of the Japan Coast Guard's base in Ishigaki City (Okinawa prefecture) and other facilities in July 2013. Mr. Frederick stayed in Japan for about one week. He exchanged opinions with officials from the Coast Guard and Ministry of Foreign Affairs and wrote his thoughts in English on Twitter.

The Japanese government held the first meeting of the "External Public Relations Strategy Planning Team" in the following month at the Prime Minister's Office and confirmed a policy of extending invitations to famous journalists, such as Mr. Frederick, and interacting with overseas individuals who have favorable views of Japan or in-depth knowledge of Japan. While this might seem to be a "valiant but doomed" strategy in the face of China's "downpour-style" public relations, Cabinet Public Relations Secretary Eiichi Hasegawa, who manages the government's public relations strategy, explains that "it is meaningless to suddenly explain territorial land and sea issues to people who are not interested in Japan." He notes that it is important to first increase the number of people with interest in Japan and thereby provide a basis for sympathizing with Japan's views.

The Japanese government is also putting emphasis on collaboration with member countries of the Association of Southeast Asian Nations (ASEAN) that are struggling with China's aggressive maritime initiatives in the South China Sea. Its efforts aim to establish an effective network of containment against China, and China is concerned about these activities.

The People's Daily, the institutional paper of China's Communist Party, railed against a quiet international conference held in Japan in September 2013. The conference entitled "Seminar on Capacity Building for Maritime Security in Emerging Countries" aimed to give assistance in strengthening the maritime policing capabilities of emerging countries. Thirteen countries attended the meeting – Bangladesh, Djibouti, Indonesia, Kenya, Malaysia, Myanmar, Papua New Guinea, the Philippines, Sri Lanka, Thailand, Tonga, Yemen, and Vietnam. Parliamentary Vice-Minister for Foreign Affairs Mr. Minoru Kiuchi, who hosted the event, emphasized in comments at the start of the conference that "Changing the status quo by force is not acceptable" in maritime matters.

The People's Daily wrote the following using excerpts from Mr. Kiuchi's comments in its Japanese-language electronic issue on September 26.

"This comment implicitly criticizes China and is promoting a maritime version of the 'China Threat' concept. It attempts to create an image of Japan as a defender of the maritime order. Japan hopes to curtail China, acquire influence in maritime conflicts and maritime security issues, and gain an advantage by establishing a moral high ground and earnestly providing maritime security assistance to related countries."

It is true that the "changing the status quo by force is not acceptable" point cited by the People's Daily is a key theme of the Japanese government in relation to maritime policy. This is because propagating this theme in international society enables Japan to continue claiming the legitimacy of its territorial rights even if China repeats provocative behavior or takes the Senkaku Islands by force. Prime Minister Abe has assumed a leading role in repeatedly voicing disagreement with "changing the status quo by force" and promoting understanding of this theme in overseas trips and on other occasions.

President Obama also stated at the Japan-U.S. Summit Meeting held in St. Petersburg (Russia) on September 5, 2013 that the U.S. is "against efforts to achieve resolutions through intimidation," demonstrating his under-standing of Japan's view. A Foreign Ministry official offered the following analysis of the President's comment: "It only took just over 10 seconds of an hour-long meeting, but had significant implications."

Who is trying to alter the postwar international order – Japan or China? The international community's stance on assertions by Japan and China is likely to strongly affect the direction of the Senkaku Islands issue.

Not relying on international entities

The Senkaku Islands issue is attracting the interest of the international community. Some Japanese politicians and intellectuals recommend using the International Court of Justice (ICJ), a United Nations entity that renders decisions on conflicts between countries.

Co-head of the Japan Restoration Party Toru Hashimoto (at the time) is one of these people. This is what Mr. Hashimoto, a lawyer, wrote on his personal Twitter account on April 27, 2013.

"One of the most effective methods would be utilizing the International Court of Justice (including the International Tribunal for the Law of the Sea)."

"Japan can decisively defeat China in the debate in a legal venue if the Senkaku Islands issue is handled by the International Court of Justice."

Advocates for utilizing the ICJ assert that "Japan's view should definitely be approved" (Mr. Hashimoto). This path also brings the benefit of clarifying Japan's stance of emphasis on rule of law to the international community.

However, the ICJ approach is a double-edged sword.

The Japanese government takes the position that the Senkaku Islands are "clearly an inherent part of Japan historically and in international law." There is risk that Japan might be seen internationally as accepting that territorial rights to the Senkaku Islands are undecided if it brought the issue to the ICJ despite already having effective control of the islands and claiming that there is no legal conflict to be resolved.

A Foreign Ministry official explains that, "This is a ridiculous policy with no benefit for Japan and just downside because even if Japan pressed China to pursue a resolution in the ICJ, China would simply use it as evidence that Japan acknowledges the existence of a conflict and that Japan hence should agree to bilateral negotiations with China."

Meanwhile, there are some government officials who believe that "China should bring a case to the ICJ." They challenge China to prove its case if it thinks that a legal conflict exists in relation to the Senkaku Islands. Shotaro Yachi, who became the National Security Advisor heading the National Security Council (Japan's NSC) in January 2014, commented at a symposium held in Tokyo on March 12, 2013 that "it would be fine to tell China to request a fair decision by the International Court of Justice."

Yet China does not appear to have any intention to use the ICJ.

Sakihito Ozawa, the Japan Restoration Party's Chairman of the Diet Affairs Committee, visited China in September 2013 and met with Tang Jiaxuan, chairman of the China-Japan Friendship Association, in Beijing's Zhongnanhai area where many Chinese leaders have their offices. Mr. Ozawa responded to Mr. Tang's repetition of China's claims to the Senkaku Islands that, "There is a difference of opinions regarding the Senkaku Islands issue. Perhaps China should take its case to the International Court of Justice." However, Mr. Tang simply answered that "this is an issue that should be resolved bilaterally."

The ICJ only begins cases if certain conditions are met – 1) an agreement exists between the parties, 2) the country bringing the suit has declared its acceptance of the ICJ's decision (accepting compulsory jurisdiction), and 3) country being sued accepts the case.

While Japan acknowledges the ICJ's compulsory jurisdiction, China does not and this means that China would not be obligated to abide by the decision in cases regarding territorial issues. China also tends to avoid court decisions by international entities so conditions 1 and 3 are unlikely to be met.

The Japanese government interprets China's aversion to using the ICJ in the following way: "China lacks confidence in its ability to win on the Senkaku Islands issue and is concerned about an adverse impact on its territorial conflicts with Asian countries for islands in the South China Sea" (Foreign Ministry official).

China also avoids court decisions and discussions handled by international entities in other cases of territorial rights issues. One example is the Scarborough Shoal in the South China Sea that was being administered by the Philippines. In April 2012, China dispatched public vessels to the nearby waters after the Philippine Navy seized a Chinese fishing boat in the area, raising tensions. While a concerned Philippines brought the case to the Court of Arbitration (international entity for conflict arbitration and mediation) under the United Nations Convention on the Law of the Sea in January 2013, China rejected the review on the basis that "Scarborough Shoal is Chinese territory." China also applied tangible and intangible pressures, such as denying attendance by the Philippine President at the China-ASEAN Expo held in China in September 2012 at the last minute.

No signs of a solution

"Cold political relations, cool economic relations"

The People's Daily and other Chinese media source have been using this expression to describe the relationship between Japan and China since acquisition of ownership of the Senkaku Islands in 2012. It means that political relations are cold and economic ties have cooled too.

There are signs of change in the economic cool-off. Exports to China rose 9.7% year-on-year to 12,628.7 billion yen in 2013, the first increase in three years, according to trade data released by the Ministry of Finance. Imports from China reached an all-time high with a 17.4% rise to 17,650.2 billion yen.

The problem is "cold political relations."

"This is very good." China disclosed a document that surprise senior officials in Japan. It issued the document as an "important statement" by President Xi Jinping as General Secretary of the Communist Party in October 2013. The document outlined core policies for Asian diplomacy under the Xi administration for use at the "peripheral diplomacy workshop," a key meeting for the Communist Party in Beijing on October 24-25, and proposed a good-neighbor policy in dealing with peripheral countries.

<China's fundamental approach to peripheral foreign policy is working closely with neighboring countries, promoting economic growth in these countries as partners, and applying ideals of intimacy, sincerity, benefit, and tolerance.>

<Advancement of good-neighbor friendly ties with peripheral countries is China's primary aim in diplomacy. It requires winning over people's hearts and encouraging warmness through emphasis on friendship and mutual help as well as equality and emotions and promotion of discussions and mutual visits.>

<We must ensure that peripheral countries benefit from China's advances and that China obtains benefits and cooperation from joint advancement with peripheral countries. China needs to encourage regional cooperation with even more effort and resolve and seek to maintain peace and stability in peripheral areas.>

However, China's attitude toward Japan is very different from good neighbor diplomacy. It was just a month after issuing this statement that

China unilaterally established an ADIZ that included airspace above the Senkaku Islands.

The Chinese Communist Party is emphasizing its history of creating the People's Republic of China after victories in the civil war with the Nationalists and the war with Japan. China positions its conflict with Japan over the Senkaku Islands as a historical issue, and this stance also makes it tougher to realize concessions and compromises.

The country with actual control is ultimately a key point in territorial issues. Japan's ability to continue the current situation of effectively controlling the Senkaku Islands is vital. Prime Minister Abe gave the following instructions after touring the Japan Coast Guard's patrol boats in Okinawa Prefecture on February 2, 2013.

"I expect difficult conditions to continue, and I would like you to persevere in your work of protecting Japan's sovereignty."

Chapter 3
Japan-U.S. Alliance and Okinawa

Okinawa is the Achilles' heel of Japan under threat from China.

Okinawa is a group of islands in a vast ocean area that measures about 400 kilometers south to north and around 1,000 kilometers east to west. It is located on Japan's westernmost national border and is a strategic point along the sea lines of communication with China and the Republic of Korea. The reality that just over 70% of U.S. military facilities and areas in Japan are concentrated in Okinawa attests to its military importance. However, Okinawa has complicated feelings toward mainland Japan, and there is a strong opposition movement against the U.S. military bases. China, which has deep historical and cultural ties to Okinawa, is strengthening its involvement in Okinawa and has even started activities that appear to make assertions to territorial rights. Will Japan be capable of defending Okinawa?

Strengthening independence movement in Okinawa

Okinawa used a "dialect tag" in past years.

The small wooden tag hanging on a string was placed on the neck of children who spoke in the local dialect at school. Dialects varied greatly by region in Okinawa, and the dialect tag was used to improve mutual understanding by unifying under a standard language. Yet some children felt intense shame and antipathy toward the dialect tag.

Yasukatsu Matsushima, a professor at Ryukoku University who was born on Ishigaki Island in 1963, was one of those people. Mr. Matsushima, who was forced to wear the dialect tag in elementary school, writes in the joint work "What is the 'Okinawa Problem'" (published by Fujiwara Shoten) that, "Japan has treated Okinawa in ways that should not be done to the same people and citizens."

He was a leading force in the establishment of the "The Association of Comprehensive Studies for Independence of the Lew Chewans (ACSILs)," which seeks to make Okinawa (Ryukyu) independent, on May 15, 2013.

The charter for establishment of the ACSILs written by Mr. Matsushima and others is filled with antipathy and anger toward the Japanese government and Japanese people.

"The Lew Chew have been colonized by Japan and the United States. Because of this the Lew Chewans have become a stateless nation, a minority people and have been discriminated against, exploited, and ruled over.

"The Japanese people have exploited Lew Chew for their own "peace and prosperity" and hope to be blessed with these benefits for their future. If this goes on, we Lew Chewan people shudder at the horror of future wars and fear we will never be able to live in peace."

While the group refers to itself as an academic association, it also accepts members from the general public other than researchers. Yet it still sets a requirement for being a member. The person must be a member of the Lew Chewan people with roots in Okinawa.

The ACSILs had about 200 members when it was established, including a member of Japan's National Diet. The diet member is Kantoku Teruya, a member of the House of Representatives elected to represent Okinawa's second district. Mr. Teruya, who belongs to the Social Democratic Party, speaks about Okinawa's independence in the following way referring to Japanese people as "Yamato" and Okinawa people as "Uchinanchu."

"The overwhelming majority of Yamato politicians have no interest in the Okinawa problem and provide 'silent agreement' to the national policy. Okinawan independence is a policy that addresses the possibility of Uchinanchus playing a central role in determining their future."

Okinawa is about the only place in Japan where there is serious discussion of independence. While it is almost entirely unknown in mainland Japan, the Okinawa independence movement has a lengthy history and deep roots.

Fuitimiti (morning)

Akoukurou (evening)

Reefwa (grinding bowl)

A group of about 10 men and women were reading through phrases from Shima Kutuba, the Okinawa dialect, from textbooks in a room at the community center. This is a study group led by Yoshikatsu Bise, a company owner from Okinawa city. It has been active at the community center once a week since 2000 with this local radio station personality as the teacher. Participants are mixed, including teachers, housewives, and others. Mr. Yoshikatsu Bise, who was against Okinawa's reversion to Japan in 1972, speaks about the study group as "preparation for independence" and goes on to explain that "A nation needs its own language. We must firmly establish our language in order to realize independence."

People capable of understanding and using Shima Kutuba are a minority in Okinawa prefecture. However, interest is growing, including passage of a local ordinance by Okinawa prefecture that declares September 18 as "Shima Kutuba Day" in 2006. The study group teacher explains the background in the following way: "A movement is starting in which people are asking what is Okinawa and what their identity is. Even if political independence is impossible, it is necessary to obtain psychological independence."

The roots of the Okinawa independence movement can be traced back to the start of the Meiji era. It began when some people who resisted eradication of the Kingdom of the Ryukyus left for China (Qing Dynasty) and called for restoration of the Kingdom. During the years when Okinawa was under U.S. military rule after the Second World War ended in 1945, while a campaign to return Okinawa to Japan gained momentum, efforts to seek independence for Okinawa, such as the formation of the "council to create Okinawa for Okinawans" led by local business people, emerged too. This council placed an opinion advertisement calling for independence with a title of "Okinawa belongs to Okinawans!" in a local newspaper in 1969 prior to Okinawa's reversion to Japan. Additionally, a group of local people founded Urumanesia, a magazine advocating independence, in 2000 when the Summit of major nations was held in Okinawa, and it continues to issue publications from time to time.

However, many Okinawan residents are not involved in the

independence movement and view it as alcohol-fueled pub talk. Okinawa political leaders comment that "this is just romantic thinking" (Okinawa Governor Hirokazu Nakaima) and "Okinawa is not going to be independent. It is part of Japan" (Ginowan Mayor Atsushi Sakima). However, it would be dangerous to simply laugh off recent Okinawa independence efforts as pub talk. China, which has started asserting territorial rights to the Senkaku Islands, is showing considerable interest in Okinawan independence.

China' shadow

The Global Times, a paper affiliated with the Chinese Communist Party paper People's Daily, voiced its support for activities by the ACSILs in an editorial on May 16, 2013, the day after the founding of ACSILs.

"We think the establishment of the ACSILs and its political aim deserve support. Okinawan independence is the foundation communicated by history and has legitimacy. If this becomes a genuine movement, it is likely to address the real interests of Okinawan people. China should provide its backing to the extent allowed by international law."

A Chinese newspaper made a point to highlight the establishment of this autonomy association, which did not attract much attention in mainland Japan, and disseminate the news worldwide through the Internet. The Global Times is strongly influenced by the Chinese Communist Party, and its remarks can be viewed as representative of the outward policy of the Communist Party.

China is trying to utilize its historical and cultural ties to Okinawa.

Fukusyu-en, which presents replicas of famous Chinese sites, is located at the corner of a residential area in the Kume district in central Naha near the prefectural office building. Visitors find a quiet garden with a Chinese-style pagoda and pond upon entering the stonework gate. The site was built in 1992 to commemorate the 10th anniversary of the conclusion of an agreement to establish friendship city relations between Naha and Fuzhou (China).

This is where Chinese people known as the "Kume Sanjyurokusei" lived after their arrival during the Ming Dynasty period. Many Kume Sanjyurokusei held official positions in the Ryukyu Kingdom's government, such as preparing diplomatic documents required for interaction with China.

It is estimated that their descendants total about 20,000 people today, and these people form the elite in Okinawa's political and business communities. Okinawa Governor Nakaima is an example. A stone monument located in front of Fukusyu-en commemorates the arrival of the Kume Sanjyurokusei. A mausoleum for the Chinese thinker Confucius (Koushi byou-kume shiseibyou) was built in June 2013, and it is managed by an organization that consists of descendants of the Kume Sanjyurokusei. The Kume district has a rich Chinese cultural atmosphere.

The People's Daily, which has focused on these ties between Okinawa and China, issued an article in its online Japanese edition on May 31, 2013 with the following coverage entitled "Review of 'Okinawa Kumemura' with a close relationship to the Ming Dynasty."

"The immigrants came from a very high political and economic status, and their descendants continue to exercise considerable influence in Okinawa today. It is widely known that Hirokazu Nakaima, the current Governor of Okinawa, is a descendant of the Kume Sanjyurokusei. The strong presence of Chinese aspects in Okinawa culture is closely intertwined with the Kume Sanjyurokusei."

Okinawa is also exhibiting interest in a stronger relationship with China.

Naha's Wakasa district located next to Kume is the entranceway to Okinawa with a main road that extends from the airport to the city area. It is also facing Naha Port that accommodates large ships. There was discussion of building two massive dragon

History of Okinawa

"The Association of Comprehensive Studies for Independence of the Lew Chewans (ACSILs)" of Okinawa held a public symposium on October 27, in which representatives of minority ethnic groups from Taiwan and Guam also participated as panelists (held at Okinawa University in Naha).

1429	The Kingdom of the Ryukyus is established.
1609	The Kingdom of the Ryukyus comes under the rule of the Satsuma Han (feudal domain).
1872	The Japanese government abolishes the Ryukyu Han and establishes Okinawa Prefecture.
1879	The Japanese government makes the Kingdom of the Ryukyus the Ryuku Han.
1945	The Pacific War ends with a land battle in Okinawa. The U.S. military occupies Okinawa following the war.
1972	Okinawa is returned to Japanese administration.
1995	A U.S. military officer commits an act of violence against a young Japanese woman. The incident draws a huge backlash from Okinawan residents.
2000	The Okinawa Summit is held.

pillars (with a diameter of three meters and height of 15 meters) at this site in 2013. Dragon pillars that bear the shape of a dragon symbolize the authority of the Chinese Emperor. Naha City, which planned the construction, estimated a cost of about 254 million yen and intends to use lump-sum grant funds for Okinawa's advancement from the national government. The plan called for using Chinese granite for the main portion with production in China.

Why does Okinawa want to spend so much to build dragon pillars? A Naha City official explained that "the city hopes to welcome tourists who visit Okinawa from Japan and other countries and boost tourism sentiment." The primary aim is Chinese tourists. In 2012, Okinawa attracted 69,500 visitors from mainland China and 268,000 Chinese tourists in total, including Hong Kong and Taiwan. Local residents had mixed reactions with some concerns that "building dragon pillars might encourage Chinese people to think that Okinawa is subservient," but also expectations that "this could be a symbol for tourism along with Fukusyu-en and Koushi byou-kume shiseibyou."

Administrative entities in China and Okinawa have close relations. Okinawa Prefecture operates offices in Beijing, Shanghai, Hong Kong, and Taipei to encourage tourism and recruit corporate activity. It also sends high school students and university students to China, and invites Chinese high school students to Okinawa.

Claiming "territorial rights" to Okinawa too

The Governor's reception office at the prefecture building displays a folding screen that presents the Chinese inscription on the "Bridge of Nations" Bell. It has an impressive size at a height of two meters and width of five meters. The folding screen's inscription was written on a bell cast by King Sho Taikyu in 1458 and includes a phrase that indicates that the Kingdom of Ryukyu "has close ties with both China (Ming Dynasty) and Japan."

However, the conquest by Iehisa Shimadzu in 1609, which was about 150 years after the inscription was written, brought the Kingdom of the Ryukyu under the control of the Satsuma domain.

The Meiji Restoration and replacement of domains with prefectures led to Japan changing the Kingdom of the Ryukyus to the Ryukyu domain in 1872 and then renaming it as Okinawa prefecture seven years later in 1879. The Japanese government ordered King Sho Utai to live in Tokyo with his noblemen. These measures starting in the Meiji period are known as the Ryukyu annexation.

However, the Kingdom of the Ryukyus paid tribute to China's Ming and Qing dynasties while also being under the rule of the Satsuma domain for many years. Tributes began in 1372 when the Ryukyu Chuzan King accepted the request from Ming Emperor Hongwu, and this was the catalyst for deeper ties with China in trade, human exchange, and other areas.

While the Ryukyu annexation sparked an issue about control of the Ryukyus between the Japanese government and China (Qing Dynasty), the matter disappeared after Japan was victorious in the Sino-Japanese War.

The Japanese government currently asserts that Japan solidified territorial rights to Okinawa at the latest when it annexed the Ryukyus. It approved the following official opinion in a Cabinet decision on June 18, 2010.

"While it is difficult to say decisively when it became part of Japan, it was certainly part of Japan at the latest in the establishment of the Ryukyu domain in the early Meiji years and subsequent creation of Okinawa prefecture."

However, some people in Okinawa argue that the Ryukyu annexation is invalid. Yasukatsu Matsushima, a professor at Ryukoku University who leads the autonomy association, similarly asserts that "it is not approved under international law and lacks validity." Chiming in with this view, China has started to openly raise questions about Japan's territorial rights to not only the Senkaku Islands, but also Okinawa.

Large-scale anti-Japanese demonstrations took place in China in fall 2010 after the incident in which a Chinese fishing boat rammed into a patrol vessel from the Japan Coast Guard near the Senkaku Islands. Akira Ishii, a professor emeritus at the University of Tokyo with a specialty in Asia and International History, was surprised to hear that the demonstrators carried banners calling for "retrieval of the Ryukyus and freeing of Okinawa." He commented that, "While it happened at the civilian level, this is the first confirmed case of China making claims to territorial rights to not only the Senkaku Islands, but also Okinawa itself."

The People's Daily carried an essay arguing that "the time has arrived to resume discussion of the Ryukyu issue that was historically unresolved" on May 8, 2013, which was one week prior to the establishment of the autonomy association in Okinawa.

The author is a member of the Chinese Academy of Social Sciences, a government-affiliated research entity, and presented the following opinions.

The Kingdom of the Ryukyus was a tributary state of China in the Ming and Qing eras.

The Japanese government annexed the Kingdom of the Ryukyus by force and renamed it Okinawa Prefecture.

The Qing Dynasty lacked the power to pursue the Ryukyu issue because of its defeat in the Sino-Japanese War. Japan seized Ryukyu along with Taiwan and other territories in the Shimonoseki Treaty concluded in 1895 after the Sino-Japanese War.

The editorial in China's Global Times paper from May 11, 2013 write that, "The Kingdom of the Ryukyus historically had a tributary state relationship with China" and "If Japan ultimately opts for an adversarial stance toward China, China should present the Ryukyu issue as a historically unresolved matter." This editorial essentially threaten to revive the issue of territorial rights to Okinawa if Japanese does not compromise in regards to the Senkaku issue.

China expressed interest in territorial rights to Okinawa immediately after the end of the Second World War. The Republic of China led by Chiang Kai-shek submitted a document entitled "territorial issue with Japan" clearly stating that "the Ryukyu Islands belong to China" to the General Headquarters of the Supreme Commander for the Allied Powers (GHQ) that controlled Japan. Chinese newspapers at the time referred to the Okinawan islands as the "Great Wall of the Sea" and emphasized the importance of controlling Okinawa from a military perspective with comments that "China has no outlet for its navy without Ryukyu."

Attitudes of the local people

What do the residents of Okinawa, a key factor, think about the Chinese stance?

There is some interesting data that sheds light on the views of Okinawans toward China – the "Survey of Okinawan attitudes toward China" conducted by Okinawa Prefecture in 2012. The prefecture requested the cooperation of 3,000 people living in Okinawa between the ages of 15 and 75 by mail and received replies from 1,187 people. It presented the results alongside of data from a nationwide survey (implemented by non-profit organization The Genron NPO in April and May, 2012), as shown below.

- What impression do you have of China?
  "Positive" "Relatively positive" Okinawa 9.1%, nationwide 15.6%
  "Negative" "Relatively negative" Okinawa 89%, nationwide 84.3%
- With which country do you feel a stronger affinity – China or the United States?
  "China" Okinawa 4.2%, nationwide 6.6%
  "United States" Okinawa 53.9%, nationwide 51.9%
- Do you expect a military conflict between Japan, China, or some other country in East Asian waters?
  "Likely to occur within a few years" "Likely to occur in the future" Okinawa 43.6%, nationwide 27.2%
  "Unlikely to occur" Okinawa 30%, nationwide 37.9%

The survey took place during the uptick in anti-Japanese demonstrations in China triggered by Japan's nationalization of the Senkaku Islands in September 2012. While the prefecture expected tough results toward China to some extent, officials were surprised to find that "sentiment is this negative." Tetsumi Takara, a professor at the University of the Ryukyus familiar with Okinawan political affairs, commented that "While they dislike the U.S. military bases, Okinawa residents naturally have negative feelings toward China applying pressure in relation to the Senkaku Islands."

However, it is precisely strong reservations toward China and fears of a war that might shake the attitudes of Okinawan residents if an event actually occurred.

The Rebuild Japan Initiative Foundation, a policy think tank headed by former Asahi Shimbun editor-in-chief Yoichi Funabashi, published "Japan in Peril? 9 Crisis Scenarios" (Shinchosha Publishing), which analyzed national crises that might confront Japan, in 2013. The book presented the following analysis of China's aim and the impact of "losing the Senkaku Islands" in a potential scenario of China armed with automatic small arms landing on the Senkaku Islands and the relinquishment of effective control to China due to a lack of effective countermeasures by the Japanese government.

"One of China's purposes in taking the Senkaku Islands would be breaking through the first island line, the Japanese archipelago, which blocks a path to the Pacific for the Chinese Navy."

"Japan's loss of the Senkaku Islands would also split the relationship between Okinawa and mainland Japan. The possibility of conflicts with the U.S. military would naturally increase due to China making the western Pacific its backyard. Okinawa, which would become sandwiched between the U.S. and China, would take a path of neutrality. The movement against U.S. military bases would intensify and call for a departure from Okinawa because the U.S. military would no longer need to defend Taiwan."

"Japan's loss of the Senkakus would sharply raise the danger of geopolitical risk. Losing the Senkakus would not only sandwich Okinawa between the U.S. and China, but also deepen the split between mainland Japan and Okinawa. The loss of the Senkakus would result in the 'loss' of Okinawa."

Mr. Funabashi, who speaks out about diplomatic and security policies, founded the Rebuild Japan Initiative Foundation after leaving Asahi Shimbun Company in 2010. He raised alarm that the loss of Okinawa would have "a dramatic impact on Japan and undermine the core of Japan's national security policy by losing the deterrent force of the U.S. military bases."

However, this type of concern is surprisingly weak in Japan.

Little sense of crisis

Yukio Hatoyama, former Prime Minister, attended a symposium held at Okinawa International University located in Ginowan City (Okinawa) on November 2, 2013. The lecture hall used for the event was packed, and some people listened from the outside through the hall's windows. Mr. Hatoyama launched into criticism of the U.S. military base in the charged atmosphere.

"We must refute the arguments being made that claim that U.S. help is vital, that the right of collective self-defense is necessary, and that U.S. military bases in Okinawa are essential because of the volatile and dangerous situation surrounding the Senkaku Islands."

His speech attracted major applause, and the audience gathered around to shake hands with Mr. Hatoyama after the symposium finished.

Mr. Hatoyama's personal view of security policy envisions "security without a permanent military presence." The Democratic Party (previously Democratic Party of Japan) advocated formation of a multilateral security framework and shrinkage and elimination of U.S. military bases in Japan at its founding in 1996. Statements at the symposium adhered to the core concept of security without a permanent military presence.

Diplomatic and security experts criticized this view as "unrealistic." Yoji Koda, a former Commander in Chief of the Self-Defense Forces, argued that "The exit of U.S. military forces from Okinawa is the same as their exit from Japan. The only one laughing if this happens will be China."

However, some officials in the Japanese government have recently starting taking the view that security without a permanent military presence might become the reality if an unforeseen event occurs. Officials at the Ministry of Foreign Affairs fear that security without a permanent military presence could immediately emerge as a reality if there is a major accident that takes human lives at U.S. military bases in Okinawa." Build-up of anti-base sentiment by local residents could cause a forced retreat by the U.S. military out of Okinawa.

Japan might face a situation similar to the Philippines if this happens. The Philippines banned the presence of permanent foreign military forces in 1987 in response to a growing movement against U.S. military bases, and the U.S. military subsequently left the country in 1992. China used this power vacuum to expand its strength in the South China Sea, and seized Mischief Reef in the Spratly Islands that the Philippines had been effectively controlling. While the Philippines desperately asked the U.S. military to return, and the U.S. has increased port calls by naval ships and conducted other activities, it is not easy to regain an island once it is taken.

The Senkaku Islands confront the same situation as Mischief Reef, and there is a growing need to seriously consider sustaining the U.S. military presence in Okinawa in order to prevent a situation that threatens Japan's national security.

Okinawa, meanwhile, deals with a heavy concentration of U.S. military facilities and areas covering 22,807 hectares, which amounts to about 74%

of all U.S. facilities nationwide. This situation naturally heightens frustration that "the burden of the bases is excessive," particularly since Okinawa Prefecture amounts to just 0.6% of Japan's entire land area.

Concentration of U.S. military bases in Okinawa reflects the geographical importance of Okinawa. Mainland Okinawa is some distance from China and the Korean Peninsula and cannot be easily subject to direct attack. It is also much quicker for U.S. military forces to respond to an incident by being in Okinawa than coming from the mainland United States. Furthermore, the U.S. military has developed facilities from troop housing to training since its occupation of Okinawa in 1945, and Okinawa's importance as a site that the U.S. military does not want to relinquish has a major impact as well.

Japanese and U.S. governments have obviously tried to reduce the burden from the bases on Okinawa. The U.S. military returned a total of over 5,000 hectares of land to the Japanese side during the period from the Okinawa reversion in 1972 through 2012. Nevertheless, U.S. military facilities and areas still account for 10% of Okinawa Prefecture's land area. The two governments agreed to return six U.S. military facilities in the southern portion of the prefecture (totaling over 1,000 hectares) in April 2013 over the next 10-16 years with the aim of further alleviation of the burden of the bases on Okinawa. The main focus of this agreement is the return of U.S. Air Station Futenma (about 480 hectares) located in urbanized portion of Ginowan City (Okinawa) and often called the world's most dangerous air facility.

Directionless Futenma issue

Ginowan City's Futenma No.2 elementary school runs adjacent to the Air Station Futenma on the other side of a fence. U.S. military planes fly over the heads of children, and this is a symbol of the difficult reality with military bases in Okinawa. School officials speak with concern about a "major catastrophe if there is an accident."

Homes are also built around Air Station Futenma, and it appears from the ground level that the U.S. military plants are skimming over the tops of condominium buildings when they land and takeoff.

A large transport helicopter operating out of Air Station Futenma crashed into neighboring Okinawa International University in August 2004. While the accident did not have any fatalities, it could easily have been a serious disaster. Other trouble since then has included a takeoff by a KC130 air-to-air refueling tanker without properly storing its hose and a transport Osprey hovering above the runway for roughly an hour because of instrument abnormalities. Ginowan City is worried that Air Station Futenma might become entrenched and continue operating at the current site and is petitioning for the transfer of the air facility by asking authorities to "understand our pain, sufferings, and anger" (Ginowan Mayor Atsushi Sakima).

The U.S. military built Air Station Futenma in 1945 during the Battle of Okinawa, and the U.S. Marines have continued using the facilities since Okinawa's reversion to Japan in 1972.

Marines stationed in Okinawa are the III Marine Expeditionary Force (III MEF) that consists of the 3rd Marine Division (ground combat element), 1st Marine Aircraft Wing (aviation combat element) and 3rd Marine Logistics Group (logistics combat element). Air Station Futenma is home to Marine Aircraft Group 36 (battle helicopters, transport helicopters, and KC130 air-to-air refueling tankers) and Marine Air Control Group 18 (air control squadron and air support (missile) squadron) under the 1st Marine Aircraft Wing.

Marines are transported directly into enemy territory and build outposts, and they also engage in guerilla war and other specialized operations. Readiness to immediately deal with an emergency situation is vital in order to carry out their duties.

The 3rd Marine Division is stationed at Camp Schwab (Nago City, etc.), Camp Hansen (Kincho, etc.) and Camp Courtney (Uruma City), and it needs an aviation element located nearby to transport troops in order to maintain immediate responsiveness. The runway at Air Station Futenma extends for 2,800 meters and can accommodate takeoffs and landings by large planes. "Futenma is a very important facility" for the U.S. military (Ministry of Defense official).

However, the Japanese and U.S. governments agreed on the return of Air Station Futenma to Japan in 1996 because of its location in the middle of a residential area and risk of a major accident occurring at any time. The two sides reviewed locations for a replacement facility in Okinawa prefecture and started focusing in the area off the coast of Camp Schwab, an existing U.S. military base, in Nago City. Yet the Japanese and U.S. governments, Okinawa prefecture, and Nago City struggled to coordinate key details, such as the exact position and construction method for the new air base. The parties reached agreement on a basic plan in 2002, and boring surveys began in 2004. Yet a fierce local opposition movement surfaced and stalled the plan for moving to the area off the coast of Camp Schwab.

Takemasa Moriya, who had a central role in handling the move issue as Administrative Vice-Minister of Defense during 2003-07, wrote in his book "Futenma: Secret Record of Negotiations" (Shinchosha Publishing) about developments during this period that "changing and making additions to negotiation terms is a common technique in Okinawa."

The Okinawa view, however, is different. A former LDP diet member from Okinawa raised questions about the government's approach. "The opposition movement had free reign due to the absence of riot police and the Japan Coast Guard. The government did not address the situation seriously."

This experience left substantial mistrust among the Japanese and U.S. governments, Okinawa prefecture, and Nago City.

Nago City is the local government entity at the center of Okinawa's northern area and faces the Pacific on the eastern coast and East China Sea on the western coast. The western coast has a concentration of city offices, resort hotels, and other major facilities, while the eastern coast is a quiet area with a scattering of small fishing ports besides Camp Schwab.

In 2006, the Japanese and U.S. governments formulated a new plan to build a V-shaped facility with two runways with a length of 1,800 meters each on the coast of Camp Schwab in the Henoko district of Nago City, and Nago City also accepted the plan. The basic concept involved land reclamation in about 160 hectares of shallow waters on the coast of Camp Schwab and building a runway connected to the island itself. This is an easier method than building a runway in waters off the coast. It also offers the benefits of hindering disruptions by the opposition movement because construction work is performed within a U.S. military facility. Furthermore, U.S. military planes fly over the water, limiting noise-related problems for nearby residents and removing danger from crashes. The agreement finally came a decade after the Japanese and U.S. governments agreed on the return of Air Station Futenma in 1996 after much uncertainty and confusion.

However, Prime Minister Yukio Hatoyama for the DPJ, which gained control of the national government in the Lower House election in August 2009, severely undermined the agreement.

Mr. Hatoyama, who was the DPJ party president at the time, bellowed from a microphone in Okinawa on July 19 ahead of the Lower House election that he rejected the effort to keep Air Station Futenma in the prefecture and move it to Nago, and intended to relocate the facility to somewhere outside of Okinawa.

"If moving the facility outside of the prefecture, at the very least, can unite everyone, then I will also take aggressive action."

The DPJ's policy chart (manifest) for the Lower House election did not mention moving the facility outside of Japan or outside of Okinawa. This is because the DPJ, which was aiming to form a government, wanted to approach the issue cautiously because the plan for moving to the Henoko district coast approved by Japan and the United States in 2006 was a "delicate glasswork" fashioned out of 10 years of meandering after the agreement to return Air Station Futenma.

Mr. Hatoyama suddenly appeared with talk of "at least a move outside of the prefecture." He had already mentioned interest in aiming for a move outside of the prefecture at the press conference upon his selection as party president in May 2009 and consciously rewrote the party's policy promise. His comments emboldened anti-base advocates in Okinawa.

The DPJ was victorious in the Lower House election, and Mr. Hatoyama, who became Prime Minister, looked into the possibility of moving the facility outside of the prefecture as he had promised. The Social Democratic Party that formed a coalition with the DPJ consented too. However, there was slim prospect of readily finding a new answer to a problem that had been causing difficulties for over a decade, and the Hatoyama government struggled with the issue from its outset.

Mr. Hatoyama participated in a Japan-U.S. Summit Meeting with President Barack Obama on November 13, 2009, and the two leaders had the following conversation.

Mr. Hatoyama said, "Please trust me," and Mr. Obama replied, "Absolutely, I trust you."

While he managed to navigate the Summit Meeting, Mr. Hatoyama lacked a specific solution, such as an alternative site. The Social Democratic Party, meanwhile, remained in opposition to the move to Nago and indicated a willingness to exit the coalition government if it returned to a policy of moving the base to a site within the prefecture. The Hatoyama government maneuvered itself into a corner, and Mr. Hatoyama felt compelled to "stake his position" on the Futenma issue in comments to a full session of the Upper House on April 23, 2010.

Mr. Hatoyama visited Okinawa a month later on May 23 and told Governor Nakaima that the government planned to move Air Station Futenma to Nago in line with Japan-U.S. agreement. This was a directionless exercise of creating a major stir that entangled the United States and Okinawa and just ending up back at the original Japan-U.S. agreement. The dissatisfied Social Democratic Party left the coalition, and the Hatoyama government collapsed on June 2.

Before his departure, Mr. Hatoyama disturbingly commented that, "the more I learned, the more apparent it became that it is necessary to have the deterrence of U.S. military forces stationed in Okinawa."

However, conditions in Okinawa changed significantly despite reaching the conclusion of "moving the base to Nago in line with Japan-U.S. agreement." Public opinion against a move that kept the facility within the prefecture reached an unprecedented level due to the catalyst of Mr. Hatoyama's comment of "at least outside of the prefecture." Newcomer Susumu Inamine, former head of the city's education department, who opposed the move beat incumbent Yoshikazu Shimabukuro, who had given approval to the move to Henoko, in the Nago mayoral election in January 2010.

These developments placed Governor Nakaima, who had demonstrated some understanding of the move within the prefecture to Nago, in a precarious position. The Governor attended a rally of Okinawans calling for a transfer of the base outside of the prefecture held in Yomitan village on April 25, 2010 amid growing pressure for a move outside of Okinawa. While Mr. Nakaima did not mention his personal view of whether the facility should move outside of the prefecture or stay within it, he stated that "I'd like to see a never give-up persistence in line with his political promise," in reference to Mr. Hatoyama's comment of "at least outside of the prefecture,"

and also that "Futenma absolutely cannot be allowed to take hold permanently." Heads and deputy heads of all prefecture municipalities attended
the rally. Everyone realized that it would be difficult to move Air Station
Futenma to another location within the prefecture.

Return of Prime Minister Abe

The 46th Lower House election held in December 2012 provided a landslide
victory for the LDP. The LDP itself won 294 seats, and the Komeito Party,
with which it cooperated during the election, secured 31 seats. These results
gave 325 seats to the LDP-led coalition. The DPJ only won 57 seats and lost
control of the government that it had taken three years earlier.

Shinzo Abe, the LDP president, received designation from the National
Diet as the new prime minister on December 26, just ahead of the year's
close, and immediately sprang into action on the Futenma move because
confusion surrounding this issue had become a thorn in the side of the
Japan-U.S. relationship.

His first step was repairing relations between the national government
and governor Nakaima. The government needed the governor's approval
of reclamation of the water surface in order to build a new runway on the
coast of Camp Schwab in Henoko, the destination for the move decided by
the Japanese and U.S. governments, based on the Act on Reclamation of
Publicly-owned Water Surface.

The government could have begun reclamation unrelated to the
governor's view if it enacted a special measures law that transferred the
governor's approval authority for the reclamation to the national government. However, muscling forward with reclamation absent the governor's
understanding clearly would have encouraged local confusion and enflamed
the opposition movement. Government officials overwhelmingly agreed
that "a special measures law was poor policy" (Foreign Ministry official),
and the only choice was somehow convincing the governor to approve the
reclamation.

Prime Minster Abe flew to Okinawa on February 2, 2013. He spoke
in a surprisingly humble manner in front of the media in a meeting with
governor Nakaima in a room at Harbor View Hotel in Naha.

"I would like to put emphasis on listening to what everyone has to say. Trust between the national government and people of Okinawa has broken down. We must build trust again from the beginning."

Mr. Abe stressed differences with the DPJ government. He promised to reach a quick solution to the Futenma move issue ahead of his first Summit Meeting with U.S. President Obama in Washington on February 22.

Some portions of the government had cautious views about rushing forward in necessary procedures for the Futenma move, such as the Defense Ministry source who warned that, "It will be difficult to build a relationship with Okinawa even though the government has changed." However, the national government proceeded with submission of application documents requesting the governor's approval of reclamation on March 22, 2013 under the firm resolve of Mr. Abe. The prime minister felt encouragement from signs of an acceptance stance in Nago following the change in administrations from the DPJ to the LDP.

The Nago Fishing Cooperative Association, which holds fishing rights to the waters covered by the reclamation, held an extraordinary general meeting and decided to give consent to the reclamation on March 11. In fact, 88 of the 90 attending members consented. This was welcome support for the national government in its pursuit of the move. A member of the cooperative in his 70's commented to the media after the meeting ended that, "There's really no choice considering the danger of the Futenma facility at its current site. Isn't it better to have the planes flying in Henoko over the ocean, rather than in that urban area, in terms of Okinawa as a whole?"

Mr. Inamine, the mayor of Nago who opposed the Air Station Futenma move, meanwhile, was displeased. He harshly criticized the fishing cooperative as "being drawn to or swayed by the bait of compensation." Nago, which has a population of just over 60,000, was divided.

Finally resolved

A key event in the history of U.S. military bases on Okinawa occurred on December 27, 2013. Governor Nakaima stated that he would approve the request for reclamation on Nago's Henoko coast submitted by the national government.

Deep wrinkles could be seen on governor Nakaima's forehead as he began a press conference at the governor's office in Naha just after 3pm. He spoke in a serious tone that, "I would like to express my opinion."

"Based on results from required reviews and implementation of all possible environmental conservation measures, I have concluded that the request meets the standards (under the Act on Reclamation of Publicly-owned Water Surface) and give it my approval."

While this decision provided a significant advance in dealing with the Futenma move issue, groups against the bases who called for rejection of the reclamation request, were angry and gathered around the prefectural offices holding red placards inscribed with the phrase "we will not capitulate." A protest sit-in filled the lobby of the first floor of the prefecture office building.

Governor Nakaima said the following to friendly prefecture council members about his decision to give the government approval: "I am aware that various Okinawans will be raising their voices. However, the Abe Government is different than past administrations. I expect it to make progress on the Futenma matter."

Governor Nakaima was born in 1939. He was a section head at the former Ministry of International Trade and Industry (MITI) and later served as president of Okinawa Electric. Mr. Nakaima became governor in 2006 with support from the LDP and Komeito Party.

Governor Nakaima headed to the U.S. ambassador's residence in Tokyo's Minato Ward at the invitation of the U.S. Ambassador Caroline Kennedy on November 29, 2013. He was cheerful and even more talkative than usual having been invited by the eldest daughter of former U.S. President John F. Kennedy and a "person attracting considerable interest" just 10 days since becoming ambassador.

He began politely with the comment that "Okinawa and the United States have close ties in political and economic areas. Okinawans generally have positive feelings toward the United States," but then recommended on the base issue that "the Japanese and U.S. governments need to take steps to lighten the burden from the bases." The ambassador responded that, "I would like to visit Okinawa and hear what Okinawans are saying. In fact, my father visited Okinawa when he served as a U.S. Senator."

The Okinawa governor possesses a political presence not seen in

Timeline of the Air Station Futenma relocation issue

1996	April 12	Japan and the U.S. reach an agreement for the full return of Air Station Futenma within 5 to 7 years.
	December 2	The final SACO report includes an agreement for relocation within Okinawa prefecture.
1997	November 5	The Japanese government proposes building a heliport off the coast of Nago city.
1999	December 28	The Japanese government passes a Cabinet resolution on the Henoko relocation.
2002	July 29	The Japanese government, Okinawa prefecture and Nago city reach an agreement on how to carry out offshore reclamation.
2006	April 7	The Japanese government and Nago city reach an agreement on a proposal for building a v-shaped runway on the coast of Henoko.
	May 1	The governments of Japan and the U.S. reach an agreement for the planned relocation to the Henoko coast by 2014.
	November 19	Hirokazu Nakaima, who accepted a conditional relocation, is elected Prefectural Governor of Okinawa.
2009	September 16	Start of the Hatoyama administration, which purported "relocation outside the prefecture and country."
2010	January 24	Susumu Inamine, of the opposing faction to the relocation, is elected Mayor of Nago city.
	May 23	Prime Minister Hatoyama reverses his position and accepts the Henoko relocation
2013	March 22	The Japanese government applies to Governor Nakaima for permission to reclaim the Henoko coast.
	April 5	Japan and the U.S. announce the possible return of Air Station Futenma in fiscal 2010.

governors from other prefectures because of the U.S. military base issue. This is why Ambassador Kennedy, who had just assumed her position, took the step of inviting him to the ambassador's residence.

The Japanese government obviously places emphasis on the relationship with the Okinawan governor too. Japanese prime ministers during the seven years since Governor Nakaima first took office in November 2006 met with him about 40 times. Prime Minister Abe met with governor Nakaima at the Prime Minister's office on December 25, 2013 and encouraged cooperation on the Futenma move issue by communicating an unusual policy of securing a budget for Okinawa's advancement of at least 300 billion yen per year through fiscal 2021.

While receiving this warm treatment, the Okinawan governor is often under pressure to reach major political decisions related to the base issue.

In 1995, then-governor Masahide Ota refused the proxy signature approving compulsory use of U.S. military base land amid strong anti-base sentiment from Okinawans in response to the rape of a young girl by U.S. military personnel. He also resisted the move of Air Station Futenma to Nago. Dissension with the government deepened, and there was even talk about the "prefecture causing a recession" because of a serious impact on the local economy by this situation, including not holding an Okinawa Policy Council meeting to discuss advancement measures.

Governor Keiichi Inamine, who defeated Mr. Ota in the 1998 election, decided to approve the move of Air Station Futenma to Henoko in November 1999 after lengthy consideration. Mr. Inamine reflected on his tenure that, "I needed a nightcap during my term." He explained the unique pressure facing the Okinawan governor in the following way: "The Okinawan governor needs to constantly be thinking about national interests and is caught in between national and local concerns."

In Japan, issues directly related to security policy between Japan and the United States are effectively left up to decisions by the Okinawan governor. A person who served as a top official in Okinawa prefecture commented that, "The Governor has a lonely position because he bears all the responsibility."

Unusual coverage by local newspapers

Governor Nakaima confronted fierce criticism within Okinawa for his major decision regarding the Futenma move.

"No Okinawan governor has ever joined with the national government and turned his back on the people's will to this extent."

A Social Democratic Party member read a resolution calling for the resignation of governor Nakaima at the Okinawa Prefecture Assembly on January 10, 2014. The governor observed glumly. The resolution passed by a slight margin with 24 members in favor and 21 members in opposition.

While the resolution is non-binding, it was the first time for the Okinawa Prefecture Assembly to pass a resolution calling for the resignation of a governor.

Local newspapers also openly called for governor Nakaima's resignation.

The Ryukyu Shimpo criticized the governor's decision as a "historical stain" and carried an editorial piece calling for his resignation in the morning edition on December 28, 2013.

"All-Okinawa sentiment favors closure and removal of Air Station Futenma and relocation outside of the prefecture as well as suspension of Osprey deployments. Resignation by this governor who betrayed Okinawans is unavoidable."

The Ryukyu Shimpo also reported the results of an emergency phone opinion survey conducted jointly with Okinawa Television Broadcasting (the survey took place on December 28 and 29) in the morning edition on December 30. Its headlines were "61% replied that they do not support approval of the reclamation" and "73.5% disagreed with relocation in Okinawa prefecture."

The Okinawa Times wrote in its editorial piece on December 28 that, "We must say that the governor abandoned his qualification as a politician who has a responsibility to represent Okinawans."

Former Defense Minister Fumio Kyuma commented regarding this type of local newspaper coverage in Okinawa that, "Harsh positions on the U.S. military base issue stand out and are fostering anti-base and anti-Security Agreement sentiment among Okinawans."

U.S. military representatives reached similar conclusions. Robert D. Eldridge, the Deputy Assistant Chief of Staff, Government and External Affairs, Marine Forces Japan (former associate professor at Osaka University), noted that, "Local journalists appear to be convinced that Okinawa and the U.S. military cannot have good relations. We want to build a relationship of trust."

Mr. Eldridge also divulged that an executive at a local newspaper stated that "we will absolutely not write anything positive about the U.S. military."

Media coverage of the base issue by local newspapers is radical.

There was also this case.

The Ryukyu Shimpo extensively covered an inappropriate remark by the Director-General of the Defense Ministry's Okinawa Defense Bureau regarding the Futenma move issue in November 2011. His response when asked about timing for submission of the environmental impact assessment required for reclamation of Nago's Henoko coast to the prefecture was "you do not tell someone that you are going to rape them ahead of time," using an example of raping a woman.

The Director-General's statement came during an off-the-record discussion (contact without providing the news source) with journalists at a pub in Naha. He requested that journalists not use remarks for articles, and the participating journalists agreed. However, the Ryukyu Shimpo journalist decided that the comments were "public in nature and affected public interest" and wrote the article. A related party explained that many Ryukyu Shimpo journalists who heard the comment asserted that the "article should be written even though comments were off the record." The article resulted in the Director-General's demotion.

The Ryukyu Shimpo, which started publishing in 1893, issues 160,749 copies per day (November 2013), and the Okinawa Times, which began publishing in 1948, issues 160,705 copies (October 2013). These two papers control almost 90% coverage in Okinawa's newspaper market. National newspapers (Yomiuri, Asahi, Mainichi, and Sankei) do not have printing sites in Okinawa and fly newspapers printed in mainland Japan to Okinawa. Nikkei outsources printing locally in Okinawa, but it only issues 5,829 copies (December 2013). Local newspapers dominate the Okinawan market due to the geographical advantage.

The national government also pays attention to the influence of local newspapers in Okinawa.

Chief Cabinet Secretary Suga traveled to Okinawa and visited local media firms on April 3, 2013. His visit aimed to promote understanding of the first-ever "Restoration of Sovereignty Day" ceremony in Tokyo on April 28. The second Abe administration decided to celebrate the day on which the San Francisco Peace Treaty that ended occupation by the allied countries after the Second World War (April 28, 1952) took effect as "Restoration of Sovereignty Day." However, Okinawans refer to this as a "day of humiliation" because Okinawa remains under U.S. military control even after the treaty's enactment. Opposition to and criticism of "Restoration of Sovereignty Day" had picked up mainly among local newspapers.

While Mr. Suga's visits to regional media offices were extremely unusual, there was no change in critical media coverage of the "Restoration of Sovereignty Day." The government held a ceremony as planned, but did not continue it in the following year.

Hiromori Maedomari, a professor at Okinawa International University and former head of Ryukyu Shimpo's editorial board, explained the coverage stance of local newspapers in the following way.

"Newspapers that do not reflect or deviate from local sentiment cannot survive. In Okinawa, people would stop reading a newspaper if it is seen as affiliated with mainland Japan, the United States, or the establishment."

Deep-rooted feelings of discrimination

"Discrimination" is a key word in understanding the "sentiment of Okinawan people" mentioned by Mr. Maedomari.

Okinawa's Deputy Governor Kurayoshi Takara wrote four numbers on a white board in his presentation at the National Graduate Institute for Policy Studies located in Roppongi (Tokyo) on November 18, 2013.

1429

1879

1945

1972

These numbers represent the years of turning points in Okinawa's history – 1429 was the start of the Kingdom of the Ryukyus, 1879 was the Ryukyu annexation when Okinawa Prefecture was established, 1945 was the Second World War when many Okinawans were killed, and 1972 was reversion to Japan.

Mr. Takara, who is also a historian, explained that there is a tendency for Okinawans to see this history in the context of "discrimination from mainly Japan."

This logic attributes the lack of alleviation of the burden of the bases to mainland Japan's discriminatory approach to Okinawa. It also blames the tragic battle in Okinawa during the Second World War and elimination of the Kingdom of the Ryukyus and establishment of Okinawa Prefecture on "discriminatory attitudes on the mainland side."

Mr. Takara made the following appeal in his presentation.

"The base issue cannot be easily resolved. It is important to understand that it involves more than just foreign policy, national security, and international politics and is related to the historical feelings of the people who live in Okinawa."

Okinawa's top political leaders have openly used the "discrimination" term in recent years. Governor Nakaima commented at the rally on April 25, 2010 calling for relocation of Air Station Futenma outside of the prefecture that, "I would like to see a sharp reduction in the excessive burden of the bases. It is clearly unfair and even seems close to discrimination viewed in terms of Japan as a whole."

Masaharu Kina, speaker of the Okinawa Prefecture Assembly, criticized the government at a rally opposing the "Restoration of Sovereignty Day" held on April 28, 2013 saying that "this once again highlights discrimination toward Okinawa." On this day, while the government conducted a "Restoration of Sovereignty Day" event in Tokyo, the Naha City office displayed a dark blue flag that expressed deep sadness.

It becomes even tougher to find a solution if the U.S. military base issue gets intertwined with the historical mindset.

Akihisa Nagashima, who served as special adviser to the prime minister on foreign policy and security affairs in the DPJ's Yoshihiko Noda administration, comments that "the intermingling of history and the problem of having to endure the excessive burden posed by the U.S. bases fosters the sentiment felt by Okinawans."

"While the silent majority in Okinawa acknowledges the importance of the Japan-U.S. alliance, Okinawa has reached the limit of being forced to accept burdens."

How should mainland Japan approach the situation in Okinawa?

A national diet member from Okinawa suggests that "if Okinawa is treated with a sense of solidarity as part of Japan, suspicions toward the mainland would not take hold." "Solidarity" obviously means sharing the burden of the bases.

Governor Nakaima met with Yoshihiko Fukuda, the mayor of Iwakuni

City located in Yamaguchi Prefecture, at the Okinawa Prefecture office on November 12, 2013. Mr. Fukuda stated that Iwakuni would accept the transfer of the in-flight tanker plane squadron from Air Station Futenma at the Iwakuni base. He is a rare case of a mainland political leader showing a willingness to share the base burden through real action.

The Okinawa governor responded happily to Mr. Fukuda's statement that "Iwakuni will do what it can."

"This is the first time I have heard this from someone outside of Okinawa."

A leading member of the local LDP organization who heard about the exchange commented to a journalist that he was "really pleased."

Major discrepancies in views of national security

Yonaguni Island is Japan's westernmost island. It is a national border island from which it is possible to see Taiwan, which is about 100 kilometers away, on a clear day and has cliffs buffeted by the "Japan Current" around its periphery. It is also only 150 kilometers away from the Senkaku Islands where Japan and China are clashing.

China fired a warning missile as part of a purported military exercise in waters off Taiwan in March 1996, expressing dissatisfaction with Taiwan's presidential election. One of the missiles landed on the water about 60 kilometers west of Yonaguni Island. Some island residents heard a thunder-like explosion and saw a column of water.

Okinawa's Yonaguni Township is very sensitive to security issues because of this situation. The Yaeyama Textbook Selection District Council (Ishigaki City, Yonaguni Township, Taketomi Township) selected the textbook issued by Ikuhosha Publishing (headquartered in Tokyo) in the textbook selection for its public middle schools in 2011. Former members of the "Japan Society for History Textbook Reform" wrote this textbook and provided extensive coverage of security issues and Japan's traditional culture.

Yono Sakihara, the head of the Yonaguni board of education, explained the reason for this choice.

"We did not want to use a textbook that takes a negative view of the

U.S. military and Japanese military. We are interested in having our children be educated as Japanese people and have a Japanese identity. This is why we selected the textbook."

However, Taketomi Township, which belongs to the same Yaeyama Textbook Selection District Council, rejected the Ikuhosha textbook because teachers criticized its insufficient coverage of the U.S. military base issue in Okinawa. Japan's Act on Free School Textbooks requires that all municipalities participating in a selection district use the same textbook. Taketomi's response violated the law, and the town did not receive free distribution of the textbook paid by the national government. Instead it distributed a textbook from TOKYO SHOSEKI (headquartered in Tokyo) using donated funds.

On October 18, 2013, the Ministry of Education, Culture, Sports, Science and Technology (MEXT) instructed the Okinawa Prefecture Board of Education to request corrective action by the Taketomi Board of Education based on the Local Autonomy Act. The relevant minister can issue a corrective request via a prefecture when a local government entity's activities violate a law, in accordance with the Local Autonomy Act. However, the Okinawa Prefecture Board of Education did not move on the request, and frustrated MEXT officials had Parliamentary Vice-Minister Michiko Ueno call the head of the prefecture board to Tokyo for questioning on November 28.

"It is very disappointing that you have not requested corrective action by the Taketomi Board of Education yet. If this continues, the Okinawa Prefecture Board of Education will also be violating the Local Autonomy Act."

Nevertheless, the Okinawa Prefecture Board of Education continued to drag its feet. A MEXT official speculated that the prefecture board appears to be worried about criticism of a corrective request by the teachers' union and local media with strong leftist views."

Major discrepancies in national security views, along the lines of Yonaguni and Taketomi townships, exist in Okinawa, and the most pronounced is the U.S. military base issue.

A number of men and women stand around "Nodake Gate" used as an entrance and exit to Air Station Futenma (Ginowan City, Okinawa). They wave placards that say "Marine Out" and "No Base" at the cars of

U.S. military personnel with Y-number license plates. They also yell through handheld microphones at cars that stop at the red light prior to driving out onto the public road.

"Hey you in the Y-number car! Are you looking?"

A man holding a placard explains that the group conducts protests twice a day (in the morning and the afternoon) on weekdays. They are mainly people involved in lawsuits against Futenma's jet roar noise calling for suspension of flights by U.S. military planes and compensation for noise damages and also include retired members of the teachers union and reformist party supporters. The man calmly explains that "it seems to really bother U.S. military personnel."

Colorful vinyl strings are tied randomly to the fence around the gate and flutter in the wind, highlighting the activities of anti-base advocates.

This type of intense anti-base activity takes place at a variety of sites around Okinawa.

In Nago's Henoko, the target relocation site for Air Station Futenma, the Helicopter Base Opposition Council against the move has two tents along the embankment on the coastline. Members sit in pipe chairs pointed in the direction of the water 365 days a year. They are monitoring the situation to ensure that the government does not make a surprise start to construction work.

"The Japanese government is ignoring the voices of Okinawa. Sacrifices in the name of "national policy" promoted by the national government are always endured by Okinawa."

This is what Council Representative Hiroshi Ashitomi explained. A female member of the group indicated that participants are roughly split between Okinawans and those from mainland Japan. The Council covers activity costs through fund-raising efforts and other initiatives.

The opposition movement against the Air Station Futenma relocation is particularly fierce among anti-base campaigns in Okinawa. In September 2004, it dispatched boats to interfere with the boring survey for the project to relocate the facility off the coast of Henoko. Toshima Kitazawa, a DPJ Upper House Diet Member who has experience dealing with the move issue as Defense Minister, commented that "the opposition people had a very strong belief that they stood up to the Japanese and U.S. government and stopped the move."

The base issue in Okinawa has deep roots back to the closing phase of the Second World War. The U.S. military, which defeated Japanese forces in the Battle of Okinawa, began building bases in preparation for an attack on mainland Japan. After the war ended in 1945, it expanded the bases in order to address the Cold War with the Communist World. Local residents struggling with war damages were helpless in the face of the U.S. military with overwhelming power. Journalist Frank Gibney wrote an article about the situation in Okinawa for Time magazine entitled "Okinawa: Forgotten Island" in 1949.

"Troops with probably the lowest morale and sense of discipline among any U.S. forces throughout the world govern local residents living in abject poverty."

While the San Francisco Peace Treaty restored independence to Japan in 1952, Okinawa remained under the rule of the U.S. military and almost nothing changed.

Residents requested rent for land being used by the military, but the amount offered by the U.S. side in 1952 was so low that it was said that "a year's rent per tsubo (about three square meters) was not even enough to purchase a bottle of Coca-Cola." The contracts also set a lengthy period of around 20 years. Many landowners refused to provide land to the military, but the U.S. military issued an eminent domain order in 1953 and seized land with "guns and bulldozers."

Base-related problems occurred throughout Okinawa, but the first case of an island-wide anti-base movement was the "shimagurumi" protest in 1956. Talk of a lump-sum land rent scheme with the potential to take land on a virtually permanent basis emerged, and a U.S. House of Representatives Survey Team issued a recommendation approving the new format, angering residents. Rallies and demonstrations throughout the island led to global media coverage of the Okinawa base issue. The U.S. military withdrew the lump-sum payment scheme and raised land rents after this fight. Toshiaki Arashiro, a visiting professor at Okinawa University, who is well-versed in the base problem, suggests that, "Success in making some change in the U.S. government's policies through the "shimagurumi" protest gave significant confidence to Okinawans."

145

Island-level anti-base movements took place numerous times after this event. Protests, later known as the "Koza riot," broke out in Okinawa City in 1970 after a traffic accident involving a drunk U.S. serviceman. Many people were injured in the ensuing riot that included burning U.S. military vehicles. The riot exposed the limitations of Okinawan rule by the U.S. military and is viewed as a catalyst for progress toward the reversion of Okinawa to Japan.

Large-scale anti-base movements continued to occur with each new incident even after Okinawa reverted to Japan in 1972, including a massive rally of Okinawans to condemn the rape of a girl by U.S. servicemen in 1995 and a major rally to call for relocating Air Station Futenma outside of the prefecture in 2010.

However, fierce anti-base movements cause counteractions too.

In Nago, dissension between the Helicopter Base Opposition Council and local residents is deepening. Residents submitted a petition to the city mayor in March 2012 requesting removal of the Council's tents located by the sea embankment. Yasuhide Miyagi, a local city council member, asserts that "the tents are occupying public space and residents cannot walk in that area." Residents from Henoko who oppose the relocation of Air Station Futenma built a prefab shed on unused land about 100 meters away from the tents and are conducting their own monitoring activities separately from the Council.

A petition with the signatures of 75,828 people calling for relocation of Air Station Futenma to Nago's Henoko area arrived at the Okinawa prefecture office on November 28, 2013. The "Council of Okinawans Seeking Removal of the Danger of Futenma Base and Consolidation and Shrinkage at the Henoko Base," a civic group chaired by Shohei Nakaji, gathered the signatures and greatly exceeded the original goal of 50,000 people. The group emphasizes the following major benefits of relocation.

- Relocating the current Air Station Futenma (about 480 hectares) to the Henoko Coast (about 160 hectares of reclaimed land on the water) would significantly reduce the area covered by bases.
- It would also eliminate the danger of Air Station Futenma located in the middle of a residential area and retain the presence of U.S. troops defending Okinawa.

Chairman Nakaji is a business person who founded a sugar

manufacturing plant in the prefecture. He offered the following appeal at a rally held at a hotel in Naha on November 24 prior to submitting the petition.

"It is insulting and inaccurate to say that all Okinawans are against the bases, the United States, and mainland Japan. Many Okinawans clearly understand the necessity of military strength to protect Okinawa."

However, it is difficult to openly voice approval of the bases in Okinawa. Kenjiro Nishida, a former Okinawa Prefecture Assembly member and an advisor to the LDP's Okinawa organization stated in his opening remarks to the rally that "the silent majority knows that Henoko is the only choice."

A self-employed man in his 40's (lives in Urasoe City) who attended the rally admitted that, "I'm afraid to express approval of the Henoko relocation amid local media reports about a fierce anti-base campaign. We are the silent majority."

In fact, "fence cleaning" volunteer activities started in the area around Air Station Futenma with intense ant-base activity. Volunteers remove vinyl strings attached to the base fence by anti-base advocates with cutter knives and scissors one-by-one on Sundays. They include families of parents and children as well as people who suffered damages in the Great East Japan Earthquake where the U.S. military engaged in relief efforts.

Yasunori Tedokon, who serves as the representative for the activities (lives in Urasoe City), offered the following comment.

"It is pointless to yell at the Americans. Building relationships as friends is more effective in enabling us to communicate our views. This should also make it easier to prevent incidents and accidents. People don't usually attack their friends."

Anti-base advocates attach strings again after their removal. Despite the back-and-forth, Mr. Tedokon explains that, "We do not scream at or raise our hands against anti-base campaign members. Our methods of pursuing peace just differ." U.S. military officials also join in the volunteer efforts with their families.

Opposition and dependence – Complicated base issue

A patient asks the doctor with a stern look.

"Doctor, am I seriously ill?"

"Please relax. Your illness is (drowned out by the roar of U.S. military planes)...desu."

"Desu, what is that? Do you mean "death"? "Death" is the English for "die", right?"

(The word "desu" is intended to mean "is" in the doctor's explanation, and comes at the end of the sentence in Japanese syntax. However, it can also sound like the Japanese pronunciation of the word "death.")

This is a comic scene from the "Futenma base" show by the FEC performing group that operates in Okinawa. FEC has been conducting performances entitled "U.S. Military Base Comedy" since 2005. Masamitsu Kohatsu, who grew up in Naha and plans, writes, and performs, notes that "people understand the situation and laugh because they deal with the base issue in their daily life."

More than 1,000 people gathered for a performance at the Okinawa City Community Center and applauded loudly. The pamphlet distributed at the performance talks about "an opportunity to laugh at and think about contradictions of the U.S. military bases and contradictions facing local residents."

"Contradictions" refers to Okinawa's tough position of discomfort with the U.S. military bases, but having to accept them for a variety of reasons.

A man in his 30's who works at a restaurant located on a U.S. military base sees the anti-base movement with mixed feelings. He has worked hard and has finally become a full-time employee, but is worried about losing his job if the bases were to be returned to Japan, and wishes that people would think about what would happen to workers like him.

The average unemployment rate nationwide was 4% in Jul-Sep 2013, and Okinawa prefecture had the worst showing at 6%. The U.S. military bases are an important employer in Okinawa. The Labor Management Organization for USFJ Employees (Incorporated Administrative Agency) hired 335 Japanese workers for U.S. military bases in Okinawa during fiscal 2012. These were highly sought positions with 5,302 applicants and a 15.8x competition ratio. Okinawa even has technical schools that support efforts to secure employment on the bases.

Land rent (military land rent) paid annually by the national government to owners of land used by U.S. military bases is a major economic factor too. Okinawa's 21 municipalities have roughly 37,000 military land owners, and average rent income per person in fiscal 2011 was about 2.18 million yen.

Classified ads expressing interest in "buying military land at a high price" often appear in Okinawan newspapers. There is a possibility of an increase in the military land rent, and the land is subject to buying and selling as a type of financial product.

An official at the Okinawa Federation of Landowner Associations for Land Used for Military Purpose describes criticism when accidents occur involving the U.S. military that, "this happens because you are supplying the base land." The U.S. military forcibly took much of the military land. However, there are numerous landowners now who depend on the land rent.

The same situation exists at Camp Schwab in Nago, the target destination for relocating Air Station Futenma. Toshiharu Shimabukuro, a former treasurer of Nago City who chairs the city's Landowner Associations for Land Used for Military Purpose, explains that, "Schwab was previously just fields and woods. Local people survived by gathering firewood and selling it in the town. It would be a very isolated village without the base. Young people can live here thanks to land rent from the base."

The national government provides Okinawa with an extensive promotion budget annually based on the Okinawa Promotion Plan formulated once every 10 years. These funds totaled 10.5 trillion yen from Okinawa's reversion in 1972 through fiscal 2012 and have mainly gone toward public projects, such as building roads and dams. Besides the promotion budget, Okinawa received 217.8 billion yen in grants for the Ministry of Internal Affairs and Communications (through fiscal 2012) given to local public entities with bases in the prefecture and 4.1 billion yen in grants from the Ministry of Defense (through fiscal 2012) for local public entities that cooperated with reorganization of U.S. military troops. The Japanese government has spent this much on Okinawa because of its awareness of the heavy burden the prefecture incurs with U.S. bases.

Economic effects from the bases are significant, including consumption activity by U.S. military personnel and others, military land rent, and salaries for base employees. Okinawa estimates the effect at about 200 billion annually in recent years, and total value since reversion to mainland Japan likely reached 6.4 trillion yen through fiscal 2012.

Okinawa faces difficult economic conditions, and income per person in fiscal 2010 was the lowest in Japan at 2,025,000 yen according to data disclosed by the Cabinet Office. This is well below the average of 2,877,000 yen for all prefectures. While Okinawa prefecture asserts that "U.S. bases located in urban areas have been a major hindrance to regional advancement," it is also true that the presence of bases has supported the prefecture economy. Okinawa continues to vacillate in its sentiment toward the U.S. bases – a blend of opposition and dependence.

Okinawa holds the key

Nago voted in its mayor's election, which was focused on whether to accept relocation of Air Station Futenma as the top issue, and results confirmed the re-election of incumbent Susumu Inamine, an opponent of the relocation to Nago's Henoko area, on January 19, 2014. Mr. Inamine received 19,839 votes, and Bunshin Suematsu, the opposing candidate (former LDP representative in the Okinawa Prefecture Assembly) advocating acceptance of the relocation obtained 15,684 votes. Mr. Inamine escaped with a victory in an election that truly split the city.

This was the fifth election for the Nago mayor since the Japanese and U.S. governments reached the agreement for a full return of Air Station Futenma. Whether to accept the relocation of Air Station Futenma or not has been the central issue each time. Advocates of accepting the relocation won up until two elections ago, but the opposition (Mr. Inamine) has been victorious since the previous election.

"Drop the Henoko relocation and go back to a review of outside of Okinawa or outside of Japan."

This is what Mr. Inamine, who won re-election, declared to journalists at his office filled with cheering supporters on the night of the election. It was just three weeks since Governor Nakaima approved reclamation of the water surface necessary for the relocation. Mr. Inamine intends to block the move project using whatever legal authority is available to a mayor, such as not approving construction of facilities used for the reclamation project. There is concern that confusion surrounding the relocation of Air Station Futenma, a symbol of the U.S. base issue in Okinawa, will continue.

Okinawa Prefecture will be holding elections for over 40 leadership and assembly positions during the year after the Nago mayoral election. The plan for reorganization U.S. bases, such as Air Station Futenma, in the prefecture will remain a central topic, and some local voices are referring to this situation as a "year-long battle" (local LDP organization official).

China is also watching this situation in Okinawa with considerable interest. The People's Daily (Japanese electronic version) carried an article on the Nago mayoral election on January 30, 2014 entitled "Okinawans sent a "No" message to the Abe government" and suggested that relocation of Air Station Futenma is "unlikely to materialize."

However, relocation of U.S. bases outside of Okinawa or outside of Japan as proposed by Mr. Inamine, the Nago mayor, might occur due to considerations on the U.S. military side.

The Ministry of Foreign Affairs forecasts that China's defense spending will roughly match spending by the United States and its military technology will advance significantly by around 2030. The core DF21 missile in China's arsenal currently has a range of about 1,500 kilometers. While this does not reach the mainland United States or U.S.-controlled Guam, it covers Okinawa and all of Japan. It is thought that China will improve its missile performance and obtain the ability to launch pinpointed attacks on U.S. bases in Okinawa and other sites by around 2020. The U.S. military might determine that "Chinese is too close" (Self-Defense Forces official) as this happens. Okinawa's strategic significance might change if the U.S. military decides to deploy in a manner that keeps a certain distance from China and the Korean Peninsula and avoids a direct attack.

RAND Corporation, a U.S.-based think tank, prepared a report in 2013 that the deployment of U.S. Marines in Okinawa and the Pacific needs to closely monitor the threat from China and anti-base movement in Okinawa. The United States is already taking steps to reorganize its troops with Guam as a strategic site in light of the enhanced capabilities of the Chinese military. The roadmap on reorganization of U.S. troops agreed with the Japanese government in 2006 seeks to reorganize and shrink U.S. bases on Okinawa and move U.S. troops to Guam, including financial assistance from Japan.

Complete removal of U.S. troops from Okinawa would not be a good outcome for Japan's overall security. Deterrence, which pressures the

151

counterpart to opt against use of military force, is an important concept in security policy, and the presence of the U.S. military in Japan is a key deterrence factor in Japan's case. An analyst at a think tank based in the United States comments that "Japan will increasingly need to take sufficient actions to stop the U.S. military from leaving." Former Defense Minister Kyuma, who is familiar with the base situation in Okinawa, notes that the Japan-U.S. Security Treaty will just become a formality if U.S. troops leave Japan and "the United States is likely refrain from involvement if something happens."

Is Japan capable of retaining deterrence as China strengthens its military pressure? Okinawa is a key factor in whether this is possible.

Chapter 4
Hidden War

Modern society is deeply dependent on computers, from electricity, gas, communications, and transportation infrastructure to military operations. Smartphones and IT consumer electronics are widely used too.

These devices are linked through the Internet and wireless systems and create a massive cyber space. However, cyber attacks that use this unseen space to steal information and inflict damage on certain counterparts are rapidly increasing. China is challenging the dominance of the United States in cyber space. Cyber attacks that appear to be coming from China and aim for security holes in the Japan-U.S. alliance have been increasing in Japan too.

Anything goes - "Unrestricted Warfare"

"The end justifies the means." Members of China's People's Liberation Army read a frightening book with this message. "Unrestricted Warfare" is a military strategy book written by two Air Force colonels (Qiao Liang and Wang Xiangsui) in February 1999 (Kyodo published a Japanese version in 2001).

Unrestricted warfare refers to a new generation of warfare that removes all boundaries and limits between wartime and peacetime and military and non-military affairs and pursues fighting that integrates "all weapons and technologies" possessed by the country. Battles are not just soldiers holding weapons but rather involve a constant effort to attack the other side in a variety of areas.

The above-mentioned book defines battlefields in "unrestricted warfare" as conventional warfare, biological and chemical warfare, space warfare, electronic warfare, guerilla warfare, terrorist warfare, diplomacy warfare, Internet warfare, smuggling warfare, drug warfare, financial warfare, trade warfare, resources warfare, economic assistance warfare, legal warfare, and media warfare.

This book writes the following using a reference to Italian thinker Niccolo Machiavelli (1469-1527) who wrote "The Prince" to define how to succeed in unrestricted warfare.

"What is the law of victory? It is very simple. It involves rigorous application of the Machiavellian approach to military matters. 'The end justifies the means.' This is the most important ideological asset left by Italian political thinkers from the Renaissance period."

Information technology (IT) is an essential weapon in the unrestricted warfare because modern society depends on IT and cannot function without IT. Possession of advanced IT capabilities makes it possible to steal secret information from a counterpart and disrupt infrastructure, communications networks, and other facilities through computer network attacks.

An official at Japan's Defense Ministry comments that "China has already begun unrestricted warfare in cyber space." China's cyber attacks started appearing in the United States, European countries, and Japan from 2003 soon after the publication of "Unrestricted Warfare."

In this year, computers came under cyber attack at the U.S. Defense Department and Army and aircraft manufacturer Lockheed Martin, and the attacks stole massive amounts of information. While authorities have not disclosed the details of the damages, investigators refer to the attacks as "Titan Rain," and concluded that China was the likely perpetrator.

Operation Aurora attacks occurred six years later during 2009 and the next year. Reports indicate that massive amounts of data were stolen from about 30 leading U.S. IT firms, including Google, Apple, and RSA Security.

Cyber attacks targeted oil companies, electric power firms, drug companies and others in November 2009. U.S.-based McAfee, a leading developer of anti-virus software, refers to these attacks as Night Dragon. It announced that the attacks stole information regarding oil field bids and other contracts worth a few billion dollars, and "we possess evidence showing that the perpetrator of the attack was based in China."

The University of Toronto based in Canada announced research results with a local think tank that warned of China's secret information gathering network stretching worldwide prior to disclosure of Night Dragon. Results confirmed virus infections of at least 1,295 computers in 103 countries and secret transmission of information to China. The catalyst for discovering the network was suspicion of China stealing emails and other information from the offices of the 14th Dalai Lama, the Tibetan Supreme Buddhist leader, disliked by China. University of Toronto researchers referred to China's information gathering network as "Ghost Net."

Cyber attacks that appear to involve China are not just stealing information. There was an incident in which the attack took control of a satellite. The U.S.-China Economic and Security Review Commission, a consultative entity for the U.S. Congress, disclosed in November 2011 that a cyber attack on the control system of the National Aeronautics and Space Administration's (NASA) Terra Earth Observation Satellite gained control of the satellite for a period of 11 minutes. The system faced two attacks – June and October 2008. The Commission cited involvement by the People's Liberation Army.

Experts in the IT field agree regarding these cyber attacks apparently involving China that "the ones that are known just represent the tip of an iceberg."

China argues back in response to criticism from the global community that "we are the victims of cyber attacks" and entirely rejects any participation in cyber attacks.

However, a special program on cyber warfare aired by CCTV, China's state-run central television station, in July 2011 contained an unexpected scene. It showed a PC screen that listed cyber attack targets in video taken at a facility of the People's Liberation Army. The list included Falun Gong, a qigong exercise group persecuted by the Chinese government. U.S. and European security experts who analyzed the video believe that it "offers evidence that China is conducting cyber attacks."

The Chinese government emphasized the necessity of joint military and private-sector technology enhancement and being prepared for cyber warfare in its National Defense White Paper issued in April 2013. China has already built its own domestic firewall (computer network defense system). This system, which is known as the Great Firewall of China as an analogy to the Great Wall of China, has a mechanism for preventing the spread of damage with forced shutdown of the connection to domestic computer networks when a server attack comes from outside China.

China has also installed a Golden Shield censorship system to monitor the Internet. Information about the Tiananmen incident, Tibetan independence, and other uncomfortable topics for the Chinese government cannot be searched in China. Search results are not given. In January 2011, it was suddenly no longer possible to conduct searches of "jasmine" and mobile phone short messaging stopped working when the Jasmine Revolution, which involved democratic demonstrations overthrowing a dictatorial government in Tunisia, took place.

An official from Japan's Ministry of Foreign Affairs explains that most likely all email transactions in China are monitored. The mails are not only read, but a virus is added to the mail that can result in discretionary operation of the PC. A U.S.-based think tank allocates a different email address than the one they normally use for researchers who travel to China. It also prohibits researchers from bringing their personal PCs to China and gives them special PCs for the trip. It promptly initializes data and programs after the researcher returns.

Danger lurking in the "world's factory"

In January 2014, at the Consumer Electronics Show in Las Vegas, the world's largest consumer electronics exhibition, Huawei Technologies, a major Chinese manufacturer of communications equipment, attracted attention with its massive booth. It announced new smartphones and had a bustling crowd.

Huawei ranks third globally in the smartphone market after Korea-based Samsung Electronics and U.S.-based Apple. It moved ahead of Sweden's Ericsson as the world's largest IT equipment manufacturer in fiscal 2012 at 220.2 billion yuan (about 3.8 trillion yen) in sales. It is a massive company that operates in over 140 countries and has 150,000 employees.

However, it is said that Huawei has a "secret side."

A special committee on information at the U.S. House of Representatives announced a research report calling for the elimination of Huawei products in October 2012. Specifically it stated that "Huawei equipment should not be used in U.S. government systems, and particularly sensing systems." Some private-sector companies have issued unusual warnings that "strongly call for finding another firm."

The Committee expressed concern about deep ties between Huawei and the Chinese government (particularly the People's Liberation Army).

Sales of Huawei Technologies

220.2 billion yuan

250 billion yuan

150

100

50

0

fiscal 2000   09   10   11   12

1 yuan=approx. 17 yen (as of January 20, 2014)

Ren Zhengfei, the current CEO, who had a career in the People's Liberation Army, founded Huawei in 1987 in Shenzhen (Guangdong). The report notes that Mr. Ren worked at the People's Liberation Army's Information Engineering Institute that teaches intelligence technology and concludes that use of Huawei's products "gives spying opportunities to China's intelligence agency."

Committee Chairman Mike Rodgers, who announced the report, commented at the press conference that "there are actual cases of Huawei products suddenly waking up at night and sending large amounts of data to China."

The U.S. government is steadily taking steps to remove Huawei products. It kept Huawei out of the emergency wireless system business in October 2011 and has stopped Huawei from acquiring a U.S. company.

U.S. Vice President Biden expressed concern about Huawei receiving an order for a high-speed wireless network in Korea to Prime Minister Chung Hong Won during his visit to Korea in December 2013. This request reflected worries about the content of communications between the U.S. military forces stationed in Korea and the Korean military leaking to China.

U.S. Senator John McCain, a leading member of the Republican Party with influence on diplomatic and security policies, submitted a comment to The Daily Beast, a U.S. news site, on January 2, 2014 with a warning that "a decision by Korea that gives major benefits to Huawei is likely to be poorly received by the United States and Congress."

The United States is not the only country with concerns. Australia excluded Huawei from a broadband communication network business for national security reasons in March 2012. The United Kingdom decided in December 2013 to strengthen monitoring of Huawei mainly through the Government Communications Headquarters (GCHQ), an intelligence agency.

Huawei supplies products used in base stations for mobile phone carriers in Japan too and sells smartphones and data communications devices. Huawei Japan, the company's local entity, became the first Chinese company to join Keidanren (the Japan Business Federation) in February 2011.

Huawei Japan asserts that the company's business "does not have any political or military relationships with the Chinese Communist Party and

Chinese government, and unfounded mistaken claims by the United States lack legitimacy." However, the U.S. government has deep concerns and it appears to have closely scrutinized transactions between SoftBank and Huawei when SoftBank acquired a U.S. mobile phone company in 2013.

China has become the world's factory through its economic advances, and Chinese firms hold a vital presence in the information and communications equipment market. Lenovo Group, a PC manufacturer, acquired the PC business of IBM, a leading U.S. computer firm, in 2005 and was the top global supplier of PCs in 2013 at about 53.77 million units (according to survey results from U.S.-based research firm IDC announced on January 9, 2014). China Mobile, a leading mobile phone company, is the world's largest mobile phone carrier with 760 million subscribers.

However, these Chinese manufacturers face similar concerns as Huawei. The report issued in October 2012 by the special committee on information at the U.S. House of Representatives cites ZTE, the world's No.6 smartphone firm in terms of market share for Jan-Jun 2013, as a company that should be excluded as a procurement source for the U.S. government, similar to Huawei. It commented that, "Questions must be raised about Chinese firms entering the U.S. telecommunications market. U.S. intelligence agencies must give warnings about threats and monitor situations."

Supply chain (parts supply network) issues are a concern too for information and communications equipment. Society uses massive amounts of equipment from consumer devices to infrastructure, but the safety of individual parts made by a variety of firms is not sufficiently monitored.

The United States confronted the following situation in around 2008. Repeated outages occurred in computer networks used by the Air Force and Federal Aviation Administration. Fires suddenly broke out in some equipment. The U.S. government's investigation found many counterfeit routers that claimed to be products from U.S.-based Cisco Systems. Routers are systems that handle data interactions among multiple networks. These devices connect PCs and other equipment to the Internet.

The U.S. government was concerned about the existence of a backdoor that allowed data to be taken from outside the system and conducted a thorough investigation mainly by the FBI. It concluded that the counterfeit routers were probably made in China.

Image of retaking remote islands

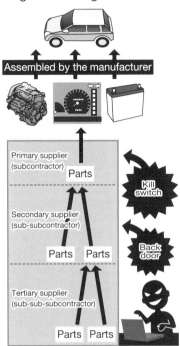

Improper adjustments to parts are not limited to backdoors. There is also a "kill switch." This approach places a part capable of shutting off the equipment's power source when a certain signal is received from outside. A successful transmission could disrupt activities of the counterpart's military forces or curtail economic activity. It is very difficult to find if an improper chip (part) or malware (problem-causing software) is added at the hardware production stage. Threats covered in movies and novels in past years have become a reality in the cyber world.

Japan obviously confronts these threats too. However, the government does not set clear standards regarding procurement of overseas products. A Defense Ministry official discloses that "the PC used at an assignment location was inexpensive but from a well-known manufacturer that assembles products in China." Japan is at risk of having its communications system undermined unless it takes a stricter view of the trustworthiness of foreign-made information and communications equipment.

Experts are calling for quick action with comments such as "it is essential to specify supply-chain security in laws and regulations" (senior analyst Toshio Nawa at CyberDefense).

Battle for dominance in cyberspace between the United States and China

Global attention focused on a 12-story building in Shanghai (China) in February 2013.

The catalyst for this interest was disclosure of a report by Mandiant, a U.S.-based information security firm, stating that this building was the site of cyber attacks against the United States by General Command Section 3 Group 2 (also known as the 61398 squadron) of the China's People's Liberation Army. Section 3 and Section 4 are considered to be cyber warfare groups.

The report's title was "APT1 – Exposing One of China's Cyber Espionage Units." Advanced persistent threat (APT) refers to cyber attacks launched against a certain counterpart for an extended period. It involves sending false mails to the target and stealing data from PCs infected by the virus.

The report estimates that the 61398 group has members totaling in the few hundreds to few thousands, including many with excellent English skills. It also suggests that it has stolen a few hundred terabytes of data from 141 entities, including the U.S. government and companies, since 2006. A terabyte is a unit of computer data volume, and just one terabyte can record data equivalent to a newspaper's morning edition for 1,000 years. There was a case in which attacks occurred over 1,764 days.

Cyber attacks on the New York Times, a U.S.-based newspaper, led to the discovery of APTs by the 61398 squadron. This newspaper struggled with cyber attacks after it reported on illicit assets worth about 2.7 billion dollars accumulated by China's Prime Minister Wen Jiabao in October 2012. Mandiant conducted the research at the request of the New York Times and discovered that the attacks were coming from the building in Shanghai.

However, Mandiant's CEO Kevin Mandia explained in an interview with the Yomiuri Shimbun that "we only uncovered about 5% of their activities."

While the Chinese government completely rejects the content of the report disclosed by Mandiant, the U.S. government started to fiercely criticize China at the same time in step with the disclosure of the report.

For example, the Defense Department wrote in the "Military and Security Developments Involving the People's Republic of China," an annual report to Congress, released in May 2013 that "China is using illegal methods to obtain military technology." President Obama told Chinese President Xi Jinping at the U.S.-China Summit Meeting held in California the following month that "resolving the cyber problem is a key factor for the future of the economic relationship between the United States and China."

Meanwhile, the U.S. government has been repeatedly conducting large-scale exercises that envision cyber attacks from China. The Cyber Storm exercise that started in 2006 is a leading example. It assumes attacks on transportation networks, chemical plants, and other sites, and involves participation by the Defense Department, State Department, National Security Agency (NSA), Central Intelligence Agency (CIA), and other major government entities, security companies, and officials from the United Kingdom, Australia, and other foreign governments. The exercises aim to achieve unified responses by related entities and friendly countries. Participation from Japan included the Cabinet Office's National Information Security Center (NISC) and the National Police Agency in 2010 and the Defense Ministry in 2013.

Break out of cyber warfare

Cyber warfare that inflicts damage on the counterpart country through cyber attacks have actually already begun.

Attacks on Estonia in April 2007 are said to be the world's first case of cyber warfare.

Estonia, one of the three Baltic States, has a history of occupation by Germany during the Second World War and then reoccupation and annexation by Soviet Union troops thereafter. It started discussing removal of a war victory monument erected by the Soviet Union in the center of Tallinn, its capital city, after restoring independence following the Soviet Union's collapse. The monument was an image of soldiers wearing Soviet Union uniforms and carrying helmets, and it symbolized brutal domination by the former Soviet Union to Estonians. However, Russia strongly resisted the removal as an "action that disparages Europe's liberators." Attacks on the computer systems of Estonia's President's office, Congress, government agencies, banks, newspaper companies, and other entities began soon after the removal.

DDoS attacks that paralyze functions by sending massive amounts of data to servers (host computers that connect PCs and other devices to the network) shut down financial institution and mobile phone services in

Estonia. The attacks persisted for roughly three weeks. Estonia is a global leader in IT usage, including being the first country ever to conduct a national election over the Internet, and has installed broadband networks through the country. These capabilities ironically amplified the damages.

This was the first case of confirmed large-scale cyber attacks targeting a certain country. While Estonia suspected involvement by Russia, the Russian government rejected the assertions. The United States and European countries dispatched IT experts to Estonia after the incident to assess the series of attacks. The incident led to Estonia becoming a central site for cyber research and the location for the North Atlantic Treaty Organization's (NATO) Cooperative Cyber Defence Centre of Excellence.

Other countries besides those with developed economies are beginning to add cyber warfare capabilities too.

A U.S. RQ170 stealth reconnaissance drone conducting surveillance of nuclear-related facilities in eastern Iran disappeared in December 2011. Iranian media reported that the Iranian military overrode the drone's communications system and forced it to land in a pasture. While military officials from various countries wondered "if that was really possible," Iran announced deployment of a domestic-made surveillance drone in September of the following year that appeared to use technology obtained from the captured RQ170.

Cyber warfare is already a reality. Richard Clarke, who worked as a special advisor to the president in the Bush administration, explained the unique aspects of cyber warfare in "Cyber War: The Next Threat to National Security and What to Do About It" (published in Japan by Tokuma Shoten Publishing), which he co-authored. Clarke highlights the ability to destroy the counterpart country, the inflicting of damage from the start of the attack in an immeasurably short amount of time, and the commandeering of computers and servers in various countries and forcing them to participate in the attack.

Fifth battlefield

"Cyber space on computers is the fifth battlefield besides ground, sea, air, and space."

The U.S. Defense Department explained in 2011 that it is adopting a policy approach that treats cyber space in this manner and a readiness to retaliate against the counterpart country with missiles and other conventional military power if the country suffers a serious cyber attack.

The United States, which has the strongest military power in the world, is exhibiting this level of concern toward cyber attacks because of advances in high-tech weaponry referred to as a Revolution in Military Affairs (RMA) and connection of many weapons to computer networks. If these networks are destroyed through a cyber attack, the high-tech weapons become paper tigers.

In fact, high-tech weapons do not fare well when confronted with computer trouble.

A cutting-edge F22 Raptor plane headed from Hickam Base in Hawaii to Kadena Base in Okinawa experienced trouble that forced it to return to Hickam in February 2007. While the F22 is known as the world's strongest fighter plane with stealth features that make it difficult to detect with radar and robust maneuverability, it encountered an abnormality in the system whereby the plane's position was displayed after crossing the International Date Line. The pilot tried to reboot the system, but this attempt did not work and the fighter returned to Hickam with the assistance of a nearby air tanker. A subsequent investigation by the U.S. military found a defect in the computer program that connects GPS located in a satellite and the fighter. While the pilot was trained in celestial navigation for flying based on positioning of the sun and stars, today's planes rely entirely on GPS to confirm location. If a similar defect occurred because of a cyber attack, even the world's best fighter "would not know where it is going" (U.S. military official).

The U.S. military is already making progress in efforts to address the fifth battlefield, including installation of a "cyber command" to deal with cyber war. The cyber command consists of roughly 900 people with a group that defends electric power plants, transmission lines, and other important infrastructure; a group that defends Defense Department infrastructure; and a group that assists military operations. The U.S. military plans to expand the command to about 4,000 members because of the heightened threat of cyber war in an "era in which a single click can destroy a country" (Chairman of the Joint Chiefs of Staff Martin Dempsey). This stance shows the extent of emphasis being placed by the U.S. military on responding to cyber attacks even with ongoing cutbacks in military spending.

President Obama called for "addressing the threat of cyber attacks" in his State of the Union speech in February 2013. The U.S. government plans to allocate a massive budget of 23 billion dollars (about 2.4 trillion yen) over four years from 2013 to confront cyber attacks.

The U.S. government is strengthening its monitoring of the Internet too. The Internet world consists of providers with ordinary users as subscribers who make mutual connections. The largest providers are known as Tier 1, and only about 10 companies worldwide fit in this category. Tier 1 providers serve in the role of relay stations for information, and other providers can exchange information worldwide through connections to Tier 1 firms. The U.S. government focuses on this aspect and engages in extensive information collection and monitoring activities with the cooperation of domestic Tier 1 firms.

Japan's NTT Communications is the only Tier 1 firm in Asia. However, the Japanese government does not have authority in domestic law to monitor communications other than criminal investigations and is not engaged in the collection of information along the lines of the U.S. government.

Governments are eager to collect intelligence, including in cyber space, due to the vital role of precise intelligence for important decisions and strategy formulation. During the Second World War, the United Kingdom decoded the content of communications from the Enigma encoding machine that Nazi Germany claimed was "impenetrable," enabling its success in the Normandy landing of June 1944 and determining the outcome of the war. It is said that "the war's outcome might have changed without the Enigma decoding."

The importance of intelligence gathering continues today. The United States has 17 intelligence agencies, including the CIA and NSA, that come under the Director of National Intelligence. The CIA gathers and analyzes intelligence obtained by spies and handles secret operations and other activities, while the NSA mainly collects intelligence using electronic equipment. The government does not disclose the number of employees and budgets for intelligence agencies, but estimates are roughly 20,000 people at the CIA and about 30,000 at the NSA.

Intelligence gathering includes illegal activities that are not disclosed in some cases. Edward Snowden, a former CIA employee, exposed a portion of NSA's information collection efforts in 2013. The materials showed that the NSA was collecting and storing phone records of ordinary citizens and tapped phone calls by foreign governments, such as Germany's Chancellor Angela Merkel. Mr. Snowden, who is accused by the U.S. government of stealing information and other crimes, worked at the CIA as a computer security technician and was also employed at the NSA's Hawaii office for three months. He is currently receiving temporary asylum in Russia.

Following disclosures by Snowden, Chancellor Merkel protested to President Obama in a phone call in October 2013 that, "It is completely unacceptable and a serious breach of trust if the wiretapping took place." The U.S. President explained that "we are not monitoring communications and do not intend to."

President Obama delivered a speech at Justice Department on January 17, 2014 amid criticism at home and abroad that announced reforms for NSA's intelligence gathering activities. The reforms stated that the United States fundamentally does not wiretap the communications of leaders at allies and friendly countries and called for commissioning storage of phone call records collected in the United States to an entity outside of the government and use of stricter viewing procedures. However, President Obama did not forget to mention the following point – "Our intelligence agencies will continue to gather intelligence on the aims of foreign governments just as what is done by the intelligence agencies of other countries."

Weapon of the Poor

Cyber warfare can inflict serious damage on a counterpart country with a single click. Furthermore, it is much cheaper than acquiring missiles, air carriers, and other advanced weaponry because it only requires talented engineers and computers. Hiroshi Ito, the research institute director at information security firm LAC (based in Tokyo), comments that "it is an ideal weapon of the poor."

Even North Korea, which struggles with an economic crisis, is placing emphasis on cyber war.

The Republic of Korea's (RoK) national parliament reported the following comment on cyber war by Kim Jong-un, the First Secretary of North Korea, in November 2013.

"Cyber capabilities are a highly potent tool that gives the DPRK military merciless attack resources along with nuclear weapons and missiles."

Nam Jae-joon, the head of the National Intelligence Service, the RoK's intelligence agency, reported this comment. North Korea's official media has not covered the comment, and the National Intelligence Service appears to have obtained it independently. He disclosed the comment, despite risk of the information source being compromised, because of "concern about the threat of cyber attacks by North Korea" (RoK government source).

Mr. Nam also provided details about North Korea's cyber war unit to the national diet. He explained that the cyber war unit has about 1,700 people with many at the Reconnaissance General Bureau, an outward operative entity. If an incident occurs, North Korea can mobilize about 4,200 engineers working on software development, including those at the state-run Korean Computer Center (KCC), as well.

North Korea trains cyber war human resources in an elite educational program. Cha Sose-Yuru, who leads an organization for North Korean emigrants, escaped to the RoK after graduating from the Command Automation University, a spy-training institute. He explains that North Korea brings top students from elementary schools around the country to Pyongyang and has them obtain expert knowledge in a "computer genius class." Universities teach programming and computer engineering too, and talented people are given assignments at the Reconnaissance General Bureau.

North Korea built this training and education system at the instructions of Former General Secretary Kim Jong-il, the father of First Secretary Kim. General Secretary Kim explained the importance of training over a decade ago in 2001 in a speech to leaders of the Central Committee of the Workers' Party of Korea.

"We must discover and train computer talents from around the country. It is enough to just study computers, revolutionary history, math, and foreign language."

"We must train true geniuses by dispelling students who do not meet standards and rewarding talented students."

General Secretary Kim went to the point of asserting that "people who are unaware of computer technology are illiterate" and was particularly focused on cyber war. While North Korea promotes military-first politics that gives a top priority to the military and approaches the United States, the RoK, and Japan as enemies, it cannot compete in aircraft and other conventional weaponry. With cyber attacks, however, it might be capable of inflicting a decisive attack against the United States and other enemies without much spending. Furthermore, these attacks do not leave much evidence, and North Korea does not have an extensive Internet system and its infrastructure facilities are not controlled by computers so it is unlikely to face serious damage even if received a counter attack to a cyber attack from the other country.

North Korea has already actually begun cyber attacks. Government entities, financial institutions, and others in the United States and Korea confronted DDoS attacks that crippled server functions by sending massive amounts of data in July 2009. The attack manipulated over 100,000 PCs infected with a virus in countries worldwide and traveled through servers in Japan. Attacks came against the RoK's Presidential office and military computer network using the same technique in March 2011 when the United States and the RoK conducted joint military exercises.

North Korea has been improving its cyber capabilities each year. Attacks on Korea's financial institutions and TV stations in March 2013 directly entered servers for security software and spread a virus to the targeted computer networks.

There is also the case of a North Korean operative selling an online game program that contained a virus to a Korean game firm. Korean prosecutors filed charges for violation of the National Security Law against a Korean national who distributed a program containing a virus purchased for $5,500 from a North Korean operative in China. The virus infected PCs that accessed the game on the Internet, and these PCs were utilized in the cyber attack managed remotely from North Korea.

Toshio Nawa, a senior analyst at security firm CyberDefense (Tokyo) described North Korea's cyber attack capabilities in the following way:

"They find weaknesses in software and make viruses that utilize the soft spots and work through system holes to cause trouble. We must admit that they possess significant development and reconnaissance capabilities."

North Korea is clearly eyeing Japan as a target for cyber attacks too. Kim Heung Kwang, the representative of the North Korean Intellectuals Solidarity group of North Korean dissidents living in the RoK held a press conference in Seoul in November 2013 to disclose that North Korea had established a cyber team targeting Japan. A leading official of the Reconnaissance General Bureau gave instructions to "expand the cyber war to the Japanese islands" and created a team with 40-50 people at the Bureau's 121 department. The team has already listed the Japanese government, R&D institutes, companies, and others as specific targets.

Pitfall for the "unprotected" Japanese government

Japan has fallen behind in preparing for the threat of cyber attacks.

"They can do that much?"

Deputy Ministers of various government agencies expressed alarm as they looked at the PC screen.

The government convened a meeting of Deputy Ministers at the Prime Minister's large meeting room on September 5, 2013. Employees from the Cabinet Office's National Information Security Center (NISC), which manages Japan's information security policy, brought in computers and gave demonstration of computer virus infections.

The infected PC starts operating with the move of a mouse linked to the PC on the commandeering side. The PC screen on the latter showed the face of the person sitting in front of the small camera on the infected PC's side similar to a videoconference.

"It is possible to listen and take images through smartphones too." After hearing this explanation, one of the Deputy Ministers wondered aloud with a stunned expression, "Maybe I'll stop using a smartphone."

The demonstration aimed to raise awareness of information security among politicians with government positions. An NISC official spoke about the dangers of smartphones at a meeting of Parliamentary Vice-Ministers held two weeks later on September 19, "It is possible to begin listening through remote operation once the GPS function confirms entry into the Prime Minister's office. Everything can be heard because of the microphone feature."

One of the participants noted "Shock at the fact that I'm carrying around a listening device."

Even the Prime Minister's office, a central institute of government, is exposed to cyber attacks. An expert in security policy was alarmed to hear that people coming to visit Prime Minister Abe at his office enter the room with their cell phones that have not been checked at all, "It is possible to place calls because radio waves are not blocked. Concern about the listening threat is way too low." The United States prohibits visitors from bringing mobile phones to the offices of senior government officials. The same practice applies to the U.S. Embassy in Tokyo.

Cyber attacks against politicians, government entities, and companies, meanwhile, are already taking place.

Masaaki Taira, an LDP Diet Member in the House of Representatives received an email in July 2013 when he was a Parliamentary Vice-Minister for METI. The email used the name of a journalist at a major newspaper firm and contained a text message that "requested an interview on economic policy and response after confirming the attached materials." However, he was unable to open the attached file. His secretary called the contact number on the email and found that it was completely unrelated food company. The journalist named as the sender existed, but did not send the email. Further investigation prompted by the suspiciousness discovered that the attached file contained a virus that sent all of the information stored on the PC to an external site. Other METI officials received the same email. They found out that this was a classic cyber attack using a "targeted email" (aims to obtain information by sending email that contains a virus). Mr. Taira was surprised to discover that "politicians and individuals" are targets.

The Japan Aerospace Exploration Agency (JAXA), a core entity for Japan's development of rocket technology, lost information to a targeted email attack too. A male employee received an email in July 2011. He opened an attachment entitled "year-end party" without suspicion because the email's main text included the name of an acquaintance. While the file contained general points, such as "contact the secretary about the year-end party," the man's PC was infected by the virus at that moment.

JAXA explains that the infection was undetected for roughly a month, and the virus steadily sent information stored in the PC to an external source. It announced in March 2012 that the leaked information "did not include sensitive data," but it sent apologies to all of the address holders to the roughly 1,000 email addresses, including business counterparts, that might have been leaked.

Even companies with advanced IT capabilities become victims. Sony encountered cyber-attacks that resulted in the loss of personal information for about 77 million people after it brought a lawsuit against a person who disclosed software that allowed the PS3 (PlayStation 3) game console to run games other than dedicated software in January 2011. It was thought that Anonymous, a group that misuses computer technologies, orchestrated the attacks. Anonymous has repeatedly attacked governments and companies since around 2006, but details about the group's structure are unknown.

An NISC survey reported that about 1.08 million cyber attacks against government entities occurred in fiscal 2012 (this is the number that was detected), putting the frequency at two attacks per minute. Volume was about twice the previous year's level.

Where are these attacks coming from?

IBM Japan disclosed analysis results for cyber attacks confirmed in Japan in the first half of 2013 (Jan-Jun) in August 2013. It found that 65.7% (two thirds) came from servers located in China. Use of servers in China obviously does not mean that all of the attacks were implemented by the Chinese government or people or criminal organizations based in China. There is a possibility that someone might be misusing Chinese servers to attack Japan. Yet it would be difficult to say that all of these attacks are unrelated to China.

IBM Japan notes that recent cyber attacks have become "more sophisticated with various techniques to prevent detection and tougher measures are required." There is danger of not even being aware that cyber attacks are taking place.

No command center in cyberspace

Prime Minister Abe made the following statement in a press conference wrapping up a trip to the Middle East and Africa in the Ethiopian capital of Addis Ababa on January 14, 2014.

"We have created a Japan-version NSC and formulated a national security strategy. We intend to strategically promote our diplomacy with a panoramic view of the world again this year within this framework."

Japan's National Security Council (NSC) was established in December 2013 and serves as the command center for the government's diplomacy and security policies. Japan launched the National Security Agency, the council's secretariat, in the following month and activities have ramped up. However, the law setting up Japan's NSC does not mention cyber attacks, and the National Security Agency does not have a dedicated division. Many experts in the cyber field say that "the absence of a section in charge of cyber activities, despite setting up Japan's own NSC, is laughable."

The U.S. National Security Council (NSC), the model for Japan's NSC, has someone in charge of cyber-related issues and an organization that deals with situations jointly with the military. The Cybersecurity Coordinator, who oversees cyber issues in the U.S. government, is a member of the NSC.

The organization with responsibility for cyber attacks in Japan is the above-mentioned NISC that was formed in 2005. It has an office in a building near the Prime Minister's office along with the Cabinet Intelligence and Research Office and other government intelligence agencies. The Assistant Chief Cabinet Secretary in charge of security and crisis management heads the NISC, and other members have responsibilities for fundamental strategy formulation, global strategy, and measures to protect important infrastructure. Japan relies on the Government Security Operation Coordination (GSOC) Team that monitors cyber attacks against government entities on a 24-hour basis and the Cyber Incident Mobile Assistant Team (CYMAT) that provide emergency responses to cyber attacks. CYMAT consists of employees with information security capabilities and knowledge, who resolve issues when government entities face system complications.

However, the NISC does not have authority to instruct government ministries and agencies regarding cyber countermeasures. An NISC person testifies that a representative at the Consumer Affairs Agency offered the following rejection when urged about strengthening measures to protect personal information.

"People die from eating jellied foods, not from cyber issues."

Furthermore, the NISC is an assemblage of seconded staff from various ministries and agencies, including the Ministry of Internal Affairs and Communications, METI, the Defense Ministry, and the National Police Agency. Many of these people return to their original workplace after about two years. Suguru Yamaguchi, a professor at the Nara Institute of Science and Technology who was involved in the NISC's establishment and served as a special adviser on information security to the government sighs with disappointment that "the rotation of staff once every two years causes the loss of accumulated knowledge at the NISC, which prevents the development of human resources with the necessary expertise."

The NISC has ambiguous powers, and the Japanese government's response to cyber issues is divided and lacks cohesion. Companies affected by cyber attacks are faced with the following myriad of options when deciding who to consult.

- Cyber Intelligence Information Sharing Network and Council on Illicit Program Countermeasures (National Police Agency)
- Initiative for Cyber Security Information Sharing Partnership of Japan (METI)
- Telecom Information Sharing and Analysis Center (ISAC) Japan (Ministry of Internal Affairs and Communications)
- Cyber Defense Council (Defense Ministry)

Companies express confusion about "where to contact if a situation actually occurs." Experts suggest that "the government needs to strengthen NISC powers and ministries and agencies need to comply when the NISC requires action."

The Japanese Government is naturally concerned about the current situation.

"Initiatives that change the whole perspective are required."

The cybersecurity strategy decided by the government's Council on Information Security Policy in June 2013 called for revamping the NISC as the "Cyber Security Center" and strengthening its authority by around fiscal 2015.

Prime Minister Abe declared at the meeting that "the Cabinet should unify to move forward with specific initiatives and aim to build safe cyber space suited to a global top-class IT nation." (Editor's note: Japan passed The Basic Act on Cybersecurity in November 2014, created the Cybersecurity Strategy Headquarters in January 2015, and passed The Revised Basic Act on Cybersecurity in April 2016. These measures broadened the scope of cyber attack monitoring to special purpose corporations and independent administrative corporations.)

Additionally, the government's "Policy on Initiatives for International Cooperation on Cybersecurity" prepared in October 2013 highlighted the importance of strengthening ties with ASEAN. Cooperative projects with various countries are moving ahead. The TSUBAME project is one example. It installs sensors in computer networks in various countries that send updates on cyber attacks and virus infections to a host computer in Japan. This effort aims to identify cyber attacks quickly through cooperation among various countries. A government official comments that "it becomes easier to formulate countermeasures if we know whether the cyber attack only targets Japan or is also targeting another country."

However, Japan confronts two major issues in its efforts to respond to cyber attacks – constitutional constraints and national awareness.

Self-Defense Forces only allowed to protect themselves

<GPS installed on a satellite suddenly stops operating on a day in 201x. GPS is a vital system for military operations and economic activities. Disruptions spread worldwide.>

<Next widespread power outages occur in Okinawa Prefecture and Misawa City (Aomori Prefecture) with bases that have U.S. military forces stationed in Japan. Financial and securities systems in the mainland U.S. experience disruptions.>

<Cyber attacks appear to be responsible for the series of troubles. While Japan and the U.S. are busy responding, warships from a certain country show up off Japan's coast...>

This is a simulation of a case of cyber attacks on Japan and the United States by a "certain country." The Canon Institute for Global Studies (Tokyo) conducted the simulation with experts and academics affiliated with the Ministry of Foreign Affairs and Defense Minister in 2012.

They predicted the following response by the Japanese government, a key point.

"The Japanese Government confirmed these conditions as an armed attack forecast situation. However, it was unable to resolve whether it could exercise self-defense against cyber attacks."

The Self-Defense Forces, which handle national defense, act in response to an order by the Prime Minister when an armed attack occurs or an imminent danger of attack exists (Article 76 of the Self-Defense Forces Act). However, it is difficult, in practice, to treat a cyber attack, which does not involve the use weapons, as an armed attack and order a retaliation by the Self-Defense Forces. This issue arises because Japan adheres to an exclusively defense security policy that limits the exercise of self-defense rights to a minimum under Article 9 of the Constitution. A Defense Ministry official comments that "Self-Defense Forces are unlikely to act unless the cyber attacks result in a loss of human life."

The Defense Ministry is preparing for cyber attacks too. It created the "Cyber Defense Team" with 100 people in the Joint Staff Office that operates the Ground Self Defense Forces and Maritime Self Defense Forces in March 2014. The team monitors Self-Defense Forces and Defense Ministry computer systems with 24-hour operations and handles virus counter measures. However, other government agency and private-sector systems are not covered by the defense because of ambiguity at this point about the legal basis on the extent of response that the Self-Defense Forces can take toward cyber attacks.

Kunihiko Miyake, a research fellow at the Canon Institute for Global Studies (former Director of the Japan-U.S. Security Treaty Division), who formulated the above-mentioned simulation, worries about the lack of a feeling of urgency about this matter in Japan and also comments that "it is important in Japan's case to understand cyber matters as military and security problems."

Cyber attacks are very likely to be a precursor of full-fledged military attacks if a war occurs in the 21st century. For example, this would involve crippling the high-tech weaponry and communications network and disrupting social foundations in the target country using cyber attacks prior to attacking with conventional weapons. In fact, large-scale cyber attacks afflicted Georgia's presidential office, media outlets, and other entities during clashes between Russia and Georgia over South Ossetia in 2008.

Israel implemented cyber attacks prior to airstrikes when it carried out airstrikes against Syria's nuclear-related facilities in September 2007. Richard Clarke, who worked as a special advisor to then-president Bush, wrote "Cyber War: The Next Threat to National Security and What to Do About It."

Clarke states that Israeli aircraft entered Syrian airspace on September 6, 2007. They destroyed nuclear-related facilities being built in Syria with North Korea's assistance, and then simply returned without incident. The Syrian military did not act at all. This was because nothing showed up on the Syrian military's radar network, which had been disabled by cyber attacks.

The Defense Ministry prepared response guidelines for the Self-Defense Forces for the first time in light of these characteristics of cyber attacks in September 2012. Japan's interpretation of Article 9 in the Constitution states that three conditions, one of which is imminent and unlawful infringement against Japan, must be met in order to exercise self-defense rights. The guidelines clarified that cyber attacks conducted as part of a military attack constitute an "imminent and unlawful infringement," and this allowed for retaliation.

However, it is difficult to identify cyber attacks ahead of time and damages spread instantaneously once they begin. This is truly a surprise attack. It is also tough to precisely determine the source of the attack because attacks are likely to utilize computer system from an unrelated third country.

Countries emphasize intimidation to keep the counterpart from engaging in cyber attacks, rather than retaliation, due to these aspects. For example, the U.S. government has officially presented a policy that it might make a preemptive strike against the counterpart if it finds signs of cyber attacks. The New York Times reported in February 2013 that the Obama administration prepared a policy that "lets the president order a preemptive attack" if there is danger of a large-scale cyber attack.

The Japanese Government, meanwhile, does not approve preemptive strikes by the Self-Defense Forces as a general rule in its interpretation of Article 9 due to the absence of an "imminent and unlawful infringement against Japan," a requirement for exercising the self-defense right. Guidelines prepared by the Defense Ministry in 2012 only permits a response once cyber attacks strike and damages occur. A former Self-Defense Forces official worries that "there is absolutely no deterrence effect toward the other country with this stance."

Cyber attacks are truly a "hidden war" and an unforeseen threat from when Japan adopted its policy of an exclusively defense security policy. However, Article 9 has become a very sensitive political issue in Japan today and thinking about this issue has effectively halted.

Constraints from human resources too

Keith Alexander, who runs the U.S. National Security Agency (NSA), appeared in a T-shirt and jeans, a rough attire that did not seem to fit the head of an intelligence agency.

The location was the "Defcon" event held in Las Vegas. It is a major global gathering where hackers from around the world compete using their technology skills. The Director appealed for cooperation with the NSA.

"You are the best resources. We need your help."

The NSA has a mission to collect intelligence using communications eavesdropping and electronic equipment. Mr. Alexander also attended the "Black Hat" international meeting of hackers held in Las Vegas in July 2013 and once again appealed to the attendees "to help us."

Computer knowledge and technical capabilities will determine the winner in the cyber war. It is not just the United States. Other countries are also earnestly trying to recruit talented hackers to join government agencies.

China utilizes highly patriotic hackers (also referred to as Honker) as civilian militia for the People's Liberation Army's cyber force, and it is thought that it assigns them to spying activities over the Internet and research into cyber attacks.

These civilian hackers make cyber attacks against enemies of China even without instructions from the government. Chinese Internet bulletin boards were full of messages about "getting Japan" in September 2012 when the Japanese government nationalized the Senkaku Islands. Many civilian hackers exchange information on bulletin boards, and they listed roughly

300 Japanese government agencies to attack. For example, hackers placed an image of the Senkaku Islands with a Chinese flag on the main web page for Japan's Supreme Court. It was also temporarily difficult to browse Defense Ministry, Ministry of Internal Affairs and Communications, and other ministry web sites. Chinese bulletin boards had many comments along the lines of "I attacked them" and "Great job."

Korea is putting a national effort into training hackers. In 2011, the government joined with Seoul-based Korea University to create the "Cyber National Defense" program and offers free tuition to students who commit to working at the military's cyber command for seven years. Russia has built cooperative relationships with about 800 hackers.

It is often said that "a good offense is the best defense" in the cyber world. Countries are striving to recruit and train hackers from the standpoint of understanding how to attack others and thereby strengthening the defense of their own network.

In Japan, however, the concept of exclusively defensive security policy leads to constraints.

The Defcon event in 2013 held games to compete in hacking capabilities, and the Sutegoma2 team of Japanese engineers and students participated. The game consists of stealing files from servers (host computers), which intentionally have weaknesses to outside attacks, given to each team.

The Japanese team put a top priority on protecting the weaknesses and shutting out suspicious communications entering the server and thereby providing defense. It placed sixth out of the roughly 900 teams in the game. While Japanese government officials monitoring the game spoke excitedly about the strong result, a U.S. hacker offered the following critique.

"The Japanese team was just defending and not taking the offensive. They won't be able to protect themselves unless they learn how to assess the counterpart's situation through attacks."

A METI official noted that "it is taboo in Japan to teach how to make attacks." METI planned to hold a "Security Koshien (Championship)" event mainly for high school students aimed at training hackers in 2003. However, it shelved the plan after strong protests by school officials and others asking "whether they wanted to train criminals" upon hearing that it included a program of competing for skills to infiltrate servers.

While METI ended up holding a similar event in the following year by reworking it as a "security camp" for burnishing computer-related skills, some parents still had inquiries about "whether it was truly alright for their children to participate."

The "hacker = criminal" image in Japan places constraint on efforts to train human resources too. Hacker originally meant someone with advanced skills related to computers and networks, while "cracker" referred to people who misuse technology for cyber attacks and other improper activities. In Japan, hacker and cracker have the same connotations. While the term "white hacker" (a "just" hacker) has started gaining use recently, there is still a negative image associated with hackers.

Japan's shortage of computer engineers is worsening each year in this environment. Yushi Okajima, an associate professor at Kanto Gakuin University who is familiar with hacking activities worldwide, expresses concern that "Japan's segment of IT engineers is steadily thinning out." He has a class on information networks at the university and explains that the number of students started dropping after a peak in around 2000. He also points out a major decline in the IT capabilities of students. Mr. Okajima attributes this change to a sharp drop in students that have experience tinkering with PCs and trying to program on their own amid rapid inroads by smartphones.

Information-technology Promotion Agency Japan, an independent administrative entity, implemented a questionnaire survey of 16,000 Japanese companies during 2011-12 that inquired "whether information security engineers were sufficient in numbers and capabilities." It estimated from the results that Japan confronts a shortfall in engineers of about 80,000 people nationwide.

Japan is likely to slip further behind in dealing with cyber challenges since it continues to face shortages in talented human resources and has weak training programs.

Tough hurdle to becoming part of Five Eyes

The Japanese Government depends heavily on the United States. Japan's gap in its abilities to deal with cyber attacks compared to the United States is "similar to the difference between a youth baseball team and the major league" (industry expert). The quickest way to prepare for threats posed by China and North Korea is teaming up with the United States, its ally.

A Japan-U.S. Security Consultative Committee ("2+2" Ministerial Meeting) took place at the Ministry of Foreign Affairs' Iikura Guest House in Azabudai (Tokyo) on October 3, 2013. The two countries agreed to have the Self-Defense Forces and U.S. military to work together in the case of a large-scale cyber attack. They also confirmed a program for Japan to learn advanced technology and experience from the United States, including dispatches of Self-Defense Force officers to the U.S. military's training courses.

"Cyber is a new focal point in the Japan-U.S. alliance."

Defense Secretary Hagel emphasized this aspect at the press conference.

The Japanese and U.S. government held the first Japan-U.S. cyber dialogue by working-level staff in May of the same year prior to the "2+2" Ministerial Meeting and announced a joint statement that called on countries to participate in the creation of new international rules for using the Internet. This effort aims to create rules with Japan and the U.S. at the forefront and thereby restrict China, North Korea, and others.

However, the alliance with the United States faces limits too.

A staff member from the Cabinet Intelligence and Research Office frequently visited the Diet Members' Office Building for the Upper and Lower Houses in Nagatacho (Tokyo) in fall 2013.

"The Act on the Protection of Specially Designated Secrets is essential for Japan to be able to obtain high-level intelligence from the United States."

The staff member brought materials to explain the necessity of an Act on the Protection of Specially Designated Secrets in order to prevent leaks of classified information. Japan passed this law with approval from the LDP, Komeito, and Your Party in December 2013.

A senior government official expressed relief that "we have moved a step close to Five Eyes."

Five Eyes is the framework for intelligence gathering activities by the five English-speaking countries – the United States, the United Kingdom, Canada, Australia, and New Zealand. These five countries use the Echelon eavesdropping network to gather and share massive amounts of phone call, facsimile, e-mail, and other intelligence obtained at overseas consular offices and bases.

Intelligence experts explain that the five countries divide projected information into "top secret," "secret," and "confidential" categories. The highest level protected information is called "four your eyes only," and this phrase became a title in the James Bond (007) series of movies. The Five Eyes name is a reference to "your eyes."

Governments of the five countries do not officially acknowledge the existence of Echelon, but the European Union's (EU) European Parliament accepted a report in September 2001 that concluded for the first time by a public entity that "there is no doubt that the Echelon global eavesdropping system exists," causing repercussions worldwide.

The European Parliament explained in the report prepared over roughly a year that Echelon started with spying cooperation between the United States and the United Kingdom during the First World War and that the five countries signed an agreement in 1948. The report notes that the United States is the central force in operating the system and that some of the massive intercepted data is diverted to industrial espionage. It mentions the U.S. military base in Misawa (Aomori Prefecture) as one of the sites for intercepting communications. Motohiro Tsuchiya, a Keio professor who served as a member of Japan's NISC, comments that "the framework of five countries remains intact even now that communications have shifted from analog to digital."

The U.S. Government monitors the activities of the Japanese government too. The U.K.-based Guardian newspaper reported in June 2013 that NSA and other agencies intercepted communications of Japan's embassies and representative teams in 38 locations, including the Japanese Embassy in the United States. A former Japanese diplomat recalls that, "The phone line would cut off when key words were mentioned in phone calls from MOFA to the Japanese Embassy in the U.S. during the period of Japan-U.S. structural talks in the 1980s. We always spoke with the assumption that our lines were being tapped after that." The U.S.-based journalist James Bamford wrote in his book "Body of Secrets: Anatomy of the Ultra-Secret National Security Agency" (published in Japanese by Kadokawa) that the NSA was tapping phone calls by the Japanese side during the Japan-U.S discussions regarding trade friction for cars in 1995.

The Japanese government did not demonstrate a clear reaction even after disclosure of this intelligence gathering activity by the U.S. government. Japan appears to have decided that it is wiser to gain admission to the Five Eyes group, rather than getting into tensions with the U.S. government. Yet a U.S. government official notes that "there are some difficulties in sharing protected information with Japan because it lags in countermeasures for dealing with cyber attacks."

Infrastructure defense left to the private sector

Falling behind in responses to cyber attacks puts the lives of the general population at risk too. This is because cyber attacks threaten electricity, gas, water, transportation networks, and other vital infrastructure for our daily lives as well.

<Internal pressure starts increasing at a feverish pace at a gas production plant. However, the device monitoring pressure shows a normal value and operators are not aware of the abnormality. A red lamp communicating the explosion danger started flashing and a siren goes off.>

This was a demonstration of a cyber attack at a "control system security center" in Tagajo City (Miyagi Prefecture) on January 22, 2014. Gas company employees from around the country carefully watched devices at the model plant installed at the center.

"It was too late to respond by the time that operators became aware."

One of the participants highlighted the threat of cyber attacks in this way.

The center is a technology research union approved by METI that was launched in March 2012. There are 23 entities that belong to the union, including Toshiba, Hitachi, and other major Japanese companies and universities, and this center conducts research to defend infrastructure from cyber attacks. Japan modeled the center on the U.S. Department of Homeland Security's facilities, and it contains seven types of model plants, including a waste water and sewage facility, a building, a thermal-fired power plant, a gas facility, and a chemicals facility.

It had been thought that Japan's infrastructure was fairly resilient to cyber attacks because many of the computer systems controlling the infra-structure are not directly connected to the Internet. However, Akio Sato, a senior researcher at Mitsubishi Research Institute who handles public relations for the center, asserts that "safety because of not being directly connected to the outside world is just a myth" since it is necessary to connect to outside networks, even if just temporarily, for program updates and maintenance management.

Even construction of a system completely shut off from the outside is not entirely safe.

The uranium enrichment facility in Natanz in Central Iran experienced an abnormality in the computer system that destroyed some centrifuges in 2010. Coverage by the New York Times explains that the source of the trouble was a virus contained in a USB memory device for data exchange that was plugged in a computer.

The United States and Israel, which wanted to halt Iran's nuclear development, jointly developed the Stuxnet virus and managed to get it into Iran's uranium enrichment facility by some method. Stuxnet is the first global cyber weapon that succeeded in destroying infrastructure and also clarified the possibility of making cyber attacks through USB memory or other peripheral devices. It is also thought that Iran inadvertently dispersed Stuxnet worldwide in the process of investigating the cause of equipment failures. There is no way of knowing when an "evolved" version of Stuxnet developed by some other country or organization might try to attack Japan.

Protection of infrastructure from a cyber attack of this nature is the responsibility of business operators in many countries, including Japan. Yet business operators are no longer capable combating such attacks in today's environment.

James Foster, a professor at Keio University who previously worked at the U.S. State Department and is familiar with cyber issues, comments that, "The goal of cyber attacks has changed from stealing information to destroying infrastructure. It is not wise to leave countermeasures up to the private sector."

The U.S. government started a review of measures to assist infra-structure defense based on an executive order by the President issued on February 12, 2013. Some ideas discussed were provision of subsidies and creating a mechanism to transfer counter-measure costs into a fee regime.

Japan listed 10 areas as critical infrastructure (information communications systems, financial systems, airlines, railways, power systems, gas systems, administrative systems, medical facilities, water facilities, and logistics) in the Action Plan on Information Security Measures for Critical Infrastructure that it prepared in 2005 and has encouraged cyber measures. It added credit systems, oil facilities, and chemical facilities more recently and is reviewing measures for operator support.

If a single infrastructure system is destroyed, the impact can spread broadly. For example, a halt of electricity supply cripples the transportation network. A Defense Ministry official comments that "just having Aegis warships and other cutting-edge facilities is not enough, Self-Defense Forces must arrive at the base in order to use them."

There is even risk of IT devices used in possession being hijacked in a cyber-attack, incurring damages, or being used in a separate cyber attack without the owner's knowledge.

Let's take the case of an automobile. Japan's Information-Technology Promotion Agency, reports that modern cars are equipped with more than 100 electric control units (ECUs) and are a bundle of IT devices.

A person related to Toyota expressed shock in seeing a video played at Defcon (held in Las Vegas) in August 2013 because it showed a Toyota Prius hybrid car having its ECUs manipulated from outside the vehicle, resulting in loss of handle and brake functionality.

Charlie Miller from U.S.-based Twitter and Chris Valasek, who works at a security services company, demonstrated the commandeering of Prius functions. While the PC used for the takeover was directly connected with a wire to the Prius in the video, experts explain that "it will be technologically possible" to achieve a takeover with wireless technology too at some point. This view takes into account wireless connections between cars with navigation systems, ETC systems, or other devices and external networks.

Smart devices that seek to improve energy savings and convenience by using network connections, such as smart home appliances, smart homes, and smart meters (next-generation electricity meters) are prone to the danger of cyber attacks. The government aims to spread use of smart meters and other devices as part of its economic growth strategy, but it is also warning about "risk of unexpected operation due to a cyber attack" for IT consumer electronics linked to networks in its Cyber Security Strategy compiled in 2013.

In fact, a cyber attack against a Korea government agency and others in March 2011 apparently conducted by North Korea manipulated the system for a surveillance camera installed at a convenience store in Tokyo and used it as a command center for instructing the attack.

Who controls cyber space?

While cyber attacks also severely affect the lives of citizens, clear international rules to manage cyber space have not been defined yet.

The Tallinn Manual prepared by the NATO Cooperative Cyber Defence Centre of Excellence is a leading example of international rules regarding existing cyber space. Experts in international law and military affairs contributed, and the report takes its name from Tallinn, the capital of Estonia where the Centre is located.

The Tallinn Manual consists of 95 items and applies existing international laws regarding war, such as the Charter of the United Nations and the Geneva Conventions, to cyber wars. It also clarifies that the country that incurs damages from cyber attacks can take suitable countermeasures and approves the collective right to self-defense (the right to stop an attack against another country by force even if one's own country is not directly attacked) for cyber space.

The Convention on Cybercrime adopted in 2001 under the leadership of the European Parliament addresses cybercrimes that involve stealing money or information. It also lists unauthorized access, communications interception, attacks on computer systems, child pornography transactions, and certain other actions as crimes and requires cooperation from countries in saving evidence, extraditing criminals, and other areas.

The Convention took effect in July 2004, and Japan is a member. However, China and Russia, which are often mentioned as the source of various cyber attacks, are not members. A person associated with Japan's police agency acknowledges that, "The convention is not functioning well in this format."

China and Russia are calling for formulation of a Convention by the

United Nations in order to avoid having cyberspace rules defined under the lead of European countries. The United Nations created the Group of Governmental Experts (GGE) on cybersecurity at the United Nations General Assembly First Committee in December 2010. Fifteen countries participated in the group, including the five permanent members of the Security Council (the United States, China, Russia, France, and the United Kingdom) and Japan, Germany, and India, and it issued a report in June 2013. However, while the report recommended "application of the Charter of the United Nations and other international laws" to cyberspace, it does not contain the specificity of content found in an official Convention.

China and Russia, meanwhile, released an "International Code of Conduct for Information Security (Proposal)" along with Uzbekistan and Tajikistan in September 2011. The main point of the proposed code of conduct is cooperation to prevent release on the Internet of information that incites terrorism and extremism and information that undermines the political, economic, and social stability of other countries. It also includes sufficient respect for the domestic laws of other countries.

The United States, European countries, and Japan want to create international rules while protecting the freedom of cyberspace. China and Russia, meanwhile, are interested in strengthening controls on cyberspace. China and other countries have reinforced these attitudes since the collapse of multiple dictatorships in the Middle East during the Arab Spring that started with the Jasmine Revolution in Tunisia. They might be concerned about the large role of information exchanged over the Internet in the Arab Spring. A top official at Japan's Ministry of Foreign Affairs comments that "Deep tensions exist between the United States and European countries and China and Russia. It is likely to take a while to create international rules."

Countries are urgently striving to prepare for cyber attacks on their own in light of these conditions, and this is a vital issue for Japan as well.

Chapter 5

Cooperation by Japan, the U.S., Australia, and ASEAN Encircling China

China is continuing efforts to treat exclusive economic zone (EEZ) areas as territorial waters. Chapter 1 looked at circumstances related to China's establishment of an ADIZ in the East China Sea. China aims to broaden this ADIZ to the South China Sea as well.

Japan and the United States subsequently agreed to New Guidelines to deal with these crisis conditions in April 2015. The guidelines enable Japan to give logistical assistance to the U.S. military even in areas separated from Japan, such as the South China Sea. This chapter reviews efforts to bolster Japan, U.S., Australia, and ASEAN relations in an effort to halt China's maritime push.

Great Wall of Sand

A pile of satellite photos provided clear evidence of China's "ambitions."

Satellites showed Chinese ships filling large amounts of sand on a shoal in the Spratly Islands located in the South China Sea to build artificial islands on March 16, 2015. China is conducting land reclamation around a coral reef on the ocean floor that is 1,000 kilometers away from its southernmost island of Hainan and reinforcing the site with concrete.

Fiery Cross Reef, the largest reef in the Spratly Islands, was a hidden reef with a majority of its presence under the water surface as of August 2014. Yet a vast portion had been reclaimed and an artificial island with a total length of more than 3,000 meters and a width of 200-300 meters appeared in a period of just over six months. China built port facilities on the eastern side and outlines of a 3,000-meter runway on the western side of the manmade island.

The South China Sea extends from China's southerly direction into Southeast Asia and is surrounded by the Philippines, Vietnam, Malaysia, Indonesia, and Brunei. These countries have competing claims to territorial rights and are contending with each other in this "sea of conflict." The South China Sea has abundant natural resources, including oil and natural gas, and provides an important sea lane between the Pacific Ocean and Indian Ocean through the Strait of Malacca. Cargo volume passing through the area accounts for roughly half of the world's maritime transportation. This is an important sea area that affects security and commerce interests for not only China and Southeast Asian countries, but also the United States, Japan, Korea, Australia, and other countries.

China is ignoring the United Nations Convention on the Law of the Sea and trying to take the South China Sea as its "own sea."

China's Foreign Ministry spokesman explains that the shoal reclamation "also aims to fulfill China's international responsibilities for rescue efforts, environmental protection, and safe navigation." Senior military officials, meanwhile, are more direct.

Deputy Chief of the Joint Staff Sun Jianguo asserted the legitimacy of land reclamations at an Asian security conference held on May 31, 2015 in Singapore with a comment that "the activity is totally within the range of our sovereignty and both legal and reasonable." He also acknowledged that the artificial islands "satisfy demand for military defense" and are military bases.

The artificial island can replenish supplies and provide maintenance to naval warships and China Coast Guard ships once it is fully equipped with port facilities and thereby enable permanent deployment of these ships to the entire South China Sea area. China will have the ability to permanently station fighters, bombers, unmanned reconnaissance drones, and other assets at the site after completing the 3,000-meter airstrip, reinforcing its air superiority throughout the entire South China Sea region. These facilities will dramatically improve China's A2AD capabilities, a strategy that calls for keeping the U.S. military at bay during military incidents. It is generally thought that China will install air defense radar and broaden the ADIZ established in the East China Sea in November 2013 to the South China Sea too at some point.

Construction of an airstrip on this scale at an uninhabited shoal is unusual. For example, the Marine Air Station Futenma located in Ginowan City of Okinawa Prefecture, attracting attention in relation to a potential transfer to the Henoko area of Okinawa's Nago City, is the station for the First Marine Aircraft Wing of the U.S. Marine Corps along with MV-22B Osprey transport planes and AH-1W attack helicopters, but only has a runway that is roughly 2,700 meters long.

China's reclamation activity in the Spratly Islands is not limited to Fiery Cross Reef. It has already built heliports in Gaven Reefs and Cuarteron Reef and there is possibility that it is building a large-scape airstrip at Subi Reef too. China has also built a structure that appears to be a control tower in Johnson South Reef, and observations have confirmed the presence of a dome structure to protect radar equipment on the Hugh Reef that has grown in surface area by about 200 times since 2004. China is steadily constructing military facilities aimed at gaining control of air space.

Admiral Harry Harris, the commander of the U.S. Pacific Fleet, criticized China's activities as "building a Great Wall of Sand" in a speech delivered in Canberra, Australia's capital city. Chinese emperors built the Great Wall as a defense line to prevent other peoples from entering the fertile central plains. The current Chinese government is building a new Great Wall out of sand in the South China Sea. However, the Great Wall of Sand has very different implications as a beachhead for Chinese outward expansion.

U.S. Secretary of State John Kerry met with Chinese President Xi Jinping in the Great Hall of the People in Beijing during his visit to China on May 17. Mr. Kerry expressed "concern" about China's land reclamation activities in the South China Sea and emphasized "the importance of easing tensions, finding peaceful solutions to conflicts, respecting international law, and curtailing actions." Mr. Xi, however, did not indicate any willingness to compromise.

"As I have stated numerous times before, the large Pacific offers sufficient room for China and the United States as major powers."

Mr. Xi clarified China's stance of broadening its interests and influence in the South China Sea while avoiding a decisive stand-off with the United States.

China's coercive approach is not just apparent in the South China Sea. There is speculation that the Great Wall of Sand might extend to the Senkaku Islands in Okinawa Prefecture where China is making territorial claims. Chinese public vessels continue incursions into the area around the Senkaku Islands. China's Zhejiang Province, a coastal area on the East China Sea, disclosed a plan on its website to build a major China Coast Guard base in Wenzhou City, which is close to the Senkaku Islands, with a budget of 3.34 billion yuan (about 66.8 billion yen using the forex rate at the time) in June 2015.

A Japanese Defense Ministry official expressed concern.

"China is testing whether aggressive expansion of sovereignty by reclaiming land in the sea works. If it succeeds, China might start showing its muscle here at any time."

Widening difference in power

A purported internal document from the Defense Ministry submitted by the Communist Party to the Upper House's Special Committee on Peace and Security Legislation on September 2, 2015 caused some commotion. It was a record of a conversation involving Chief of Staff Katsutoshi Kawano, the top leader of the Self-Defense Forces, during a visit to the United States in December 2014.

Mr. Kawano noted that "the Ministry could not find the same document," but acknowledged that "there was a document on the same topic." While ruling and opposition parties criticized sloppy document management that let the confidential information leak out, the meeting's content deserves attention.

Mr. Kawano had the following exchange with Scott Swift, Navy Staff Director for the office of the Chief of Naval Operations, at the U.S. Department of Defense on December 18, 2014 according to proceedings from the meeting.

Swift: "The Senkaku issue must be understood as an issue with China, not just a matter of the Senkaku islands. It is important to factor the presence of 2-3 Chinese submarines in the Indian Ocean into the overall picture."

Kawano: "The Abe government is cooperating with the Philippines, Vietnam, and other ASEAN countries from a standpoint of rejecting changes by China to the status quo using force."

Swift: "India is making a variety of port calls to Vietnam and others when it conducts exercises in the South China Sea. Shouldn't Japan make strategic port calls too?"

Kawano: "Japan is currently dispatching Maritime Self-Defense Forces to the Republic of Djibouti to deal with maritime piracy and is implementing strategic port calls during this dispatch."

Swift: "Shouldn't Japan be sending a message by making all port calls at ports that are not on the path, such as Singapore and Kuala Lumpur?"

The meeting shows the U.S. military, which is increasingly concerned about China ramping up activities in the Indian Ocean, in addition to the East China Sea and South China Sea, requesting further "strategic port calls" by the Self-Defense Forces. The exercise of "freedom of air and sea navigation" by the Self Defense Forces' destroyers and P-3C patrol planes, along with the U.S. military, in the sea area where China is trying to expand its interests also clarifies the presence of the Japan-U.S. alliance.

Sea lane security is one of the top priorities for Japan, which relies on crude oil, natural gas, and other imports, in protecting the livelihood of its people, and the long navigation path from the Indian Ocean to the South China Sea and East China Sea is a lifeline for the Japanese economy. Japan's use of two Maritime Self Defense Forces' destroyers for international anti-piracy efforts in waters around Somalia (Africa) is part of "the need for Japan, as a beneficiary of sea lanes, to make a direct physical contribution" (top official from the Maritime Self Defense Forces).

While the United States has picked up its surveillance and monitoring in the South China Sea, China is steadily moving forward with the creation of "existing facts" that "change the status quo with force" as seen in Chapter 1. The United States is exposing the limits of its strength as a superpower as expressed by President Obama in his comment that "the United States is not the world's police officer." The United States required the cooperation of Japan, its alliance partner who shares the same values, in order to confront

China in the Asia-Pacific region where the U.S. model advocating democracy and rule of law and the Chinese model of rewriting the status quo through authoritarianism are clashing.

Cannons fired 19 times, signifying treatment as a state guest, while Kimigayo played in the background at the White House lush with fresh greenery on April 28, 2015.

President Obama vigorously praised Prime Minister Abe at the welcome ceremony ahead of the Japan-U.S. Summit Meeting.

"President Eisenhower greeted Prime Minister Nobusuke Kishi, the grandfather of Prime Minister Abe, here at the White House in 1960. Today we are welcoming Prime Minister Abe with whom we have worked to expand our alliance. He is leading Japan in taking on a new role in the world."

Mr. Abe responded that "my government has made revitalization of the Japan-U.S. alliance a top priority for its diplomatic policy" and declared that "the relationship between our countries has become stronger than ever, and our alliance has recovered with vigor."

Mr. Obama personally showed Mr. Abe around the Lincoln Memorial on April 27, upon his arrival in Washington on the day before the meeting, and the two leaders interacted in this context for about 20 minutes. Mr. Obama closely aligns himself with President Lincoln who is known as the "father of emancipation." Mr. Lincoln is a symbol of freedom and democracy for the U.S. people as well.

The walk was not in the original schedule and came together as a sudden proposal from the U.S. side. The United States also prepared an opportunity for Mr. Abe to speak to a joint session of the U.S. Congress, a first-time event for a Japanese prime minister. Mr. Obama, who takes a business-like approach, is not a good fit with his liberal tendencies for the conservative Mr. Abe. Yet his unusually warm treatment reflected a major change in the assessment of Mr. Abe who is steering a cooperative course with the United States in security matters.

Mr. Abe took on revisions to Japan's security legislation that approved the limited use of collective self-defense rights in order to counter China's growing coerciveness toward the Senkaku Islands. The new Japan-U.S. defense cooperation guidelines finally confirmed by the two sides on April

27, 2015 strengthened the deterrence of the Japan-U.S. alliance in dealing with China's maritime initiatives. The new guidelines facilitate seamless cooperation between Japan's Self Defense Forces and the U.S. military from peaceful times to incidents. They also expand cooperation between Japan and the United States, which had been limited to the area around Japan, to a global level.

This policy fits with the "rebalancing policy" that places emphasis on the Asia-Pacific promoted by Mr. Obama (refer to Chapter 1 for details).

"You have revived the Japanese economy, and Japan is contributing to the world in security matters. Thank you, Shinzo."

Mr. Obama highly praised Mr. Abe's initiatives at the press conference after the summit meeting. He also harshly criticized China for its attempts to change the status quo in the East China Sea and South China Sea through force.

"We cannot underestimate the amount of tension being created by China's activities related to maritime and sovereignty issues. This (China's) method is wrong."

The Soviet Union, which previously faced off with the United States in the Cold War period, placed a nuclear-powered submarine equipped with submarine launched ballistic missiles (SLBM) in the Sea of Okhotsk north of Hokkaido and secured a "card" of being able to conduct a nuclear attack against the mainland U.S. without interference from the U.S. military. China similarly aims to make the South China Sea into a "special area" that is not hindered by the U.S. military and obtain an SLBM card against the mainland U.S. This is a view presented by many security experts.

Strong concerns exist that U.S. nuclear capabilities would provide less deterrence and it would no longer be possible to prevent China's coercive maritime ambitions if China's strategy becomes a reality. The scenario of the Chinese military advancing to the Senkaku Islands is likely to appear more realistic too.

Mr. Abe looked closely at Mr. Obama's eyes as he made the following comment in the Japan-U.S. summit meeting.

"Military capabilities of the Southeast Asian countries in the South China Sea are very weak. This is why the U.S. military and the Japan-U.S. alliance have such important roles."

Mr. Obama nodded in agreement and noted "I understand this."

The military capabilities of ASEAN countries competing with China for territorial rights in the South China Sea are completely outclassed by China, as indicated by Mr. Abe. Materials prepared by the Defense Ministry in May 2015 show that China has 892 military ships with gross displacement of about 1.42 million tons, 2,582 operational aircraft, and over 370 maritime law enforcement boats under the China Coast Guard.

In contrast, Vietnam has 94 military ships with gross displacement of 37,000 tons, 97 operational aircraft, and over 34 ships in the coast guard, the Philippines has 80 military ships with gross displacement of 47,000 tons, 26 operational aircraft, and 58 ships in the coast guard, and Malaysia has 208 military ships with gross displacement of 58,000 tons, 71 operational aircraft, and 189 ships in the coast guard.

Totals for the three countries are just 382 military ships with gross displacement of 142,000 tons and 194 operational aircraft. China leads by almost 10-fold just using a simple calculation of the numbers.

Additionally, China has been increasing its national defense spending at a roughly double-digit annual pace simply in disclosed values since 1989 (refer to Chapter 1 for details) and is making significant qualitative advances in recent years by developing next-generation fighters with stealth capabilities, building air carriers on its own, and deploying new anti-ship ballistic missiles.

Defense Ministry materials concluded that "qualitative and quantitative differences in military power are pronounced" between China and countries that border the South China Sea. A "power vacuum" has emerged because the military power of countries on the South China Sea is virtually non-existent if compared to China's overwhelming military strength.

Changing the status quo in the East China Sea

China is similarly making incursions into a "power vacuum" in the East China Sea.

P-3C patrol planes under Fleet Air Wing 1 of the Maritime Self Defense Forces (Kanoya Air Base in Kagoshima Prefecture) monitor sea regions daily. China is steadily developing a gas field near the intermediary line in the East China Sea that is equidistant from the coastlines of Japan and China.

P-3C planes confirmed that China restarted gas field drilling activities in June 2013. China built new sea platforms in waters on the Chinese side of the intermediary line and accelerated gas field development efforts.

Seafloor gas field development begins with test drilling using mobile drilling equipment and moves to full-fledged drilling with a stationary platform after discovery of an appropriate site. Japan's P-3C observations discovered an increase in stationary platforms. China had four platforms prior to May 2013 and increased platform volume fourfold during two years with another three sites in 2013 (from June), five sites in 2014, and four sites in 2015.

Japan's Nansei Islands and mainland China are located in close proximity with the shortest distance at 180 nautical miles (about 333 kilometers). Exclusive economic zones with priority rights to seafloor resources (EEZs extend 200 nautical miles (or about 370 kilometers) from the coastline) claimed by Japan and China are overlapping. While Japan is calling for use of the intermediary line between Japan and China as the border for the EEZs of the two countries, China asserts that the boundary should be near the Okinawa Islands. The two sides have not resolved this discrepancy in views. An undefined border means that the area around the intermediary line is a "disputed sea zone." Yet China has started developing new gas fields despite this status.

The Japanese government disclosed China's platform installations on July 22, 2015. Chief Cabinet Secretary Suga criticized China's actions at a press conference stating that, "It is extremely regrettable that China is unilaterally developing resources, even if it is located on the Chinese side of the Japan-China intermediary line, at a time when the border has not yet been finalized." Mr. Suga shared that Japan repeatedly protested to China by raising the issue and requesting that China halt development activities at the Japan-China Summit Meeting held in Beijing in November 2014, the Japan-China Foreign Ministers' Meeting in March 2015, and Japan-China Summit Meeting in the following month. It previously had not disclosed this information.

China began to develop gas fields in the East China Sea in the late 1990s. In November 1998, China built mining facilities and started production at the

Pinghu gas field, which is located about 70 kilometers on the Chinese side of the intermediary line. It subsequently developed the Shirakaba (Chunxiao), Kashi (Tianwaitian), and Bajiaoting fields located near the intermediary line, and the Shirakaba field crosses the intermediary line and extends to the Japanese side. Criticism from the Japanese side increased due to strong likelihood that China's mining activities at the site are stealing natural gas from the Japan side as if "through a straw."

In response, the Japanese and Chinese governments began negotiations on joint development around the intermediary line. They started negotiations on a treaty to realize joint development after reaching an agreement in June 2008 to let Japanese companies participate in the Shirakaba development and designate a joint development zone in the sea area that crosses over the intermediary line.

However, the incident in which a Chinese fishing boat rammed a patrol ship from the Japan Coast Guard in waters around the Senkaku Islands in September 2010 derailed the negotiations. The Chinese side, which claims territorial rights to the Senkaku Islands, suspended tasks as a retaliatory measure. Treaty negotiations have not resumed since then owing to further cooling off in the Japan-China relationship amid anger from the Chinese government toward nationalization of the Senkaku Islands by the Japanese government in September 2012. China is accelerating its development of gas fields in the East China Sea while the treaty negotiations remain on hold.

China's gas field development creates problems that go beyond just the issue of taking natural gas from the Japanese side. The more serious threat is national security.

Japan's Defense Minister Gen Nakatani explained at a meeting of the Lower House's special committee on peace and security legislation on July 10, 2015 that the Chinese side might install radar and a helipad for takeoff and landing by helicopters and reconnaissance drones. This development is a concern for the Defense Ministry.

"China could enhance surveillance and other capabilities in the East China Sea if it proceeds to utilize the platforms for security purposes and gain a greater understanding of activities by the Self Defense Forces."

While China established an ADIZ that includes Japan's airspace above the Senkaku Islands in the East China Sea in November 2013, observers noted that the Chinese military did not have capabilities to monitor the entire ADIZ area with radar. However, it is unclear whether these platforms are equipped with terrestrial radar equipment. Platforms concentrated around the intermediary line are located precisely at the median between the Japan-side edge of China's ADIZ and the mainland's coast line and hence enable monitoring of airspace that could not be covered using existing terrestrial radar located in mainland China. This positioning gives China the ability to monitor activities by the Self Defense Forces as suggested by Mr. Nakatani.

China disclosed the national defense budget for 2015 that sets a 10.1% year-on-year rise in spending to 886,898 million Chinese yuan (about 16,850 billion yen based on the forex rate at that time). Japan's defense budget, meanwhile, calls for a 2% year-on-year increase to 4,980.1 billion yen in fiscal 2015 (including expenses related to U.S. military forces stationed in Japan). China's budget is roughly 3.4 times larger just at disclosed values. China is headed toward expansion of its budget to four times Japan's level in five years and almost seven times in 10 years if it continues to increase defense spending at this pace.

Mr. Abe made the following comment regarding China's plans to pursue maritime advances with support from enhanced and modernized military capabilities at a meeting of the Lower House's special committee on peace and security legislation on May 27, 2015.

"The emergence of China, its activities in the East China Sea and South China Sea, and cyber attacks, terrorism, and extremism truly extend beyond national borders. The era in which a country could protect itself on its own is over."

Collaboration with ASEAN countries

Back in the South China Sea, a P-3C patrol aircraft from Japan's Maritime Self Defense Force flew in airspace over Palawan Island in the Philippines near the Spratly Islands on June 23, 2015. This was the first joint exercise by the Maritime Self Defense Force that envisioned a search for a distressed ship. The Maritime Self Defense Force's announcement described the purpose of the exercise as "improving humanitarian assistance and disaster rescue skills and strengthening friendly ties with the Philippine Navy."

A separate hidden aim is encouraging modernization of equipment used by the Philippine military. The P-3C is equipped with radar, electronic warfare support equipment, infrared dark vision systems, and other cutting-edge submarine detection equipment. It can also be outfitted with torpedo and anti-ship missile weaponry. The Maritime Self Defense Force has about 70 of these aircraft, putting it second after the U.S. military's roughly 200 planes, and has accumulated a significant amount of operational capabilities thus far.

BNI-2A patrol planes from the Philippine military that participated in the exercise are not equipped with radar and significantly trail the P-3C in actual capabilities. The Maritime Self Defense Force side communicated the P-3C's performance and method of using the system for submarine detection to the Philippine side in the exercise. A spokesman for the Philippine Defense Ministry commented two days after the joint exercise that "we have an interest in procuring P-C3 planes," expressing a forward-looking stance toward a rollout of new patrol planes.

Southeast Asian countries must try to encourage China to refrain from its reckless maritime pursuits by raising their deterrence against China. This also benefits Japan as it confronts pressure from China in the East China Sea.

On June 4, prior to the exercise, Mr. Abe met with Philippine President Benigno Aquino at the State Guest House in Moto-Akasaka (Tokyo). This was the sixth Abe-Aquino Summit Meeting since the launch of the second Abe Cabinet at the end of 2012.

Mr. Abe is actively arranging meetings with Mr. Aquino who is resolutely standing up to China in relation to territorial issues in the South China Sea and welcomed Mr. Aquino with the highest-level reception as a State Guest this time.

"Japan hopes to strengthen cooperation with the Philippines in all areas as a strategic partner that shares ideals and goals and contribute to the stability and prosperity of the region and international community."

This is what Mr. Abe emphasized at the meeting. Both leaders agreed to start negotiations for an agreement on transfers of defense equipment in order to promote defense cooperation in the maritime security field. The talks aim to arrange the sale of defense equipment developed by Japan to boost the Philippine's maritime surveillance capabilities that are lacking.

Mr. Abe announced a plan to provide the Philippines with 10 patrol ships utilizing overseas development assistance (ODA) with the aim of improving the capabilities of the Philippine Coast Guard on his trip to the Philippines in July 2013. China is deploying large patrol ships at a rapid pace, and the China Coast Guard presented a goal of having a fleet of more than 50 large ships in the over 1,000-ton class by 2015. It is likely to deploy many of these ships in the East China Sea and South China Sea, and this makes assistance to Southeast Asian countries, which only have older-style patrol ships a pressing issue.

Japan Marine United, a Japanese shipbuilding firm, concluded an official contract for construction of 10 patrol ships with the Philippine government two years after Mr. Abe's proposal. Mr. Abe welcomed the contract at the sixth Summit Meeting and proposed more discussions to further enhance the surveillance capabilities of the Philippine Coast Guard.

Mr. Abe selected the Southeast Asian countries of Vietnam, Thailand, and Indonesia for his first overseas trip after the launch of the second Abe Cabinet. He spent a year visiting all 10 ASEAN countries located along China's periphery and is strengthening cooperation in the security field.

Mr. Abe met with Vietnam's Prime Minister Nyugen Tan Dung at the Prime Minister's Office on January 16, 2013 and commented with vigor that, "Japan intends to follow a path of peace with ASEAN and play an active role in easing tensions and promoting prosperity in the region amid major changes in the strategic environment in the Asia-Pacific region."

Vietnam has incurred intimidation with force from the Chinese side, such as severing of a survey cable being used by a resources discovery vessel of state-run oil firm PetroVietnam by a Chinese fishing boat in the South China Sea in November 2012. Anti-China demonstrations broke out in Hanoi, and relations with China worsened. Mr. Abe launched diplomatic efforts in Southeast Asia with Vietnam and others aimed at building a network of partners encircling China.

Mr. Abe held another meeting with Mr. Dung in December 2013 during the Japan-ASEAN Summit Meeting conducted in Tokyo and indicated interest in beginning discussions on provision of patrol boats to the Vietnam Coast Guard. This initiative aims to enhance Vietnam's maritime surveillance capabilities, similar to the effort with the Philippines, and curtail China's activities in the South China Sea. Foreign Minister Fumio Kishida visited Hanoi about eight months later in August 2014 and signed an agreement to give six used boats worth 500 million yen to Vietnam after meeting with Vietnam's Deputy Prime Minister and Foreign Minister Pham Binh Minh.

Revival of U.S.-Philippines cooperation

The United States moved to strengthen ties with ASEAN too. The new military agreement signed with the Philippines on April 28, 2014 laid the groundwork for a resumption of stationing U.S. troops in the Philippines, a symbol of the rebalancing policy. This is evidence of Mr. Obama's call for "emphasis on Asia" and taking a leading role in the region.

"Our commitment to defend the Philippines is ironclad and the United States will keep that commitment, because allies never stand alone."

Mr. Obama expressed resoluteness to cooperate on security matters in a speech delivered in front of about 400 U.S. and Filipino troops at a Philippine military facilities in the suburbs of Manila where he was visiting on the day after signing the military agreement. He added firmly that, "It is vital to ensure support for international law, defend freedom of navigation, and prevent interference with trade. Conflicts (regarding territory) must be resolved peacefully and without intimidation or coercion."

The new agreement approved use of Philippine military bases by U.S. troops. While U.S. troops will not be permanently stationed at bases in the country, they can have access for troop rotations and deployments of fighter planes and ships.

China expanded its sphere of influence in the South China Sea backed by military force after the U.S. military pulled out by 1992 as explained in Chapter 1. The new agreement seeks to strengthen the presence of the U.S. military.

"This assistance agreement confirms our promises to mutual defense."

President Aquino highlighted this key outcome of the agreements at a press conference after the signing ceremony. Likely sites for reintroduction of the U.S. military after the past full exit include the former U.S. naval base in Subic, which is located in the northern part of the Philippines and is a convenient site for monitoring the South China Sea.

The United States and the Philippines have an alliance relationship. The U.S.-Philippines Mutual Defense Treaty concluded in 1951 creates an obligation to jointly engage in defending the treaty partner in the case of an attack from a third country. However, the Treaty did not envision assistance from the Philippines if the U.S. mainland faced an attack or an attack against the Philippines by a third country. It primarily sought to let the U.S. military use Philippine bases as supply sites for activities in Southeast Asia, the Indian Ocean, and other locations, including the Vietnam War and the Gulf War in the Middle East. The Philippine bases gave the United States an important foothold to secure the safety of sea lanes in the South China Sea where the U.S. Navy operated.

The defense obligation based on the U.S.-Philippines Mutual Defense Treaty is attracting renewed interest in recent years because of the pick-up in China's military expansion and maritime initiatives in recent years.

In April 2012, China dispatched two fishery patrol ships and engaged in a stand-off with Philippine Navy ships after the Philippine ships restricted the activities of eight Chinese fishing boats anchored at Scarborough Shoal (Huangyan Island) in the Macclesfield Bank (Zhongsha Islands) located to the west of Luzon Island in the Philippines. The Chinese side positioned ocean patrol boats from the State Oceanic Administration and Chinese navy boats around the fishery patrol ships. The tense unpredictable situation lasted for over two months.

The Philippines ultimately backed down and removed its military ships, avoiding a clash. Since then, China established effective control over Scarborough Shoal. How would the U.S.-Philippines Mutual Defense Treaty function if a similar situation emerged and it involved a military clash between the Philippines and China? While the United States takes the position that territories in the South China Sea do not come under the scope of the defense obligation, the Philippines has expectations that the United States will come to its defense. There is a discrepancy in views between the United States and the Philippines. The possibility of actual intervention by U.S. forces in a military clash between the Philippines and China is low, but the United States must broaden its military cooperation with the Philippines in order to maintain trust in the U.S.-Philippines alliance.

The Balikatan joint military exercise conducted regularly along the coast of the Philippines by troops from the United States and the Philippines in April 2015 consisted of about 12,000 troops, or roughly twice the amount from the previous year, and was the largest exercise for the past 15 years. The content of the exercise changed to address China's maritime initiatives. While past exercises mainly targeted public safety, such as dealing with the Islamic extremist group Abu Sayyaf located in the southern Philippines, the primary purpose now is responding to external threats – namely, China's maritime campaign.

The United States implemented Cooperation Afloat Readiness and Training (CARAT) with the Philippines in the sea to the east of Palawan Island two months later. CARAT is a bilateral sea exercise that the United States has conducted with the Philippines, Brunei, Indonesia, Malaysia, Singapore, Thailand, and other countries. The U.S. military utilized the cutting-edge Fort Worth littoral combat ship (LCS), which was deployed at the base in Singapore in December 2014, for its first CARAT exercise in this event.

The Fort Worth measure 119 meters in length and 18 meters in width and has about 3,000 tons of displacement and can navigate nimbly at speeds of over 70 kilometers per hour. It performs well at mine clearing and anti-submarine battle activities in shallow waters along coasts. The Japanese government is reviewing possible deployment of highly mobile LCS that could make a large contribution to the defense of outlying islands, such as the Nansei Islands including the Senkaku Islands. The U.S. military's use of the Fort Worth in this exercise aimed to send a warning to China that it has the means to engage in the defense of outlying islands jointly with the Philippines. The Fort Worth made a port call and refueled at Subic Bay, the likely location of a re-stationing of U.S. troops, after the exercise, high-lighting the return of the U.S. military to this sea area.

Asian friend

Mr. Abe is strengthening collaboration with Australia too, besides the United States and ASEAN countries, amid strong awareness of the increasingly difficult security environment facing Japan and concern that "a single country cannot sustain peace alone." He sought friendly ties well beyond the past level that could be called a "quasi alliance" with Australia.

Mr. Abe became the first Japanese prime minister to deliver a speech to Australia's parliament on July 8, 2014. He made the following appeal after speaking favorably about the success of Japan and Australia moving beyond the past history of battles in the Second World War and building a "new special relationship."

"Let us join together all the more in order to make the vast seas from the Pacific Ocean to the Indian and those skies open and free. In everything we say and do, we must follow the law and never fall back onto force or coercion. When there are disputes, we must always use peaceful means to find solutions. These are natural rules. I believe strongly that when Japan and Australia, sharing the common values, join hands, these natural rules will become the norm for the seas of prosperity that stretch from the Pacific Ocean to the Indian."

Mr. Abe has pressed forward with efforts to strengthen relationship with countries that share the same value in light of China's maritime ambitions. The phrase "in everything we say and do, we must follow the law and never fall back onto force or coercion" clearly referred to China's behavior.

Mr. Abe and Australian Prime Minister Tony Abbott have an excellent relationship that is considered by officials supporting Mr. Abe to realize the "closest mutual understanding among global leaders," and Mr. Abe received unusually warm treatment, including hospitality at an unofficial dinner hosted by Mr. Abbott on the day before the Parliament speech and an extended review of Australia in a five-hour trip on the official government plane from the capital of Canberra to a tour at an iron ore mine on the day after the speech.

Mr. Abbott referred to Japan as Australia's "friend in Asia" in September 2013 after becoming Prime Minister and visited Japan as his initial destination on the first trip in East Asia in April 2014.

Mr. Abbott started the Summit Meeting with Mr. Abe with the following comment.

"Terrible things occurred (in the war), but it is not necessary that Japan alone must continue apologizing."

He referred to the issue of historical views causing friction between Japan and China, RoK, and others. Mr. Abe was confronting isolation in the international community regarding the historical view, including fierce anger from China and the RoK after his visit to Yasukuni Shrine at the end of 2013 and "disappointment" criticism even from the United States.

Mr. Abe had a brief 10-minute conversation with Mr. Abbott at the Global Economic Forum's Annual General Meeting (Davos Meeting) held in Davos (Switzerland) in January 2014, according to a Japanese government source. Despite the shortness of their contact, Mr. Abbott positively told Mr. Abe that "Japan has accumulated one of the most respectable histories in the world following the war."

While Mr. Abbott is known for his favorable stance toward Japan, no other foreign dignitaries went this far in understanding the historical context amid ongoing repercussions from the Yasukuni Shrine visit. Kevin Rudd, who was prime minister before Mr. Abbott, was previously a diplomat with a career that included working at Australia's embassy in China and put emphasis on bolstering ties with China. The relationship between Japan and Australia stalled during his term. The vote of confidence in Mr. Abe from successor Abbott undoubtedly helped in rebuilding the relationship between Japan and Australia.

While comments from Mr. Abbott were some of just a few providing back-up for Mr. Abe regarding the historical view issue from the international community, the Japanese government did not officially disclose the content. It took this stance of refraining from disclosure because Mr. Abbott would have definitely confronted harsh criticism in visits to China and the RoK that Mr. Abbott had scheduled after the Summit Meeting in April. The Abe administration did not try to publicize that "Japan has friends too" and instead selected a path of quietly building a genuine relationship of trust with a country that has common values.

Japan-U.S.-Australia triangle

Closer ties between Mr. Abe and Mr. Abbott contributed to rapid progress by cooperation in the security field between Japan and Australia.

The following is a symbolic example.

Mr. Abe held a special meeting of the four-minister meeting of the National Security Council (NSC) at the Prime Minister's Office on April 7,

2014 prior to the Japan-Australia Summit Meeting at the State Guest House in Moto-Akasaka (Tokyo) and invited Mr. Abbott as a first-ever foreign-leader guest. Contents of meetings, including proceeding records, by the NSC, just launched in December of the previous year, are fundamentally not disclosed.

At the meeting, Mr. Abe started by explaining that "Japan and Australia share universal values, including freedom and democracy, and strategic interest in peace and stability in the Asia-Pacific region." Mr. Abbott then smiled while commenting that "It is an honor to be selected as the first-ever foreign leader to attend an NSC meeting. I hope to further strengthen cooperation with Japan." During the roughly one-hour meeting, Mr. Abbott exchanged views on conditions in the Asia-Pacific region, particularly in respects to China, with Mr. Abe, Deputy Prime Minister and Minister of Finance Taro Aso, Chief Cabinet Secretary Yoshihide Suga, Foreign Minister Fumio Kishida, and Defense Minister Itsunori Onodera.

Mr. Abe was probably thinking about the close friendship between former Prime Minister Junichiro Koizumi and former U.S. President George W. Bush. In May 2003, Mr. Abe, who was then Deputy Chief Cabinet Secretary, accompanied Mr. Koizumi to the United States and was present when Mr. Koizumi attended a regular presidential briefing given by the U.S. Central Intelligence Agency (CIA) at Mr. Bush's invitation and heard classified information.

Mr. Abe and Mr. Abbott agreed at their meeting to hold Australia-Japan Foreign and Defense Ministerial Consultations ("2+2"), the first in roughly two years, in June and to begin negotiations on a framework for joint development of defense equipment and technology. The joint development initiative followed Cabinet approval in April of the Three Principles on Transfer of Defense Equipment and Technology.

The Three Principles on Transfer of Defense Equipment and Technology, which replace the "Three Principles on Arms Exports" that fundamentally prohibited exports of defense equipment and technology, let Japan export defense equipment, including weapons and related technologies, on the condition of rigorous management by the counterpart country if it contributes to Japan's security and international peace. Specifically, the new principles envision exports of equipment used in surveillance, rescue, transport of people and goods, and mine sweeping on the seas to countries located along Japan's sea lanes. Some examples are the Maritime Self Defense Force's US-2 rescue flying boats made by ShinMaywa Industries (Hyogo) and the Ground Self Defense Force's field communication system supplied by NEC (Tokyo). Equipment exports are international cooperation that factors in the emergence of China.

The Three Principles on Transfer of Defense Equipment and Technology also created a path for joint development of defense equipment by Japan and Australia.

Australia is a major resource country, including iron ore and coal, and its economy relies on sea transportation of mineral resources and agricultural goods to other countries. The South China Sea provides a sea lane to Japan, China, and the RoK, which account for roughly half of its trade, and also to Southeast Asia. While having naval capabilities that can extend to the South China Sea is a top priority for national interests, Australia has not achieved much progress in modernization of its naval forces.

Australia is particularly interested in the Maritime Self Defense Force's cutting-edge submarine technology. The Maritime Self Defense Force, which does not possess nuclear submarines, developed unique submarine construction technologies over many years.

Submarines that are difficult to detect are effective at surprise attacks against enemy ships. With advanced submarines, it is possible to prevent incursions by air carriers, destroyers, and frigates from the rival country. Vietnam, which is embroiled in a territorial conflict with China in the South China Sea, purchased six cutting-edge Kilo-class submarines from Russia. The Kilo-class submarines are equipped with torpedoes and anti-ship missiles that fly at a low-level above the water. Observers indicate that these submarines will provide effective deterrence against China's maritime ambitions.

A submarine's concealability is extremely important, and propellers on the Maritime Self Defense Force's submarine developed by Japan offer global top-level noise suppression. The six submarines currently in Australia's fleet, meanwhile, are older-style vessels with performance shortfalls and slated for retirement by the late 2030s, and their replacement is an issue. Australia is interested in jointly developing a successor submarine based on the Maritime Self Defense Force's Soryu technology and a fighting system from the United States.

The Soryu submarine uses a diesel engine and possesses advanced capabilities for submergence depth, traveling distance, and quietness. Standard displacement is about 3,000 tons, the highest level globally for a conventional-drive format that does not use nuclear power. The price for this type of submarine is roughly 50 billion yen. The Defense Ministry booked construction costs for an 11th submarine that uses the latest lithium-ion battery technology for the batteries in its budget requests for fiscal 2015.

However, considerable resistance exists within the Japanese government to exports of submarine technology that represents an "array of top secrets." Even some voices in the Maritime Self Defense Force raised questions about "whether it is appropriate to transfer Soryu technology, a precious assemblage of Japan's technologies, to Australia, which is not an official alliance country." Yet Mr. Abe overcame this cautious view and instructed the government to proceed with joint development of a submarine with Australia. Mr. Abe signed an agreement regarding joint development of defense equipment at the Japan-Australia Summit Meeting held in Canberra in July 2014.

The United States, which is promoting a policy of "emphasis on Asia" welcomes closer ties between Japan and Australia, which are both U.S. allies, as an important contribution to stability in the Asia-Pacific region.

The Obama administration has been stationing U.S. Marines in Darwin, which is located in northern Australia, during April to October each year since 2012 as a periodic deployment. Mr. Obama announced this plan, which creates a four-site rotation including Okinawa Prefecture, Hawaii, and Guam, at the U.S.-Australia Summit Meeting in November 2011. In 2014, as part of the third deployment, the United States also dispatched the Marine Air-Ground Task Force (MAGTF), which has a high readiness level for conflict incidents and other situations, from California and CH-53 large transport helicopters used by the Marines in Iraq and Afghanistan. Total headcount reached about 1,150 troops, a roughly six-fold increase from the 200 troops in 2013, and the 2016 deployment is targeting further expansion to about 2,500 troops.

Darwin faces the Timor Sea and is a strategic site as a gateway to

Southeast Asia. Ships wanting to navigate the Pacific Ocean and Indian Ocean while circumventing the South China Sea must pass through the waters of the Timor Sea and Arafura Sea. Deployment of U.S. Marines in Darwin, which faces this sea area, gives the United States control over this strategic point. The United States deployed LCS vessels in Singapore, which borders the Malacca Straits that connect the South China Sea and Indian Ocean in April 2013 and is steadily building a capacity to contain China within the South China Sea.

Japan, the United States, and Australia share concerns about China's maritime ambitions. Mr. Abe, Mr. Obama, and Mr. Abbott held the Second Japan-U.S.-Australia Summit Meeting, the first in seven years, in Brisbane (Australia) in November 2014 and issued a joint press announcement that highlighted reinforcement of security and economic collaboration among the three countries.

The joint announcement stated that collaboration among the three countries is "founded on an unshakeable base of shared interests and values, including democracy, open economies, rule of law, and peaceful resolution of conflicts."

Mr. Abbott proposed joint development of a submarine based on the Soryu model that also includes the U.S. military's fighting system to the Japanese and U.S. leaders at the Summit Meeting and confirmed Australia's interest in an effective "Japan-U.S.-Australia joint development."

However, Mr. Abbott lost to Malcolm Turnbull, the former Communications Minister, in an emergency party head election by Australia's Liberal Party on September 14, 2015, and had to resign. While Mr. Turnbull, the new prime minister, belongs to the same party as Mr. Abbott, he takes a more flexible stance toward China than Mr. Abbott in diplomacy. This change has increased uncertainty about the direction of Australia's development of the next-generation submarine.

Mr. Abe congratulated Mr. Turnbull on becoming prime minister in a telephone talk on September 18 and explained his desire for "further advancement of the Japan-Australia relationship in a broad range of areas, including security and the economy." Mr. Turnbull responded by expressing "interest in working with Prime Minister Abe to promote stability and prosperity in the Asia-Pacific region."

While collaboration among Japan, the United States, and Australia is vital to addressing China's military expansion, it is not easy to keep all three countries on the same page.

Deterrence from security legislation

Japan passed security-related legislation that substantially changes its security policy at an ordinary Diet session in September 2015. The law, which primarily approves limited exercise of collective self-defense rights, has important implications for expansion of defense cooperation between the Self Defense Forces and U.S. military and enabling more effective and dynamic activities. It also supports development of a maritime security network encircling China through cooperation with the United States, Australia, ASEAN countries, and others.

Discussion of the security legislation bills extended over roughly four months and addressed military clashes on the Korean peninsula, mine laying in the Middle East's Strait of Hormuz, and conflicts in the South China Sea.

"A certain country is conducting land reclamation in the South China Sea. While I would like to refrain from specifically describing the scope of this legislation, the government intends to utilize the legislation if a situation occurs."

At a meeting of the Lower House's special committee on peace and security legislation, which was reviewing the security legislation on May 28, Mr. Abe was asked about the regional scope of "situations with an important influence" for provision of logistical assistance by the Self-Defense Forces to the U.S. military or others. He suggested that the legislation takes into account the South China Sea while avoiding mention of China.

This means that Self Defense Forces will be allowed to transport goods for the U.S. military to Southeast Asia and supply fuel to U.S. ships outside of the conflict sea area if a conflict breaks out between China and the U.S. military in the South China Sea and the Japanese government confirms that it is a "situation with an important influence."

The preface of the security-related legislation clarifies "Three New Conditions for Use of Military Force" as basic guidelines for limited exercise of Japan's collective self-defense rights – 1) when an armed attack against

Japan occurs or when an armed attack against a foreign country that is in a close relationship with Japan occurs and as a result threatens Japan's survival and poses a clear danger to fundamentally overturn people's right to life, liberty and pursuit of happiness (survival threat situations), 2) when there is no other appropriate means available to repel the attack and ensure Japan's survival and protects its people, and 3) use of force limited to the minimum extent necessary.

Whether the scope of collective self-defense rights extended to conflicts in the South China Sea was a major point of contention.

How will the Self Defense Forces respond if China engages in a conflict with a neighboring country and lays mines in the South China Sea? When asked this question at the May 28 meeting, Mr. Abe responded that, "it is difficult to envision this action (clearing mines laid in the South China Sea) because it is fundamentally possible to circumvent the South China Sea."

At the committee's meeting on June 5, a member of the Democratic Party asked about the possible use of the "survival threat situations" condition to support exercise of collective self-defense rights if a conflict occurred in the South China Sea. Gen Nakatani, Minister in Charge of Security Legislation (Defense Minister), stated that "it is a legal possibility if the situation satisfies the three new conditions for exercise of self-defense rights," leaving room for potential application.

The possibility of dispatching Self Defense forces to clear mines in the South China Sea cannot be completely ruled out. This is the stance of the Japanese government.

Tetsuo Kotani, a Senior Research Fellow at The Japan Institute of International Affairs, explains that "The possibility of China laying mines in the South China Sea in a battle with a nearby country is greater than a crisis involving Iran in the Strait of Hormuz. Not every country can handle mine clearing, and the United States does not have sufficient capabilities for mine clearing in the South China Sea and is interested in relying on Japan. Japan should retain the option of declaring a "survival threat situation" because the South China Sea is an important sea lane."

In fact, the U.S. military has high expectations for activities by the Maritime Self Defense Force in the South China Sea. Harry Harris, Commander of the U.S. Pacific Fleet, commented in a press conference with

Japanese media outlets in June 2015 that the United States "welcomes" surveillance activities by Maritime Self Defense Force ships and patrol planes in the South China Sea. Mr. Kotani comments that, "China is getting ready to begin operations with strategic nuclear-powered submarines that carry long-range ballistic missiles in the South China Sea, and it is essential to monitor these operations. However, the U.S. military cannot sufficiently monitor the South China Sea because of budget cuts, and it would be very helpful to the United States if the Maritime Self Defense Force, which has global top-class surveillance capabilities, conducts monitoring and thereby enhances the reliability of the U.S. nuclear umbrella."

Mr. Abe was careful to avoid directly naming China in the Lower House deliberations for diplomatic reasons, but repeatedly referred to the "China threat" in the Upper House review. He spoke candidly about the threat at a meeting of the Upper House's special committee on peace and security legislation on July 29 that "China is rapidly and broadly strengthening its military capabilities. This is a concern for the international community."

He also noted that "China has increased its military spending 41-fold over 27 years." Mr. Nakatani commented that "The Self Defense Forces scrambled 464 times in response to Chinese planes during fiscal 2014."

The government provided specific figures more often during this review to highlight the seriousness of the China threat and necessity of the legislation.

The Japanese government seeks to put some type of brake on China's maritime initiatives by passing the security legislation and strengthening ties with the United States, ASEAN countries, and Australia. However, there is no way of turning back the clock on China's landfill reefs in the South China Sea and stationary platforms in the East China Sea.

U.S. Secretary of State Kerry called for "three halts," mainly directed at China, regarding conditions in the South China Sea at the ASEAN Regional Forum's (ARF) Ministerial Meeting in Kuala Lumpur, Malaysia's capital city, on August 6, 2015.

"What is really necessary now is refraining from land reclamations, major construction, and militarization."

Mr. Kerry criticized China's behavior and warned against further actions at the ARF venue that involves participation of the Philippines,

Vietnam, and other ASEAN countries as well as Japan, China, Australia, and others, and Japan, the Philippines, and others agreed with Mr. Kerry's opinion.

China's Foreign Minister Wang Yi, however, directly rebutted this opinion and did not show any interest in Mr. Kerry's proposal.

"The three halts are not effective. What is the specific content of the halts? There is absolutely no agreement among the various countries."

China proposed cooperation measures with 10 items aimed at broadening security, economic, and other cooperation with ASEAN countries and reinforced its appeasement approach to ASEAN countries. Attitudes toward China's offensive clearly differ among ASEAN countries. General Tanasak Patimapragorn, Thailand's Deputy Prime Minister and Minister of Foreign Affairs, welcomed China's proposal on behalf of ASEAN and spoke favorably about a "relationship beyond friendship."

Many ASEAN countries rely on China's economic power, and it was evident that a united front cannot be achieved even with an attempt by the United States to exercise leadership. Cambodia, which is close to China, initially argued that China's land reclamations in the South China Sea should not be mentioned at all in the joint statement at the ASEAN Foreign Ministers' Meeting. While ASEAN countries share "concern" about China's aggressive maritime initiatives, they are putting priority on cohesion ahead of the launch of the Economic Community at the end of 2015. A Malaysian diplomat explained that "While it might be correct, there is nothing to gain from fighting with China. Diplomacy is the best way to work things out."

Even the vital Obama administration is not completely rejecting formation of a "new relationship of great powers" between the United States and China that China has been proposing for a while. This approach calls for deepening cooperative ties on problems where the United States and China have common interests.

While Mr. Obama clearly stated at the press conference after the Japan-U.S. Summit Meeting on April 28, 2015 that the U.S. defense obligation based on Article 5 of the Japan-U.S. Security Treaty extends to the Senkaku Islands in Okinawa Prefecture and demonstrated the strong bond between Japan and the United States in dealing with China to the world, he also added that "I do not see a strong Japan-U.S. alliance as a provocation (against China)." This point aimed to soften the message toward China.

China reclaimed land around Fiery Cross Reef and is building an airstrip that extends 3,000 meters in the South China Sea. The biggest concern for Japan and the United States, however, is land reclamation at Scarborough Shoal where China pushed out the Philippines in 2012 and has taken effective control. China seized control of the Paracel Islands after winning a battle with South Vietnam in 1974 and subsequently built a 2,400-meter long airstrip on Woody Island in order to establish air supremacy in the northern part of the South China Sea. China will create a massive triangle of military sites in the South China Sea if it proceeds with land reclamation at Scarborough Shoal.

These facilities will give it air supremacy over the northern half of the South China Sea. Interference with navigation in the South China Sea for the U.S. Navy's Carrier Strike Group would be a major setback to the global strategy of the United States. It would also present a serious issue for Japan with its reliance on a sea lane in the South China Sea.

However, the international community's ability to deter China is weakening.

Chapter 6

The Ruthless Economic Battle between Japan and America's TPP and China's AIIB

It was long ago that the Asia-Pacific region came to be called "the center of global growth." Now the United States, the world's largest economy in terms of gross domestic product (GDP), and Japan, the third-largest, are engaged in an intense dispute over sovereignty with number-two China.

On the economic front as well—finance, trade and the like—China has kept a distance from the American-led international system and is steadily taking steps to expand its influence in the Asia-Pacific region. An example is the establishment of the Chinese-led Asian Infrastructure Investment Bank (AIIB).

Japan and the United States have fought back against China by getting the Trans-Pacific Partnership (TPP) signed. Can the TPP place a check on China, which wants to push aside the U.S. and become the leader of trade in Asia? This chapter will examine what happened behind the scenes during the TPP negotiations led by Japan and the United States, and the creation of the Chinese AIIB to resist the economic order of Japan and the West.

A key milestone

On April 21, 2015, U.S. President Barack Obama expressed alarm over China's actions when he said in an interview with an American TV station that if the TPP negotiations are not concluded, then China will write the rules in a growing region of the world and the United States will be shut out.

The Obama administration, which has advocated a "rebalance policy," is shifting its military and diplomatic focus from the Middle East to the Asia-Pacific. It is meant as a correction of the excessive attention that U.S. national security policy paid to Afghanistan, Iraq and other places in the Middle East following the terrorist attacks of September 11, 2001. If China continues to be allowed to take provocative actions in the East China Sea and the South China Sea, the Western Pacific will eventually become the Chinese Sea. Sensing an impending crisis, President Obama urged the early signing of the TPP as a core tenet of the rebalance policy.

The TPP was born from the P4 agreement that was concluded between New Zealand, Singapore and two other countries. This treaty came into effect in 2006. The aim of the TPP is to limit tariffs on industrial and agricultural goods, as well as to write rules for a high level of fair and transparent trade and investment.

President Obama expressed his great determination to support the TPP when he gave a speech at Suntory Hall in Tokyo's Akasaka district during a visit to Japan in November 2009. He said, "The United States will also be engaging with the Trans-Pacific Partnership countries with the goal of shaping a regional agreement that will have broad-based membership and the high standards worthy of a 21st century trade agreement." Afterward, Australia, Peru, Canada and Mexico joined the TPP talks, bringing the total number of parties to the negotiations, including Japan, to 12. If the agreement is ratified, it will create a massive economic zone accounting for just under 40% of global GDP.

But first I would like to take a behind-the-scenes look at the TPP negotiations.

The TPP is a pact under which nations around the Pacific Ocean would eliminate tariffs on the import of agricultural and industrial goods, write common rules to facilitate investment and trade and strengthen ties between their economies. Japan and the United States account for approximately 80% of the combined GDP of the 12 nations who aspire to open their markets beyond what past agreements have achieved. It is obvious to anyone that Japan and the U.S. are spearheading the effort to make the TPP a reality.

Prime Minister Abe is trying to escape a long bout of deflation and put Japan on the path to growth through his set of economic policies known as Abenomics. The "three arrows" under Abenomics are massive monetary easing, expeditious fiscal spending and a growth strategy to draw out the dynamism of the private sector. The first and second arrows of monetary easing and fiscal spending have produced results for now, but the growth strategy that is the third arrow has been ineffective and has yet to accomplish its purpose. Prime Minister Abe characterizes the TPP as a "pillar of economic strategy" which he expects will increase export and import volume and stimulate the economy.

The original goal for reaching a compromise in the TPP talks was November 2011, but that target for finding a consensus was pushed back time and again.

Japan, the United States and the other parties to the talks all have a thorough understanding of the need to reach an agreement on the TPP soon. Even so, progress in the negotiations proved elusive due to sharply conflicting interests.

If we take agricultural products as an example, exporting nations want to export as much of their own goods as they can. Therefore, in the TPP talks they sought to eliminate tariffs levied by importers or reduce them as closely to zero as possible. On the other hand, importers were reluctant to agree because reducing tariffs would strike a blow to their domestic agriculture.

Every country has goods that are "sensitive" in that liberalization and an increase in imports is likely to hurt a domestic industry. Japan characterizes rice, wheat, beef and pork, dairy products, as well as sugar cane and other sweet crops, as "five sacred cows" that should be protected with tariffs. The 12 parties include advanced nations like Japan, the United States and Singapore, as well as emerging countries such as Vietnam and Malaysia. It is rare that their interests coincide, and even in bilateral talks an extremely complex set of equations must be solved simultaneously in order to reach a final agreement.

Talks between Japan and the United States during President Obama's trip to Japan on April 23-25, 2014 were the key to the TPP, as they resulted in a substantial basic agreement.

Obama arrived in Japan on the night of the 23rd and joined Abe for dinner at the counter of Sukiyabashi Jiro, an up-scale sushi restaurant in Tokyo's Ginza district. There the two leaders talked over sake.

Abe explained to his counterpart that Japan had already enacted significant cuts to tariffs and that any further major reductions would strike a terrible blow to Japan's domestic farming.

Obama asked Abe whether or not he was an agricultural reformer.

The Japanese had expected that having the two leaders speak candidly while dining on sushi would bring them closer together. However, Obama, known for his businesslike attitude, immediately jumped into the topic of the TPP and got so detailed as to bring up specific numbers concerning pork tariffs.

During Obama's visit to Japan, Akira Amari, the Japanese minister in charge of the TPP talks, and United States Trade Representative (USTR) Michael Froman met separately to work out the basics of an agreement that would gradually lower the Japanese tariff on beef imports from the current 38.5% to "above 9%" and gradually reduce the tariff on pork from a maximum of 482 yen per kilogram down to 50 yen. On April 25, the final day of Obama's stay, after the announcement of a joint declaration by Japan and the United States, Abe was proud to state, "This marks a key milestone in the TPP negotiations and will inject fresh momentum into the broader talks."

However, the settlement of other issues was postponed. These included the conditions for implementing emergency import restrictions (i.e. safeguards) that would raise tariffs should imports of American beef and pork suddenly increase. Other outstanding issues were what to do about the tariff-free import ceiling for American rice and U.S. tariffs on Japanese automobile parts.

Different approaches proved problematic

Half a year after Japan and the United States came to a substantial basic agreement, the parties to the talks were concerned about whether they could reach a broad agreement by the end of 2014, which was already three years later than initially envisioned. Officials held a ministerial meeting on the TPP in Beijing, China on November 8, 2014, but the mood was already downcast even before this round of discussions had commenced. The reason for this was simple: there was absolutely no sign that Japan and the United States would come to a consensus in bilateral talks.

Just before a November 3 meeting, White House Press Secretary Josh Earnest said during a press conference in Washington, D.C., "I do not anticipate that there will be a significant breakthrough in trade talks while the President is traveling in Asia." At a press conference on the 4th, Mr. Amari said it would be quite difficult to come to a broad consensus at the ministerial meeting in Beijing.

At the ministerial meeting, the 10 nations besides Japan and the United States engaged in negotiations while keeping an eye on the progress of the bilateral talks between the other two. Unless these two key parties had the will to reach a consensus, then there was no prospect of wrapping up the negotiations.

We have to go back about a month before the ministerial meeting to discover the problem behind the bilateral talks. On September 23-24, Amari met with Froman in Washington, D.C.

The Japanese expected the U.S. to offer a specific proposal on how far to lower tariffs on auto parts imported from Japan (the majority of which are currently set at 2.5%). However, Froman answered that there would be almost no cuts. A person involved in the negotiations said that Amari was furious at this "ridiculously asinine proposal" for Japan and unleashed a tirade.

"I came here because you said we would wrap up the negotiations. So long as you have no intention of doing so, then I will not meet with you anymore."

Amari immediately stood up and left the stunned Americans in attendance.

The differing Japanese and American approaches had produced a grave problem.

In talks on agricultural products, the Americans had agreed to Japan's demand to leave in place tariffs on the five sacred cows. Therefore, they believed Japan would in turn listen to American demands to leave auto part tariffs in place as much as possible.

The Japanese had a completely different idea about this. In the negotiations to this point, Japan had been put on the defensive and pressed to concede to demands to significantly lower tax rates on agricultural goods and on the creation of special import ceilings. The only area where Japan could win by going on the offensive was automobiles. Amari revealed to close aides prior to his meeting with Froman that "if we can't win anything with automobiles even though we have been bloodied over agricultural products, then the opposition parties in the Diet will thrash us."

After breaking off the discussion with Froman, Amari walked over to the Japanese embassy in Washington. There he made a phone call to Prime Minister Abe and reported on how the meeting had collapsed. He was ready to resign from his post as minister if Abe rebuked him and ordered him to compromise with the U.S. Amari was tense. After concluding his report, Abe thanked him and said, "That will be fine." Unanticipated relief washed over Amari.

Yet this was not the end of the talks between Japan and the United States, who held the key to the TPP negotiations. Two days later, on September 26, Abe visited the U.S. to attend the United Nations General Assembly. At a New York City hotel he met with Vice President Joe Biden. A meek Froman was beside Biden, taking notes.

Abe said to Biden, "We need to meet halfway if we are to conclude the negotiations." Before their meeting, there had been no plan to discuss the TPP. This unexpected remark kept up appearances in front of Biden while also making a call to action to Froman, whose talks with Amari were inconclusive.

Froman, known as a skilled lawyer, probably anticipated such a scenario. He immediately jotted down the key points so that Biden could make a counterargument.

But Biden ignored the note. Keeping pace with Abe, he faced the Japanese prime minister and said he understood it was difficult for Japan and the United States to proceed with their talks, and that they should work hard to come to an agreement. He then looked at Froman next to him and teased him by suggesting the USTR may have a different opinion. It was a rare remonstration, there in Abe's presence, of Froman, who had not dropped his hardline stance against Japan. As vice president and an official who is close to Obama, Biden understood that allowing the TPP to fail was unacceptable. Froman, who remained quiet, became red in the face.

The Abe-Biden meeting was a *de facto* handshake of reconciliation over the abruptly interrupted Amari-Froman meeting.

However, even if Japan and the U.S. were willing to make progress with the TPP negotiations, it would not be a path easily taken, considering the domestic situation in each country.

For the states participating in the TPP talks, the strength of each one's administrative foundation is a major factor determining whether they can shake up the negotiations as they please. The Obama administration in particular has been buffeted by wariness over the TPP in America. The Republican Party, which controls the U.S. Congress, has many members whose base of support comes from labor unions. They are very concerned that lowering tariffs on Japanese cars and auto parts by enacting the TPP will hurt the U.S. auto industry. American industry groups were demanding the immediate removal of Japanese tariffs levied on agricultural products like beef, pork and rice. In the negotiations thus far it seemed fairly certain that Japan's 9% tariff on beef and a pork tariff of 50 yen per kilogram would remain, which increased the dissatisfaction among American trade groups. Concerned about a low support rate, Obama found himself in a difficult position to make daring concessions in the TPP talks.

Planetary alignment

After breaking off talks in September 2014, Amari told Froman in no uncertain terms that "my words are the words of the prime minister." Froman, who is known as a tough negotiator, softened his attitude and said that he trusted Amari and wanted to work together with him. That being said, Froman did not do much to alter his tough negotiating stance. During talks Amari repeatedly said, "If we don't compromise, then we can't call this a negotiation. When we begin to compromise, then we'll find an agreement."

With the Japanese government assuming that the TPP negotiations would conclude during 2014, Prime Minister Abe was secretly planning a trip to the United States in January 2015. His calculation was that on the 70th anniversary of the end of World War II, he could beat China and South Korea—who are united in playing the "history card"—to the punch by showing the world the robust partnership between Japan and the United

States on both security and economic issues. However, the two countries' stalled talks on the TPP made it impossible to come to a broad agreement on the pact by the end of 2014, and the planned January 2015 trip to the U.S. was shelved. Instead Abe decided to make his foreign trip to the Middle East.

Ironically, the thing that sped up the TPP negotiations was the U.S. mid-term elections that were held on November 4, 2014. The Republican Party gained majorities in both the House of Representatives and the Senate, thus putting Obama's Democratic Party in the minority. With the Republicans, proponents of free trade, in control of Congress, the U.S. government became more supportive of the negotiations.

When Katsuyuki Kawai, a member of the LDP serving in the lower house of the Diet, visited the United States in January 2015, he was surprised at how suddenly the atmosphere concerning the TPP had changed in the U.S. Congress. That was because Republican lawmakers who had shown little interest in the TPP until the year prior were expressing sudden enthusiasm for the pact. By gaining control of a majority in both houses, he received the impression that "the ruling party in Congress has begun to sense its responsibility." Until then, the Republican Party was constantly opposing the Obama administration, but now that they had seen a chance to take back control of the government, they calculated that they could promote themselves as a responsible political party if they cooperated on expediting the TPP.

It was at this time that the Japanese government also felt that the Obama administration had become more serious about the TPP than it had been before. The Japanese embassy in Washington received information that the National Economic Council (NEC) had issued assignments to top officials and had begun working on ways to work with the majorities in Congress. Froman, the USTR, set up a special office for working with Congress. Surprise and hope spread among members of the Japanese government's negotiating team, as they believed that Obama, who is well-known for being poor at working behind the scenes, was going to be more earnest now.

Soon after, from late January to early February 2015, Assistant USTR Wendy Cutler and Takeo Mori, Japan's Ambassador in charge of Economic Diplomacy, held meetings on automotive sector tariffs. According to a source with knowledge of the talks, Cutler said at the time that the "planets have aligned."

A planetary alignment, when multiple planets in the solar system form a direct line pointing at the Sun, is an expression used to refer to an incredibly rare situation. Obama, a lame-duck president who had two years left until the end of his term in office in January 2017, began a final push to make the TPP part of his "legacy." His administration took a more cooperative stance for the fleeting time before the opposition Democrats and the Republicans geared up for the presidential election campaign beginning in late 2015. This was the last chance to set the stage in America so as to conclude the TPP negotiations. It was at this time during the talks that Cutler showed some flexibility on auto parts tariffs, while the Japanese were relieved that "perhaps the negotiations will not break down over automobiles."

While the TPP negotiators began to see some light at the end of the tunnel, members of the U.S. Congress suddenly began turning their attention to the fate of the Trade Promotion Authority (TPA) Bill. In the United States, Congress has the authority to revise the content of trade deals that have already been agreed to with other countries, but if Obama gained TPA, then Congress would have to take an up-or-down vote on trade agreements the administration concludes. This would weaken Congress' influence while giving the administration greater power to negotiate. This was a weapon that Obama needed to have in order to pass the TPP.

As it seemed less likely that the TPP talks would come to a consensus, the U.S. government seemed to be more divided, with the minority Democratic Party in Congress protesting more loudly against the pact and the majority Republican Party backing the administration.

On February 19, 2015, Chairman of the House Ways And Means Committee Paul Ryan and other Republican lawmakers met with Prime Minister Abe at his residence during a visit to Japan. As a member of the majority party, Ryan gave his reassurances that he wanted to make the TPP happen and would submit the TPA Bill to the House during the spring. He added, however, that gaining congressional approval would not be easy and that there are many views among lawmakers. He cited the example of the free trade agreement the United States signed with several Central American countries. In 2005, when the pact was ratified, it only passed the House by a slim two-vote margin.

Obama was facing very strong opposition to the TPP from within his Democratic Party. One opponent was Nancy Pelosi, a top Democratic lawmaker and House Minority Leader, who paid a courtesy call to Prime Minister Abe on April 3, 2015.

Abe said to Pelosi, "We are going to create a new and free economic zone in the Asia-Pacific region. I would also like to tell you about the significance of Japan and the United States taking the lead in creating such an economic area. In addition to developing regional economies, the TPP holds strategic significance in that it will also contribute to security." Pelosi responded that the United States also wants to create a clear path forward, but she indicated that prospects were grim since at present there were many hills and valleys on the road ahead and that it would not necessarily be easy to traverse. Afterward, Pelosi publicly expressed to Obama her opposition to the TPP talks.

A tough gap to bridge

At one point, the impression was that the TPP is a national strategy that is intimately connected to security, in addition to U.S. trade and investment policy.

On April 8, 2015, U.S. Secretary of Defense Ashton Carter broached the topic of the TPP during remarks at a joint press conference with Japanese Minister of Defense Gen Nakatani.

He said, "As Secretary of Defense, I never forget that military strength ultimately rests on the foundation of the economy. That's one reason why the Trans-Pacific Partnership or TPP is so important for both our countries and probably one of the most important parts of America's rebalance."

It is unusual for an official in charge of military policy to stray so far into economic policy in a public setting. This event alone was a sign that the Obama administration was very determined to make the TPP happen. In a hurry to conclude the negotiations on the treaty, the administration was vociferously touting the TPP's significance.

Meanwhile, the Japanese were receptive to the sudden American reversal on setting a deadline for concluding the TPP talks.

In late April, a major event approached for Japan and the U.S.: Prime Minister Abe's visit to the United States.

Koya Nishikawa, a lower house Diet member and former minister of agriculture taking the lead on TPP policy within the LDP, made inquiries with top officials in the TPP Task Force on the latest concerning the negotiations.

"The negotiations began with a gap as wide as the Amazon River, and then it narrowed to around the width of the Yellow River. Around how wide is it now? About as wide as the Kanda River?"

When Nishikawa posed this question, one of the task force leaders gave this reply after giving it a bit of thought:

"I think you could say it's about like the Tone River."

The Kanda River, which flows through residential areas of Tokyo, is as narrow as 10 meters at one point and has a total length of 322 kilometers. The Tone River is one of the biggest in Japan and stretches as wide as about 1 kilometer. In other words, a gap between Japan and the U.S. was still a difficult one to bridge.

When Abe made his trip to the United States, the Japanese and U.S. governments did not initially envision a scenario in which they would come to an agreement in their bilateral talks. That is because the TPA Bill had not been passed in the U.S. Congress. The Republicans, holding a majority in Congress, needed to make a show out of entrusting President Obama with negotiating authority by passing the TPA. According to this script, Obama would conclude the TPP talks thanks to the generosity of the Republican Party. But if he reached a compromise in the bilateral talks with Japan before the passage of the TPA, then the Republicans would lose face and the momentum for passing the bill would be lost.

On the other hand, if no progress was made in these bilateral talks, then the other 10 countries participating in the TPP negotiations would lose their motivation to conclude a treaty. During a summit meeting between Prime Minister Abe and President Obama on April 28, they went no further than innocuously confirming their present position of welcoming any major developments in the bilateral TPP negotiations. After their summit, a top official in Japan's Ministry of Foreign Affairs expressed quiet confidence: "The bilateral talks are really going well. We just can't show it because we need Congress to pass the TPA."

Successfully concluding the bilateral talks also required consensus among all 12 parties to the TPP negotiations in order to make the treaty a reality. Several issues still stood in the way of reaching this full consensus.

In the broader TPP talks, there was difficulty in writing rules on intellectual property that would strengthen protections such as patents and copyrights. The United States was in disagreement with other countries over how long to protect data on biopharmaceuticals so that the companies developing the drugs can maintain a monopoly. There are global drug makers located in the United States, and the U.S. government wants to protect that industry's interests. Hence, the Americans wanted a period of 12 years, while Japan wanted eight years. On the other hand, the many countries that distribute cheaper generics insisted on a period of five years or less.

Meanwhile, emerging countries like Malaysia and Vietnam objected to insistent American demands for the "reform of state-owned enterprises" so as to make these entities compete on a level playing field with foreign companies.

Froman told Japanese government officials accompanying Prime Minister Abe on his April 2015 visit to the United States that a conclusion to the TPP negotiations would come in "maybe June." He went on to add, "But Malaysia is a problem."

When fixating on the reform of state-owned firm, the United States has China's presence in mind. Because China was established as a communist state, there are many state-owned enterprises in that country. State-owned firms shielded by special privileges granted under the protection of the Communist Party had been the seeds of China's economic development, and they have continuously swelled in size. The Chinese leadership is struggling to draw out the dynamism of the service industry in urban areas and elsewhere in the private sector by enacting reforms affecting state-owned firms. The U.S. envisions China joining the TPP someday in the future. At that time, the Americans fear that Chinese state-owned enterprises will become *de facto* non-tariff barriers that will block the entry of American companies into the Chinese market. It was not going to be easy to reach a compromise on the reform of state-owned enterprises in the TPP negotiations in a way that would eradicate this source of trouble and prepare the trade zone for the future entry of China.

During his visit to the United States, Prime Minister Abe gave a speech to a joint session of Congress on April 29. The tensions over the TPP within the U.S. Congress were palpable. Watching over the speech, Foreign Minister Fumio Kishida noticed that the lawmakers of both houses, who had all joined together to give the prime minister a standing ovation, immediately exhibited split reactions once Abe began talking about the TPP. After his speech, Abe said to a close LDP lawmaker, "Obama told me beforehand that only half the lawmakers would clap when I talked about the TPP. He was right. There was little clapping."

An unsuspected ambush

Japan and the United States saw June 2015 as a turning point toward reaching an agreement on the TPP. That is because from the second half of 2015 onward, the hostility between America's two main political parties would intensify in the run-up to the presidential election in November of the following year. President Obama was not worried about his image as he tried to win over lawmakers. For example, during the G7 summit of advanced economies that commenced in Elmau, Germany on June 7, he invited lawmakers opposed to the TPP onto his personal jet, Air Force One, to get up close and personal and persuade them to vote "yes."

Japan was equally earnest, as any further delays would be impermissible.

Worried about an "exit strategy," the Japanese began working behind the scenes to win over domestic interests. On the night of June 3, Koya Nishikawa dined with leaders of the Central Union of Agricultural Cooperatives (JA-Zenchu). The union is opposed to the principle of tariff elimination in the TPP. Having a background in agriculture and fisheries, Nishikawa initially said he was "opposed to the TPP." However, Prime Minister Abe directly charged him with coordinating with farmer organizations, thus placing him among those working to move the TPP negotiations forward. JA-Zenchu thus considered him a sworn enemy.

Despite finding himself in a kangaroo court, Nishikawa declared that "from now on I will meet with you once a month." In order for the agricultural and fisheries budget to come out a winner upon the conclusion of an agreement in the TPP talks, all the parties involved needed to come together and establish a common position. It was not a time for them to fight amongst each other.

On June 24, the U.S. Congress, after many twists and turns, enacted a law granting President Obama TPA. He became the first U.S. president in eight years to have such authority. The other parties to the TPP talks responded by beginning preparations to play their trump cards. On June 6, Amari wrote a message on a bamboo decoration hung during the Star Festival at the entrance of the dormitory for Diet members in Tokyo's Akasaka district. That message was a prayer for "the early conclusion of the TPP talks." Based on the expectation that a ministerial meeting would be held in Hawaii on July 28, Amari said at a press conference on the 7th that "all countries share the desire to reach a final consensus at the ministerial meeting."

The Japanese had greater hope now that the ministerial meeting in Hawaii would be where a final settlement to the talks would be achieved. "We can now reach out and touch the ribbon at the finish line with our hands." That is what Prime Minister Abe said as he indicated his high hopes for an agreement during a speech at a Tokyo hotel on July 9. However, Abe added that "the final day of a negotiation is the most difficult one." The accuracy of that statement would be proven in an unwelcome way.

In the TPP negotiations, if one country could not conclude individual talks on the elimination of tariffs with the other 11 states, then no broad consensus could be reached. According to a source involved in the negotiations, Canada said that in bilateral talks they had not gotten as far as a general proposal. Hence, this was the greatest impediment toward reaching a broad agreement. Canada's reluctance was largely due to restraint stemming from the general election to be held in October and a desire to avoid deliberations on tariffs deemed likely to affect Canadian farmers.

Yet upon observing the enthusiasm of Japan and the United States and their willingness to consider an agreement that leaves out Canada, America's northern neighbor finally began to stir itself to action. Ahead of the ministerial meeting, a meeting of chief TPP negotiators was held in Hawaii on July 24. Although the Canadian delegation had from the outset taken a hard-nosed negotiating stance, they soon came to compromise along realistic lines. After the first day of negotiations, a Japanese government official commended Canada for "finally taking things seriously."

However, an unexpected "ambush" of sorts by a country other than Canada was taking shape: New Zealand, the world's largest exporter of dairy products.

New Zealand refused to engage in bilateral talks with Japan, the United States or other countries on dairy product tariffs; their stance was consistently standoffish. While the United States insisted on a 12-year period of protection for biopharmaceutical data and emerging countries argued for a period of five years or less, New Zealand suggested a compromise of "seven or eight years." However, New Zealand demanded that Japan, the United States and Canada vastly increase their imports of New Zealand dairy products as a condition for concessions.

The amount by which New Zealand demanded that these three other countries increase their imports was considered unrealistic in that it would "exceed the amount of New Zealand's total exports." Japan's negotiations with New Zealand over its dairy products were antagonistic. Chief negotiator Hiroshi Oe, who has a reputation for being a stubborn negotiator, at one point was unable to stop himself from shouting out, "Stop messing around!"

On the evening of July 30, during the ministerial meeting, Froman served as the chair, but the participants jumped from topic to topic and were unable to agree on a common theme, giving the impression that the discussions would be inconclusive. The 12 countries decided to postpone coming to a broad agreement in the immediate future and to make a fresh start at the next ministerial meeting. Japan and the United States were off-balance, as they had not anticipated that New Zealand would prove to be an obstacle.

"It's become a bit difficult" to reach a broad agreement.

Nishikawa was charged with gathering information on the ground during the ministerial meeting in Hawaii. Late on the night of the 30th, he telephoned Chief Cabinet Secretary Yoshihide Suga to report on the situation.

"We have been unable to find common ground with the United States, Canada and New Zealand. Right now only the chief negotiators are meeting, and in the end we were unable to hold the ministerial meeting at night. If they don't meet all night tonight, then we won't be able to release a conclusion tomorrow, so it's a pretty tough situation."

Suga was nearly speechless, as he had assumed a broad agreement would be made. All he could say was, "Why...?"

During a joint press conference at the close of the ministerial meeting on the 31st, Froman touted the results of their talks, saying that they had made significant progress and that he was more certain than ever that the TPP had come within reach. Amari emphasized that "we can reach an agreement if we hold one more ministerial meeting." Meanwhile New Zealand's minister, Tim Groser, gave the impression there were still strong disagreements when he stated that it would be difficult for New Zealand to accept a problematic agreement.

Japan and the United States made a mistake sizing up New Zealand when they discounted the country's situation and its people's pride. New Zealand is a major producer of dairy products, which account for approximately 30% of its total export value. The importance of dairy to New Zealand becomes starker when one considers that automobiles, the best-known product of Japan, only make up roughly 15% of its total export value. With a population of only around 42 million people, New Zealand had grown its economy by promoting free trade and increasing exports. New Zealand made a strong push for eliminating tariffs in the TPP negotiations as well and the Japanese negotiators considered it a "fundamentalist country" when it came to free trade.

With no other industry worthy of such notice as dairy, New Zealand is also a country that can only play offense, not defense. In other words, the only competitive product New Zealand sells to other countries is dairy; it has no other domestic industry in need of protection. Furthermore, New Zealand is a member of the P4 agreement (the predecessor to the TPP) with Singapore, Chile and Brunei. Thus, New Zealand took pride in being an initial member of the TPP negotiations.

When asked by reporters at the joint press conference whether New Zealand would withdraw from the negotiations, Groser responded that New Zealand was one of the first countries to begin engaging in the TPP negotiations. He asserted that New Zealand would not withdraw from the talks and would not be pushed out. That was how easy it was for New Zealand to crush the optimism of the other participating states that assumed when it came time to wrap up a full agreement, New Zealand, a weaker nation, would then hush up.

A settlement agreement from a drifting crisis

It was not until the morning of August 1 that Abe learned that the broad agreement had been postponed at the ministerial meeting in Hawaii. When he received the report from his secretary, the prime minister, disappointed, blurted out, "What, they didn't do it?" That afternoon, he commented on the failure to reach a broad agreement at the ministerial meeting by saying, "I want to do everything I can until the meetings finally lead to a consensus." Despite this assertion, the prime minister was in fact growing impatient.

Reaching a compromise through the negotiations would mean that the then unreleased details concerning tariff reductions for rice, wheat, dairy and the other "five sacred cows" would be made public, which would likely lead to a backlash from Japan's agricultural industry. The Committee on Agriculture, Forestry and Fisheries, a joint committee of both houses of the Japanese Diet, had already adopted a resolution to "defend tariffs at all costs," while the opposition parties were hounding the ruling coalition on the issue. Even so, if the treaty were ratified in an extraordinary session of the Diet in the fall of 2015, attention would then shift to how to deal with the implications for domestic agriculture. The idea of the government and the ruling parties was to publicly promote initiatives to strengthen Japanese agriculture by securing sufficient funding for these measures in the fiscal 2016 budget.

However, if the negotiations did not conclude and the treaty's ratification had to wait until the ordinary Diet session set to convene in January 2016, then the situation would change completely. Since budget deliberations are the top priority during an ordinary session, discussions on treaties would likely be pushed back until April or later. Depending on the situation, the ruling parties could focus their energy on the upper house elections scheduled for July while working to avoid inciting objections to the TPP. The Abe cabinet had to avoid crossing a treacherous bridge, as its approval ratings had fallen steeply due to repercussions from Diet deliberations on the national security bills.

The LDP has a bitter memory of when an upper house election was swayed by agricultural policy. It was in 1989, when, on top of Prime Minister Sosuke Uno's extra-marital affair, the big Recruit corruption scandal that rocked Japanese politics and the introduction of a consumption tax, the import of beef and oranges was liberalized, thus inviting a backlash from farmers. Together, these developments combined to strike a direct blow to the LDP. The party was only able to win three out of 26 single-member districts. It was a landslide defeat, after which the LDP has never held an absolute majority in the upper house.

The early conclusion of the TPP negotiations was an unconditional must for the Abe administration. There had already been major progress toward a broad agreement in the talks between the participating countries, and 25 of the total 31 treaty articles had been settled. Yet the travails of the final mile continued.

Japan and the United States had considered "excluding New Zealand," but unless New Zealand voluntarily announced withdrawal from the talks then the country could not be forced out. However, because the requirement for the treaty to come into force is that the total GDP of all signatories be at least a certain percentage of the GDP of all 12 parties to the talks, it could come into effect without New Zealand's ratification. Japan took an antagonistic negotiating stance toward New Zealand, which it said "accounts for only a small percentage of the total GDP."

Yet the Japanese were very much of the opinion that "the biggest reason is that the U.S. did a poor job setting the stage." Based on the content of its bilateral meetings on the automotive sector with Japan, the U.S. arranged to talk behind the scenes with Canada and Mexico. That is because these three countries are the members of the North American Free Trade Agreement (NAFTA). When the meetings in Hawaii commenced, however, the Americans did not engage in direct discussions with them. This is how Japanese foreign ministry officials explain the Americans' inattention to detail.

"In their past bilateral free trade agreement (FTA) negotiations, no matter how bad things get, in the end the Americans are always certain they will get their way. They thought it would work that way in multilateral negotiations, too."

On August 6, Amari met with Prime Minister Abe at his residence and informed him that he expected it would be difficult to hold a ministerial meeting in August as hoped. Amari himself had intended to hold such a meeting that month, but arrangements were not possible because the United States and other participating countries had already begun taking their summer recesses.

Amari did not know what to do with his anger over the utterly uncertain outlook. On August 10, Amari posted the following message on his website's Diet Report page, where he wrote about the broad agreement's postponement.

"What every country found odd was that the strong insistence that America always shows was absent this time. They seemed lifeless and resigned to giving up. ... America, the chair of the meetings, prevaricated and didn't give details, but they didn't have the mental or physical ability to keep on going when the negotiators refused to take a break."

These constant expressions of dissatisfaction with the United States reportedly caused a temporary controversy within the U.S. government. A divide was growing between Japan and the United States, whom one would normally expect to join forces and tackle the drifting TPP crisis head-on.

But the way toward a broad agreement in the TPP negotiations was not completely blocked off. Japan was working to promptly reconvene the talks, which created the momentum for holding a TPP ministerial meeting in Atlanta, Georgia on September 30 and October 1. Beforehand, on September 25, a Meeting amongst Main Ministers on the Trans-Pacific Partnership (TPP) was held at Prime Minister Abe's residence. There he pushed Amari and the other officials present by saying, "The end of the negotiations will be the hardest part. I hope to make this ministerial meeting the last ministerial meeting."

Before he departed for Atlanta, Amari was asked by reporters at Narita Airport about what would happen if a consensus were not reached at this ministerial meeting. He did not hide his trepidation: "I think it will be in danger if we end up procrastinating for years."

In his preparations for the ministerial meeting, Amari narrowed down the main points of contention to three issues: protections for biopharmaceutical data, expanding imports of dairy products and rules on the procurement of auto parts.

The issue for which Amari saw an immediate opportunity was auto parts. A problem pertaining to automobiles was the "rules of origin" that determine whether a completed automobile is eligible for eliminated or reduced tariffs, depending on how much of its parts come from TPP member states. While Mexico and Canada, where many parts factories are located, argued that around 60% of the parts should be procured from TPP states, Japan demanded a rate of about 40%. Because the 12 negotiating parties saw the light of opportunity to reach a broad agreement covering the entire scope of the negotiations, they extended the ministerial meeting's schedule for another day and decided to keep on going until October 2.

Although they were on the verge of a broad agreement, the "labor pains," so to speak, persisted. With regards to the protection period for biopharmaceutical data, the situation was still the same: the United States insisted on 12 years to sufficiently protect the profits of pharmaceutical companies developing new drugs, while emerging countries were on the other side of the issue, along with Australia, arguing for five years or less so that less expensive generics could be used soon.

Anticipating the situation, Amari carefully prepared some common ground over biopharmaceuticals.

"What do we do about biopharmaceuticals?"

After arriving in the U.S. on September 29, the day before the ministerial meeting, this is what Amari said to Australian Minister for Trade and Investment Andrew Robb at Nakato, a renowned Japanese restaurant in Atlanta's suburbs. Robb had been a friend of Amari's for 20 years, ever since they had gotten to know each other when Amari visited Australia as a young lawmaker.

As the two shared *shochu* during their meal, they quickly came to agree on suggesting "effectively eight years" to finally settle the dispute. The "effectively" is the key component. Since emerging countries are fine with regulations providing five years for a monopoly on sales, they could create such rules soon. Having them then extend that to eight years as soon as possible was the clever yet ambiguous compromise offered by Japan. As they sat on their knees on tatami mats in their private room, Amari expressed his desire to be cooperative in working toward a broad agreement, to which Robb replied that he hoped this would be the last time they had a meeting on the subject.

As the 2nd rolled around, significant progress was made in the negotiations on the data protection period: in a breakthrough, the United States, which had until then been resolute, offered a new proposal of an effective eight-year period. It was meant to narrow the gap between Australia and the emerging countries that were arguing for five years or less. There was no other choice but this scheme cooked up by Japan. On the 3rd, the USTR, who had seen the light, suggested to the other countries that they again extend the meetings until the 4th so they could try to find consensus on the troubling issue of biopharmaceuticals.

A settlement on import ceilings for dairy products was also coming closer at that time. Right at the tail end of the negotiations, the parties decided to make new TPP low-tariff import ceilings for butter and skim milk, which they set at 60,000 tons of raw milk equivalent, to be raised to 70,000 tons in the sixth year or later. The consensus was reached on rules of origin for automobiles, under which eligible automobiles would be manufactured with at least 55% of their auto parts manufactured within the TPP zone. They also agreed to set the data protection for biopharmaceuticals to an effective eight years. All the remaining puzzle pieces had been put together.

The 12 parties to the negotiations held a joint press conference on October 5, where they announced they had reached a broad agreement. The TPP negotiations that commenced in March 2010 took five-and-a-half years to conclude. It was at this moment that countries representing around 40% of global GDP decided to create a massive economic zone.

However, the broad agreement was not won thanks solely to the 12 countries' negotiators. On the 5th, President Obama issued a statement following the agreement: "We can't let countries like China write the rules of the global economy. We should write those rules..." At a press conference on the 6th, Prime Minister Abe revealed his relief that they had beaten China to writing the economic rules of the region when he said, "[I]n the case that China chooses to participate in this system in the future, [it] will make a large contribution to the security of Japan and the stability of the Asia-Pacific region."

China, which was not present at the negotiating table, was the architect in the shadows that had driven Japan and the United States, the key players in the talks, toward an agreement.

Challenge to the economic order

As the TPP negotiations limped along, China was publicly challenging the global financial order led by Japan and the West.

This financial order is a system centered around the World Bank and the International Monetary Fund (IMF), which were established in 1944, during World War II, at a conference in Bretton Woods, New Hampshire attended by America and other Allied powers. This order also includes the Asian Development Bank (ADB), whose largest financers are Japan and United States. The leadership positions in these institutions are essentially fixed: the leader of the World Bank has always been American, a European has headed the IMF, and a Japanese national has been at the helm of the ADB.

Regardless of the fact that China surpassed Japan to become the world's second-largest economy by GDP, the country has been very dissatisfied with the fact that it has been unable to secure top spots at these institutions and project its message in accordance with Chinese economic might.

Chinese President Xi Jinping released a plan for the Asian Infrastructure Investment Bank (AIIB) in October 2013 in order to construct a Chinese-led international financial system. The purpose of the bank is to meet rapidly growing demand for financing of infrastructure projects in Asia, while another goal is to make effective use of the $4 trillion in foreign currency reserves China has built up.

Furthermore, China worked with other BRICS countries, among them Russia and India, to establish the New Development Bank. The bank's founding ceremony was held at its headquarters in Shanghai, China in July 2015. The institution has a total capitalization of $50 billion, with each country contributing $10 billion. AIIB, as its name suggests, invests in infrastructure in Asia while the New Development Bank invests in infrastructure of emerging countries. At the end of 2014, China put up $40 billion to establish the Silk Road Fund.

President Xi is also advocating his "One Belt, One Road" project to create an expansive economic zone by connecting China and Europe over land and sea. The two components of this project are the Silk Road Economic Belt linking China and Europe over land via Central Asia, and the 21st Century Maritime Silk Road to promote economic cooperation in coastal countries from Southeast Asia to Europe. It is a grandiose plan that targets these two economic areas to promote the construction of railways, high-speed rail, power plants and more in the emerging countries of Asia. The AIIB is an essential tool for the financial support China needs in order to create this economic zone.

It would not go too far to say that internal Chinese politics also played a role in the establishment of the AIIB. China is a representative of the world's emerging countries, and the momentum of its economy, which had put up an annual growth rate of over 10%, is now starting to show signs of weakening. The Chinese economy grew at a clip of 7.3% in 2014, but there are whispers within China and abroad that these figures were inflated because the Chinese manipulated the statistics. Heavy industry that had been accustomed to rapid growth is suffering from excess production, creating a serious glut in materials directly involved in building infrastructure, such as steel, cement and glass.

There was also an event which aroused serious suspicions that the Chinese economy is slowing down: for three straight days, from August 11-13, 2015, the renminbi tumbled in value.

Advanced countries like Japan leave it to markets to determine currency exchange rates. In China, however, every morning China's central bank, the People's Bank of China (PBC), announces a "standard value" for the renminbi-dollar exchange rate. Trading that day is limited to a band within 2% above or below the standard value, thus exerting tight control over the value of China's currency. On August 11, the PBC announced it would change its calculation method, which in effect initiated a devaluation. The standard value on the 11th was 6.2298 renminbi to the U.S. dollar, pushing the yuan (as the renminbi is otherwise known) down 1.85% versus the dollar over the prior day. It was the lowest level in approximately two years and four months. The three straight days of declines brought the currency's value down by around 4.5% from the standard value.

There is no doubt that the renminbi was overvalued prior to its tumble. The U.S. economy continued to improve and an interest rate increase was on the horizon. In contrast, the Chinese economy was slowing down. Even so, the standard value had been pretty much fixed at around 6.11 renminbi to the dollar. Market observers were critical, suggesting that "the authorities might just be setting whatever value they want."

The People's Bank of China explained that due to the situation, it had changed its calculation method in line with the wishes of the market because "the effective exchange rate of the renminbi has strayed from market expectations." For certain, the renminbi had been largely pegged to the U.S. dollar, so it must be said that this policy was a step toward "marketization."

However, it is clear that the true aim was to provide a boost to exports by trading the yuan at a cheaper rate in an attempt to stimulate China's economy. By playing their trump card of devaluing the renminbi, the Chinese leadership shocked markets into thinking that "perhaps China's economy is actually worse than we thought." This was the main culprit behind large but temporary losses for stock markets in Japan and other Asian countries, as well as in the West.

In contrast to weak projections for the Chinese economy, demand for infrastructure in other Asian countries is strong. According to the IMF, the outlook for the 2015 GDP growth rate in Asia's developing/emerging countries exceeds 6%, which is high compared to the 2.0% rate forecast for advanced nations.

Asia's infrastructure needs investments to the tune of $800 billion a year. It will be difficult for existing international financial institutions like the World Bank and the ADB to meet emerging countries' demand for capital. On top of that, the ADB conducts stringent reviews to determine such things as whether loan recipients are controlling emissions of environmental pollutants and whether they have the ability to actually repay their loans. According to Thailand's Minister of Finance, Sommai Phasee, there is growing discontent among Association of Southeast Asian Nations (ASEAN) members because they have been unable to receive the loans they expected: "We need much more in the way of funding sources. If the AIIB creates competition with other financial institutions (like the ADB), then that will be good for emerging countries."

The AIIB has played a tremendous role in building bridges. On one side are Asia-Pacific countries in need of new infrastructure in the center of global growth. On the other is China, which is looking overseas for a path to growth to stand in for its stagnant domestic market. The AIIB perfectly serves both sides' interests.

A shock out of the U.K.

A bitter diplomatic fight broke out over joining the AIIB, with China trying to bring in as many countries as possible and Japan and the United States attempting to stop them. However, the resulting overwhelming victory for China was, in a sense, to be expected.

The first to bow to China were the 10 ASEAN member states. Nine of them, Indonesia being the exception, signed the AIIB charter in October 2014. The turning point was the ease with which Vietnam and the Philippines joined the bank, as they are embroiled in a dispute with Beijing over sovereignty rights in the South China Sea. The month after, Indonesia also signed the charter, which spread a sense of defeat within the Japanese government. The ASEAN states even went so far as to employ various channels to approach EU member states about joining the bank as well. The ASEAN member states were all of the opinion that "the participation of advanced nations is essential" to raising the ratings of AIIB bonds.

After China lured ASEAN to its side, one focus of Japan was on what Australia, which Japan considers a "quasi-ally," would do. After strengthening security ties in the Asia-Pacific region with Japan and the United States, Australia had become a party to the TPP negotiations. Australian Prime Minister Tony Abbott was one of the foreign heads of state who thought of Prime Minister Abe as someone they can get along with. He expressed a negative view of the AIIB in late October 2014 when he said "it's got to be a multilateral institution with the kind of transparency and the kind of governance arrangements that, for argument's sake, the World Bank has."

The situation suddenly changed thereafter, however.

Prior to the Group of Twenty Summit held in Brisbane, Australia beginning on November 15, Abe made a confidential phone call to Abbott from his residence.

Prior to their conversation, Eiichi Hasegawa, one of the prime minister's aides, explained the situation in Australia thusly:

"The price of iron ore bound for China has fallen and the economic situation in Australia is grim. Somebody who wants infrastructure built in Asia cannot say 'No' to the AIIB spurring demand for iron ore. I think Abbott is in a tough position right now."

Hasegawa's dire prediction hit the mark. In their conversation, Abbott said he was uncertain about whether or not to join the AIIB. Empathizing with Abbott's difficult circumstances, Abe responded, "In the end, you should do what is best for you, Tony."

On March 25, 2015, Abbott announced that Australia would join the AIIB. He had called Abe a little while before to inform the Japanese prime minister of his decision.

According to U.S. Secretary of the Treasury Jacob Lew, President Obama considered the AIIB a challenge to American leadership and approached ally South Korea to persuade them not to join the Chinese-led institution. However, during an information session held in Beijing in September 2014, China pressed South Korea to join the bank under the condition that it "sign the charter." Eventually, South Korea caved to Chinese pressure and decided to join the AIIB. The American efforts came to naught.

As they played defense, the biggest shock for Japan and the United States came on March 12, 2015. On this day, the British Chancellor of the Exchequer announced that the U.K. would join the AIIB. Britain was the first G7 member state to announce its participation.

Britain had been leaning toward joining from a fairly early stage. A major factor behind this decision was that in return for being a part of the AIIB, Britain would be the first major Western country to issue sovereign bonds denominated in the Chinese renminbi. As a Japanese Ministry of Foreign Affairs official put it, "The U.K. was impressed by the gift from China and consumed it. The power of Chinese money has changed the status quo."

The key person in Britain behind the country's joining the AIIB was Chancellor of the Exchequer George Osborne. According to sources, Osborne shook off repeated efforts by U.S. Secretary of the Treasury Lew to change his mind on joining the AIIB, and the U.K. Foreign & Commonwealth Office was worried about hurting Britain's relationship with the United States. Osborne declared that in order to create more jobs, it is important to increase exports to countries with high growth rates like China. In addition to issuing renminbi-denominated sovereign bonds, Britain also decided to hold some of its foreign currency reserves in renminbi.

While preparing for a general election in May, the Cameron administration had also allowed a referendum on Scottish independence. The administration was standing on unsteady ground. Predictions by British public opinion research firms immediately prior to the election indicated a neck-and-neck race between the two major parties: the Conservatives and the largest opposition party, Labor. The Conservative Party was hoping for support from the business community, as exemplified by the London financial district, or "the City" as it is otherwise known. The Manifesto issued by Prime Minister David Cameron's ruling Conservative Party emphasized stronger ties with China by mentioning that "exports to China more than doubled since 2009."

The Conservative Party exceeded expectations by winning an outright majority in the general election. Cameron reappointed four key Cabinet members, including Osborne, who was also appointed to the Cabinet's number-two post: First Secretary of State.

The repercussions from the shock out of the U.K. continued. The floodgates opened on March 17 when Germany, France and Italy all announced they would join the AIIB. Deputy Chief Cabinet Secretary Katsunobu Kato was nearly speechless: "For Europe to collapse so quickly..."

Volkswagen, Germany's largest automaker, gets about one-third of its sales volume from the Chinese market. Areva, a major French company that deals in nuclear power, is also intent on strengthening ties with China. From a business perspective, China was certainly not a country to be ignored by European states. They tended to believe that even if Chinese hegemony conquered Asia, it would have little effect on distant European nations.

Because China set the end of March 2015 as a deadline to join the AIIB, a number of countries announced their decision to join to avoid missing the bus. They did so because they were concerned that if they did not receive the benefits of being a founding member, then it would put them at a competitive disadvantage against other countries. Turkey also announced its intent to join on March 26.

Clueless at the Prime Minister's residence

On March 31, the deadline to join the AIIB, Prime Minister Abe received updates at his residence from officials including Vice Minister Tatsuo Yamasaki from the Ministry of Finance and Deputy Minister Yasumasa

Nagamine from the Ministry of Foreign Affairs. The prime minister told his people to "remain calm" and deal with the situation prudently.

Most officials within the Japanese government initially thought that AIIB membership would be limited to developing countries in need of financing to build infrastructure. The Ministry of Finance, which was most directly charged with dealing with this matter, informed Abe of information indicating that "no G7 nations will join the bank." However, once the way was opened, four out of the seven—Britain, France, Germany and Italy—announced they would join.

Abe had been one step behind for the entire process. He expressed his dissatisfaction to his close aides, saying, "Neither the Ministry of Finance nor the Ministry of Foreign Affairs were able to get any information. The only thing they got right was that 'the U.S. won't join.'" Both the finance and foreign affairs ministries, panicked over Britain's shocking decision, offered up an excuse: "Britain didn't consult with the United States about joining, either."

Former presidents of the ADB find positions in the Ministry of Finance. There were growing suspicions within the prime minister's residence that "maybe they love their posts in the finance ministry so much that they didn't bring up any bad news and just reported negative information about the AIIB."

German Chancellor Angela Merkel and Prime Minister Abe had a telephone conference on April 1. At the time the details of the conversation were withheld from the media. During a meeting prior to the conversation, Abe asked, "Will she ask Japan to join as well?" Aides including a finance ministry official expected otherwise. Abe was told, "There's no reason why she would say that." During the phone call, however, when Abe asked Merkel to "act deliberately" and delay joining the AIIB, Merkel made a counterproposal: "England and France are going to join, too. Europe acts together, so Germany will also join. Why doesn't Japan join, too?"

Hence Abe's complaint. One of the prime minister's close aides was visibly astonished at the finance ministry officials' lack of insight.

Vice Minister of Finance Yamasaki, who was tasked with handling AIIB affairs, decided to turn in his resignation that July. This post generally has a two-year term, but decision-makers in Tokyo's Kasumigaseki district decided to accept the replacement only one year into his term.

While a flood of countries were announcing their decision to join the bank, the Japanese government's suspicion even turned toward the United States, as Japan wondered whether the Americans would also join and abandon their ally. On April 13, Prime Minister Abe met secretly with Kevin Maher, the former director at the U.S. State Department's Office of Japan Affairs. At that time Abe disclosed his concerns, saying, "When Xi Jinping visited the U.S. in September, did America say it would join the AIIB? If so, it would be a major blow to Japan (who would be left out)."

China believed that if they could draw South Korea, ASEAN member states and other Asian countries into the AIIB, then they could whittle away at Japanese and American influence in the Asia-Pacific Economic Cooperation (APEC) zone and also throw a wrench into the TPP negotiations proceeding under Japanese and American guidance. A cool-headed analysis will show that for Japan and the United States, who were placing critical importance upon the TPP negotiations, joining the AIIB never was an option. However, the Chinese momentum even caused Abe, who was already aware of this fact, to lose confidence.

Meanwhile, whether or not the Chinese were aware of the agitation arising between Japan and America, China aggressively approached both these countries about joining the AIIB. It would seem the Chinese aim was to build trust in the AIIB by approaching advanced nations in the same way they had approached ASEAN states.

A group was created in early 2014 to prepare for the establishment of the bank. It was headed by Jin Liqun, former Vice Minister of Finance of China. China's biggest pundit on international finance, he majored in economics at Boston University and is a former Vice President of the ADB. Jin was later selected as the first President of the AIIB. According to a source, when Jin and his entourage visited Japan, he approached Japanese government officials by saying, "We can prepare an appropriate place for you at the AIIB." Afterward as well, top Chinese officials continued whispering reassurances that "even if you miss the bus after the March deadline passes, we will arrange another bus for Japan."

Yet the transparency of the AIIB's administration was lacking; whether there would be a permanent governing board was even unknown. It is also

plausible that the bank could be used to finance the construction of additional ports for the Chinese navy, which is rapidly enhancing its blue water
capabilities. According to a Ministry of Foreign Affairs official, the Japanese
government was cynical: "In short, China wants to do whatever it wants."

The "debt sustainability of borrowing countries" was also seen as a
problem. If the bank invests in projects with lower prospects of borrowed
funds being paid back, then it could end up with bad debt. The Japanese
government estimated that if Japan joined the bank, then at most it would
cost approximately $3 billion. A senior Ministry of Finance official whose
duties were related to the AIIB attested at the time, "It would be impermissible to just throw away taxpayer money." Foreign Minister Kishida said to
his close aides, "Even if Japan contributes funds, we're still not going to have
much of a say. As a country in the Asia region, Japan is not in a position to
put China into our debt just by injecting a little capital."

Japan goes on a counteroffensive

China's Ministry of Finance announced the 57 founding members of the
AIIB on April 15, 2015. The size of this group is comparable to the 67 countries and territories that have acceded to the ADB. Furthermore, over half of
the 12 parties to the TPP negotiations decided to join the Chinese institution.
On this day, Chief Cabinet Secretary Suga of Japan emphasized at a press
conference that the number of AIIB members was "within the range we
expected," but Japanese officials were not inclined to accept this figure at
face value. Even Xi Jinping, the AIIB's chief promoter, revealed to Prime
Minister Abe during a summit on April 22, "We did not expect to win this
much understanding."

Although the Japanese had acted slowly, now they went on a counterof-
fensive. The ADB, which supports infrastructure projects in the Asia-Pacific
region, put together reforms to its lending operations on April 22 so as to
significantly speed up the relevant procedures. The AIIB issues loans quickly
so as to meet the high demand for infrastructure in emerging countries.
Hence, the ADB decided to put up a fight by streamlining its own operations.
A loan from the ADB requires procedures to study and analyze a project in
order to determine whether it coincides with the values of the institution

and if the loan can be expected to be repaid properly. While in some cases these procedures took two or so years, the ADB decided to transfer authority to personnel stationed in applicant countries and otherwise take steps to cut the process down by about half a year.

During a press conference at the ADB's annual meeting in Azerbaijan on May 2, the bank's president, Takehiko Nakao, announced that the institution would increase the approved annual amount for loans and grants in 2017 to approximately $20 billion, marking an increase of about 50% over 2015 levels. This policy will increase ownership equity and facilitate investment and lending by integrating the Asian Development Fund, which provides grants and loans at very low interest rates to poor countries, with Ordinary Capital Resources used for financing offered to middle-income countries. Efforts such as cooperative financing were projected to increase the value of the ADB's annual assistance to roughly $40 billion.

On the following day, May 3, the ADB convened the Partnership Forum for Nepal in Azerbaijan. There the bank announced an additional $300 million in assistance for Nepal. Participants at the forum also decided to hold a conference on assistance, led by Japan and the ADB, to help Nepal recover from the massive earthquake that had struck the country. A source at Japan's Ministry of Foreign Affairs said the purpose would be to "show how we are different from China by providing high-quality assistance in a timely manner."

Furthermore, Prime Minister Abe announced during a speech in Tokyo on May 21 that Japan would invest around $110 billion over the five years running until 2020 in order to support the building of high-quality infrastructure in Asia. This was an increase of 30% over the amount of assistance provided in the previous five years, which was roughly $85 billion. Aides to Abe confessed that "we had decided from the get-go to put up a number bigger than the AIIB's." In his speech, Abe said Japan will reform "the practice of asking local governments for guarantees." He was also apologetic, while at the same time taking aim at the AIIB when he referred to the "cheap, but shoddy" approach that had not fulfilled expectations in Asia.

The Mekong-Japan Summit Meeting was held at the State Guest House in Tokyo's Akasaka district on July 4. The conference was attended by the leaders of Japan and five Southeast Asian countries that lie along the Mekong River

(Thailand, Vietnam, Cambodia, Laos and Myanmar). There, Prime Minister Abe announced Overseas Development Assistance (ODA) for the other five countries amounting to 750 billion yen over three years, beginning in fiscal 2016. The amount of ODA before this time, announced once every three years, was over 500 billion yen in 2009 and most recently 600 billion yen in 2012. This new package of aid is far greater in value than any of its predecessors. In a joint statement, the leaders announced that in addition to assistance in building up industrial infrastructure, further intangible assistance would be provided to, for example, make that infrastructure more advanced and to develop human resources. Supporting independent regional economic growth marked a distinct differentiation with the AIIB, which observers consider to be more focused on building infrastructure at low cost.

Meanwhile, the 57 founding members of the AIIB convened at the Great Hall of the People in Beijing on June 29 to sign the bank's charter. According to the agreement, China has the greatest voting right at 26.06%, as calculated according to how much each country has invested in the institution, among other factors. This also means that China can block decisions on important matters that require a consensus of 75% or greater. China's percentage of shares is much higher than those of the top holders in the ADB (Japan: 15.7%) and the IMF (USA: 17.7%). Having invested $29.7 billion in the AIIB, China accounts for nearly 30% of the AIIB's capital. China, which holds a *de facto* veto on the most important decisions, is expected to not assign a permanent director at the headquarters in Beijing and to decide on resolutions in a more "transient" manner via email or other such means.

During a group photo following the signing ceremony, Xi Jinping was all smiles as he stood in the middle of the representatives from the 57 countries. During a press conference, he asserted, "We will push existing international financial institutions to respond more appropriately to global economic changes and the demands of member countries."

However, there was no sign of a representative from Taiwan at the signing ceremony. It would seem this was due to reluctance on China's part, which under its One-China policy requires that Taiwan participate in international organizations under the name Chinese Taipei. As Japan and the United States had feared, this was a departure point for what was anticipated to be arbitrary Chinese administration of the AIIB.

Chapter 7

China Needs to Learn from Showa History

Previous chapters reviewed China's repeated threatening behavior in the East China Sea and South China Sea and Japan's efforts to contribute to maintaining stability in the Asia-Pacific region while cooperating with the United States, Australia, and ASEAN countries.

Despite its strong military emergence, China does not appear to be ready to directly challenge the United States, which still retains the position of global superpower. It is likely interested in avoiding clashes with the United States.

If this is the case, China has something it can learn from Showa history, particularly Japan's political and diplomatic history just before the start of its war with the United States in 1941.

Why was Japan unable to avoid a war with the United States? President Xi Jinping and other Chinese political leaders and officials of the People's Liberation Army can obtain insight and techniques for avoiding a U.S.-China conflict from an accurate understanding of the historical process and mistakes of Japan's political and military leaders.

Point of no return

Key catalysts that led Japan to war with the United States in the Pacific, or events that pushed the situation to a point of no return, were the Tripartite Pact by Japan, Germany, and Italy signed in September 1940 and the advance into Southern Indochina (French Indochina; now Vietnam, Laos, and Cambodia) in July 1941.

The United States took retaliatory action of banning oil exports to Japan due to anger over the Southern French Indochina advance that established a military site in today's Ho Chi Minh City (former Saigon), and Japan, which relied on the United States for 90% of its oil, faced a situation of "either waiting for a collapse or taking action" and decided to go to war with the United States four months later. The Southern French Indochina advance was a direct trigger for the Japan-U.S. clash.

Japan's political and military leaders at the time were not aware that the Southern French Indochina advance would create the worst-case result.

For example, the secret war transcripts written by the General Staff Office's war leadership team noted three days prior to the invasion on July 25 that "we believe there will not be an export ban if our troops stop at the Southern Indochina advance." The team also wrote on the following day (July 26) after the United States announced a freeze on Japanese assets aimed at halting the advance that, "We do not expect a total ban and think the US is likely to hold off. While it might happen at some point, we do not think the timing is close."

Japanese officials determined that "There would not be a total ban as long as the advance only went as far as Southern Indochina. Even if it happened, the timing would be later."

In fact, however, the United States proceeded with a total ban on oil exports to Japan on August 1 after Japanese troops advanced into Southern Indochina on July 28.

Why was Japan certain that the United States would not ban exports? This was a misreading of the counterpart's stance due to a belief that "the United States should accept an advance up to Indochina."

Ryuzo Sejima, a military officer who served in the staff office of the Imperial Headquarters, wrote in "Realities of the Great Asia War" (PHP

Books) that, "A total ban on exports to Japan by the United States meant the start of a war between the two countries. We did not expect President Roosevelt, who understood this point, would take this step." Toshitane Takada, the No.1 Section Manager for Military Affairs at the Department of the Navy, one of the main advocates in the Navy favoring a war between Japan and the United States also noted in post-war testimony that, "We thought the United States would not be angry up to the point of the advance into Southern Indochina. This came as a surprise." (Yomiuri Shimbun War Responsibility Reexamination Committee "From Marco Polo Bridge to Pearl Harbor: WHO WAS RESPONSIBLE?" Chuko Bunko).

Japan impressed by Germany's success

What led Japan at the time to make such a dangerous move with the advance into Southern Indochina? There is just one reason. It strongly desired the oil in the Dutch East Indies (today's Indonesia).

It is necessary to shift the narrative from Asia to conditions in Europe to understand the background.

In Europe, Nazi Germany, under the leadership of Adolf Hitler, formed a Non-Aggression Pact with the Soviet Union in August 1939 and invaded Poland in September, the next month. The United Kingdom and France, which had turned a blind eye to Germany's occupation of Czechoslovakia in 1938, finally declared war against Germany, and the Second World War began.

In Japan, Prime Minister Kiichiro Hiranuma abandoned his Cabinet with the comment regarding the Germany-Soviet Union Non-Aggression Pact that "conditions in Europe are mystifying," and Nobuyuki Abe, his successor as prime minister from the military, issued a statement that Japan would not be involved in the European war.

Germany stopped its activities for the time being, and the U.K. and France did not take action despite having declared war. The two sides glared at each other for a while. The equilibrium broke about seven months later in April 1940.

Germany invaded and quickly took control of Norway and Denmark with its Blitzkrieg operation. It overwhelmed the Netherlands and Belgium in May and carried through with this momentum to invading France and taking Paris in June. Germany had truly conquered mainland Europe and was only missing the United Kingdom, an island country. Germany's rapid successes strongly impressed Japan.

Ambitions in French Indochina and the Dutch East Indies

Japan concluded the Japan-Germany Anti-Comintern Pact in 1936 and Italy joined in the following year to establish the Japan-Germany-Italy Anti-Comintern Pact. However, the Japanese Navy maintained a cautious stance toward having this arrangement develop into a military alliance among the three countries. Three naval officials – Navy Minister Mitsumasa Yonai, Administrative Vice-Minister Isoroku Yamamoto, and Military Affairs Bureau Head Shigeyoshi Inoue - strongly resisted this direction under the first Fumimaro Konoe Cabinet. This stance reflected their concerns about agitating the United States and an increased likelihood of war with the United States if Japan formed a tripartite alliance. Mr. Yonai commented at the time that, "the Navy is not ready for war with the United States."

The Army, meanwhile, led the arrangement of the Japan-Germany Anti-Comintern Pact, partly aimed at removing the involvement of Germany, which had been militarily assisting China under Chiang Kai-shek in China, and argued for conclusion of a tripartite alliance. It saw the Soviet Union as a hypothetical enemy country and thought it could control movements by the Soviet Union, which feared a pincer attack, by teaming up with Germany. However, Mr. Konoe dissolved his Cabinet in response to feuding by the Army and Navy, and the subsequent Germany-Soviet Union Non-Aggression Pact rendered a tripartite alliance to curtail the Soviet Union meaningless and this problem disappeared. Yet the situation changed dramatically after Germany's impressive gains during the spring to summer 1940.

Japan was not simply entranced by "Germany's strength." The pressing issue of who would control French Indochina and the Dutch East Indies, which had been colonies of France and the Netherlands, after these countries fell to Germany played a major role. The Dutch East Indies, a major production site for militarily vital strategic materials such as oil and rubber, was a key place that Japan, which relied heavily on the United States for oil, greatly desired.

France formed the Nazi-leaning Vichy government after its fall to Germany. These developments led to the decision by Japan to conclude the tripartite alliance and make a military advance into French Indochina with Germany's backing. The U.K. and France had been using the area around the Chinese side of French Indochina as a route to transport weapons and goods to Chiang Kai-shek's Chongqing government (Chiang supply route), and the advance into northern Indochina aimed to sever this supply route. The Mitsumasa Yonai Cabinet that followed the Abe Cabinet collapsed in July 1940 under pressure from the Army due to the passive stance toward a tripartite alliance. The second Konoe Cabinet formed as the successor decided to move into northern French Indochina and conclude the Tripartite Pact in September 1940 under Foreign Minister Yosuke Matsuoka.

However, conditions differed from the Nazi-leaning French Indochina government in the key Dutch East Indies. The Netherlands created an exile government in London, and the Dutch East Indies government naturally assumed a strong stance against Japan too in light its Tripartite Pact with Germany. Foreign Minister Matsuoka started negotiations for oil purchases with the Dutch East Indies government in September 1940, but the talks struggled. This situation inspired a different concept of "using a military threat."

Shigeru Fujii from the Navy Military Affairs Bureau (author's note; member of the No.2 section) discussed the idea of advancing into Southern Indochina as a way of acquiring control of rice, tin, rubber, and other resources and establishing a face-off with the Dutch East Indies that would likely improve their attitude and thereby provide access to oil to Akiho Ishii (author's note; member of the Army Ministry's Military Affairs section), and Mr. Ishii agreed. The aim was a coercion effect from a peaceful advance to the South." (Sumio Hatano, "Staff Officers' Pearl Harbor" Asahi Sensho).

Misreading of the U.S. response

The advance into Southern French Indochina obviously had the implications of laying future groundwork due to the importance of this location as a

Maximum sphere of influence of the Empire of Japan, and
French Indo-China and the Dutch East Indies

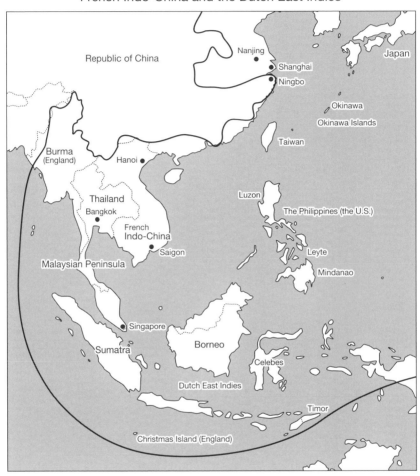

military site for a start in hostilities with the United Kingdom and the United States at some point. This is because Southern French Indochina put Japan's fighter planes within attack reach of not only the Dutch East Indies, but also the United Kingdom's Malay (today's Malaysia and Singapore) and Burma (today's Myanmar) and the Philippines under U.S. rule.

Yet the target of the advance into Southern French Indochina at least for the Konoe Cabinet (third Konoe Cabinet) in July 1941 was intimidation against the Dutch East Indies. Both the Army and Navy agreed that, "Further military advances would only occur if Germany beat the Soviet Union and then landed in mainland Britain and put the United Kingdom on the verge of surrender or if Germany's trade disruption strategy pushed the United Kingdom into a desperate position" (above-mentioned "Staff Officers' Pearl Harbor"). This is why, as seen in comments by Ryuzo Sejima and Toshitane Takada, the Konoe Cabinet and the Army and Navy were not expecting the United States to proceed with a total ban on oil exports to Japan that would directly lead to a war and expressed surprise (Takada).

From the U.S. perspective, however, the advance into Southern French Indochina naturally came across as "the final stage of leap toward a large-scale attack into the Southwest Pacific" (then Secretary of State Cordell Hull).

Ikuhiko Hata, who specializes in modern history, wrote in "Path to the Pacific War, War Outbreak Diplomatic History 6 – Southern Advance" (Asahi Shimbun) that "it is not unusual for the United Kingdom and the United States to view Japan's advance into Southern French Indochina, which put it within bombing range of Malay and Singapore, as a shocking move comparable to having a knife at their throat" and added that "it was too much of disconnect to be explained as simply an adverse cycle of accumulated misperceptions and mutual distrust that commonly occurs in international politics."

Unexpected start of economic sanctions

China should be able to learn many lessons from Japan's critical mistakes prior to the war.

It is most important to avoid excessive emphasis on obtaining resources and interpreting conditions in a way that suits one's own interests, as happened in Japan's case. The things that you want – Dutch East Indies for prewar Japan and Senkaku and Okinawa in the Nansei Islands and the Spratly Islands and other locations in the South China Sea with geopolitical value for today's China – are also something that the counterpart absolutely does not want to give up. This obvious point is often forgotten among one's own ambitions.

Another lesson of Showa history is that the counterpart might act differently than expected. A good example is the view of Japan's advance into Southern Indochina, which aimed to put pressure on the Dutch East Indies and obtain oil, as a direct threat by the United States.

Furthermore, economic pressure on Japan itself was unexpected by Japan.

Economic sanctions against Japan by the United States began with a ban on steel scrap exports to Japan right after Japan's conclusion of the Tripartite Pact in September 1940. The United States steadily strengthened economic pressure on Japan by adding steel and ferroalloy to the export ban list in December 1940 and then expanding it further to copper, bronze, zinc, and nickel in January 1941 and radium and uranium in February. Yet the United States was still excluding oil. The Japanese side interpreted this stance favorably as "the United States is not banning oil because it is not interested in war with Japan." The United States was able to apply these economic sanctions because it notified Japan of termination of the Japan-U.S. Treaty of Commerce & Navigation formed in the Meiji Period in July 1939 and the treaty expired in January 1940.

Why did the United States decide to abandon the Japan-U.S. Treaty of Commerce & Navigation at that timing? In fact, this was not at all expected by Japan.

A customs officer for the Northern China government friendly to Japan was assassinated in the British concession of Tientsin (Tianjing) three months prior to the treaty departure notification. The British concession was an excellent place for anti-Japanese guerillas to hide. While the assassins were immediately arrested, the United Kingdom refused to hand them over to the Japanese military. In response, the Japanese military closed off the British concession and Japanese troops conducted stringent searches of British people entering and leaving the concession at checkpoints, including some public strip searches.

This was the period of intense confrontation between the Army and Navy regarding formation of a tripartite alliance in the Hiranuma Cabinet. At the same time, pro-military organizations held a "People's rally against the United Kingdom" in the Hibiya area of Tokyo that was packed with slogans such as "Let's denounce the United Kingdom with its policy of assisting Chiang and interfering with the goals of our sacred war (author's note; Japan-China war)." Crude harassment of British people with strip searches also sought to foment "pro-Germany, anti-U.K." sentiment in Japan and increase support for a tripartite alliance.

Neville Chamberlain, the United Kingdom's Prime Minister, initially reacted strongly against the behavior as "unacceptable humiliation," but ultimately switched to an appeasement stance and agreed to fully accept the actions of the Japanese military in the Tientsin British concession on July 24. The United States suddenly sent Japan a notification of its termination of the Japan-U.S. Treaty of Commerce & Navigation two days later on July 26.

Shinji Sudo, Professor Emeritus at Kyoto Sangyo University, wrote the following in "Pearl Harbor <Surprise Attack> Debate – Conspiracy Theory, Delayed Notice, War Outbreak Diplomacy" (Kodansha Sensho Metier)."

"The Japan-United Kingdom meeting (author's note; regarding the Tientsin Incident) served as the direct trigger for departure from the Treaty, but that was not the only reason. President Roosevelt, who had been considering ways to stop Japan's initiatives in China since July 1937 but held off because of the likely negative reaction from Japan and domestic isolationist views, finally lost his patience."

Isn't there some resemblance between China, which is repeatedly taking coercive actions in the South China Sea and Senkaku Islands, and the Japanese military's anti-U.K. movement?

"Let's defeat the Philippines and Vietnam one by one. "Little Japan" is not a concern." Isn't China forgetting about the presence of the United States as it reviews "the best way to halt" China's recent "arrogant" actions? Isn't the United States likely to "lose its patience" at some point?

Shinichi Kitaoka's five conditions

The author is not the only one arguing that "it's China who needs to learn from Showa history."

Shinichi Kitaoka, Professor Emeritus at the University of Tokyo and President of the International University of Japan, listed the five following conditions that led Japan into a military expansion in an article for the Yomiuri Shimbun (morning edition on September 22, 2013).

(1) Belief that "geographical expansion guaranteed national security and prosperity"
(2) View that "counterparts are weak"
(3) Conclusion that "international society is powerless and lacks the strength to impose sanctions"
(4) Weak control of the military by politicians
(5) Loss of freedom of speech

He also explains that, "These conditions do not apply to Japan at all today. Japan is not a peaceful country because of Article 9, but instead because of more fundamental factors supporting the prosperity of modern Japan." He then goes on to make the following points.

However, the five conditions apply to today's China to a considerable extent.

First, China is pursuing activities to obtain resources around the world. The concept of security is a driving force for expansionist maritime activities, and there is also a desire to enhance national prestige.

Second, China has confidence in its military advantage in East Asia.

Third, China does not show any signs of concern about sanctions from the international community and often takes actions that ignore international law. In fact, it is difficult to impose sanctions against a permanent member of the United Nations Security Council. China also uses its massive economic clout to silence countries that are critical.

Fourth, there are growing concerns that China's activities in recent years indicate that government control of the military is weakening.

Fifth, it is very difficult to criticize the government in China.

He comments that, "I do not expect China to invade nearby countries. But it has substantially more factors working in this direction than Japan, which has no prospect of starting a war."

This is a very accurate analysis. Dangers from the fourth condition (weak control of the military by politicians), in particular, certainly should be something that leaders of China's Communist Party (besides those with PLA careers) can learn from Showa history.

Is there any sense in just blaming class-A war criminals?

China has been using history to the greatest possible extent in anti-Japan propaganda, as explained in Chapter 1. It compares Japan from the Second World War years to the Nazis and is trying to create the impression that the dichotomy of "defeated countries/Japan" and "victorious countries/China and the international community" still exists today.

Given this background, it is unlikely that China will refrain from "historical" propaganda and this campaign can be expected to continue repeatedly.

However, it is not prudent for China to believe its own propaganda and actually think that just the seven people, including former Prime Minister Hideki Tojo, who received the death penalty at the International Tribunal of the Far East (Tokyo War Crimes Trial), or the 14 class-A war criminals jointly enshrined at Yasukuni Shrine, drove Japan down the path to war.

While China is not the only one exhibiting ignorance on this point because some leftists and liberals in Japan completely reject Japan's prewar history, it is obvious from just looking at a few Showa historical materials that war blame should not be placed just on class-A war criminals.

Two key sources of the point of no return for the Pacific War were the Tripartite Pact and the Southern French Indochina advance, as explained above. The former took place under the second Konoe Cabinet, and the latter came under the third Konoe Cabinet. Hideki Tojo, who the Chinese treat as a Hitler-like figure, became prime minister in October 1941 when the Japan-U.S. relationship was already beyond repair.

Furthermore, Mr. Tojo knew that the Emperor strongly desired to avoid war and worked to stop the war to the very end. While Akira Muto, head of the Army Ministry's Military Affairs Bureau, sought to sidestep war with the United States at the request of Mr. Tojo, fierce pro-war advocates were the General Staff Office's Operations Head Shinichi Tanaka, Operations Manager Takushiro Hattori, and Logistical Manager Masanobu Tsuji. Mr. Tanaka and the other war advocates fiercely attacked Mr. Muto. The secret war transcripts written by the General Staff Office's war leadership team noted on October 21 that "The Army Ministry has been pressing more for diplomatic efforts recently […] This suggests the maneuvering of Bureau

Head Akira Muto" and on October 22 that "Is anyone damaging our national interests by ignoring the request of our division to halt diplomatic efforts and instead following the strategy of Bureau Head Muto?" Yet Mr. Muto received a death sentence at the Tokyo War Crime Trial, just as Mr. Tojo, and the three war advocates survived after the war. Mr. Tanaka was even a witness for the prosecution side.

No one from the Navy received a death sentence at the Tokyo War Crimes Trial. Yet it was the Navy, not the Army, that led the advance into Southern Indochina. The First Committee, which included Shingo Ishikawa, the Navy Military Affairs No. 2 Section Manager, and Sadatoshi Tomioka, the Navy General Staff Operations Manager, as core members, explained to top Navy officials in June 1941 that "we reached a conclusion with considerable confidence to act" regarding the acquisition of oil from the Dutch East Indies. Osami Nagano, Commander of the Navy General Staff […] aggressively argued for the Southern French Indochina advance based on this recommendation. Mr. Nagano died from an illness during the Tokyo War Crime Trials and was one of the 14 class-A war criminal jointly enshrined at Yasukuni Shrine. Yet Mr. Ishida and Mr. Tomioka did not face trials and wrote autobiographies after the war.

Difficult to stop a large rolling stone…

A careful review of events at the time makes it very clear the extent to which trying to place all the blame on class-A war criminals is divorced from reality.

Furthermore, China's attempts to treat Hideki Tojo as a Hitler-like figure, while obviously propaganda, are comical.

In his book "Showa Commanders" (Tosho Shuppan), Tahei Takamiya, Asahi Shimbun's Army Ministry journalist, writes about Mr. Tojo's faint-heartedness. He describes the timing right after the decision to retreat when it became clear that Japan was losing the Battle of Guadalcanal.

"It was around January 1943 on a morning with a cold dry wind outdoors. Unusually he spoke for more than an hour in a face-to-face session in a Japanese-style study at the Prime Minister's residence. Mr. Tojo spoke with pride that 'this works really well in warming things up' in reference to used envelopes filled with pine needles being utilized as fuel due to the shortage of coal to burn in the stove. If pine needles are left alone, they rot. This way they function as chopped wood, and it is better to utilize envelopes this way rather than selling them to waste handlers, particularly since they could have information that should remain confidential. While this is a great idea, the normal pattern would be moving straight into an argument that it would be better to put more energy into improving war results instead of spending time on this, and a reply from the prime minister to 'leave and don't come again' or 'I'm leaving and won't come the next time you ask.' This morning, however, he was strangely subdued and had a meek response of 'I don't need to hear it from you. I am thinking of things.'"

"Fighting a war is similar to rolling a large rock down a hill. It is possible to stop it with the strength of a few people if it has only moved the first 50 centimeters or at most about a meter. If it goes two meters or five meters, however, it takes a few tens or few hundreds of people to stop. If it goes further, the rock will travel to the bottom of the hill or as far as it can go."

"While it is unfortunate, there is a possibility of ultimately losing if this pace continues."

"I don't want to let that happen, but this might be the outcome."

He had a somber look. I was unable to tell him to give up quickly if this is the situation. Mr. Tojo closed his eyes for a while and then just moved on to a different topic.

"You might think the Prime Minister is someone great. Yet Tojo the person is a man just like any other. This man becomes spectacular because of the trust received from the Emperor. It is like being a moon. The moon is a cold object and does not have its own heat or light. It reflects light from the Sun, and this light makes it visible to the earth. One choice would be resigning and having someone figure out responsibility. Yet I cannot request this right now. It is best to remain quiet and endure while the Sun is still shining light."

He also said something else that was unrelated to the previous comments.

"Things are not going well with the Navy. We cannot fight a battle with conflict between the Army and Navy. Even if things are agreed at the top, problems occur as the message moves lower. Nothing can be done. The Army Minister's prestige has declined."

It was a sad message of self-deprecation.

How can Mr. Tojo, who expressed a loss of confidence due to fatigue from conflict between the Army and Navy, be placed in the same category as a true dictator with complete control of Germany?

Japanese people can fully understand the "large rock" example. The parties putting the "large rocks" into motion changed each time. Kanji Ishiwara, a staff officer of the Kanto Army, put a rock into motion in the Manchurian Incident (1931). A key figure in the Lugou Bridge Incident (1937), which led to the full-fledged war between Japan and China and was resisted by Mr. Ishiwara, was Akira Muto who spoke of 'using Mr. Ishiwara's activity in the Manchurian Incident as a model.' While Mr. Muto sought to avoid war on the eve of the outbreak of Japan-U.S. hostilities on a mission from Mr. Tojo, as Mr. Tojo mentioned, Japan was already at a point where it "needed a few tens or few hundreds of people to stop."

Can President Xi Jinping control the military?

Is China's Communist Party leadership sufficiently in control of the People's Liberation Army, mainly driven by the Navy, that has strengthened military capabilities and gained confidence?

Looking at the presence of PLA officials in the Communist Party's Central Military Commission (CMC), while President Xi Jinping, a civilian, chairs the CMC, the two vice chairs are both military people (Fan Changlong and Xu Qiliang) and the other eight members are also from the military. Is it possible to control the military with this type of lopsided structure?

An event occurred in January 2011 that suggested civilian control might not be working with China's military.

The Chinese Air Force timed the first test flight of the Chengdu J20 next-generation stealth fighter to take place during a visit to Beijing by the Obama administration's former U.S. Defense Secretary Robert Gates. Mr. Gates asked about the message being sent at a meeting with then President Hu Jintao who also chaired the CMC. Yet Mr. Hu was completely unaware of the test flight and received the news from a senior military official attending the meeting.

Even the U.S. Naval Academy's Toshi Yoshihara advocating

reinforcement of defense capabilities in the Nansei Islands as explained in the previous chapter made the following comments in an interview with the Yomiuri Shimbun (morning edition on April 3, 2013).

China's Communist Party and the military reportedly formed an agreement after the Tiananmen Incident in 1989. It calls for "the military to focus on strategic planning unrelated to politics and allocation of resources to the military by the party and government." This arrangement gave autonomy to the military for weapon development and formulation of military doctrine (core principles).

Yet political issues occur too. It is unclear whether President Xi Jinping can reject an aggressive operation presented by a military commander on the basis that "it is not a wise political choice."

If this is true, the situation seems very similar to the relationship between politicians and the military in prewar Japan.

There are many other concerns too. While diplomats and bank executives readily jump on the military bandwagon and engage in anti-Japan criticism such as the "Japanese are Nazis," there is a risk that this could antagonize domestic public opinion. Aren't political and military leaders at risk of narrowing their maneuverability by stirring up "Internet rightists" in China that repeatedly make aggressive posts on the Internet?

There are so many dangerous resemblances between China and prewar Japan.

It is time to learn the lessons of Showa history if Chinese leaders have any feelings of uncertainty reflecting in the current situation. This is honest advice to the Chinese people.

Avoid appeasement and alienation

Japanese people also must learn the correct lessons from Showa history.

The use of "correct" addresses the danger of taking an approach that just advocates "peace," along the lines of leftists and liberal forces.

What should be correctly learned from Showa history?

The first lesson is that appeasement runs the risk of encouraging the counterpart to go further.

While U.K. Prime Minster Chamberlain's appeasement toward

Germany's occupation of Czechoslovakia, which resulted in the subsequent division of Poland by Germany and the Soviet Union, is a well-known case, something similar happened on the eve of the Japan-U.S. war outbreak. The event was Japan's advance into Northern French Indochina in September 1940. The French Indochina government initially strongly anticipated intervention by the United States when it received the request from Japan to accept the advance. Yet President Roosevelt did not move at all. Appeasement by the United States at that time contributed to Japan's misperception that "the United States is likely to accept advances up to Southern French Indochina."

If Japan and the United States take an appeasement stance toward China in seeking solutions in the case of a Japan-China clash over the Senkaku Islands, it could result in a more dangerous situation. Efforts must be made to ensure that China never misperceives that "the United States will not intervene even in a move up to Okinawa." This means preparing sufficiently to protect the Senkaku Islands.

The second lesson is doing what is necessary to avoid dissonance between Japan and the United States.

In prewar Japan, the Army believed that "the United Kingdom and United States were separable" and took a tougher stance just toward the United Kingdom. For example, the Japanese military conducted strip searches of British people at checkpoints while excluding U.S. citizens during the Tientsin concession incident that triggered the U.S. departure from the Japan-U.S. Treaty of Commerce & Navigation.

China is probably thinking of ways to "avoid situations that result in genuine involvement by the United States and keeping conditions at a level that just involves Japan." While China is likely to hold back from military action in the Senkaku Islands as long as it believes that the United States will act in accordance with the pledge to "apply Article 5 of the Japan-U.S. Security Treaty (obligation to defend Japan) to the Senkaku Islands, the danger comes if it determines that the "United States will not act." It is best to be prepared for a crisis in the Senkaku Islands at any time.

The conclusion from these lessons is that Japan's diplomatic and security strategy toward the Senkaku Islands and Okinawa should seek to bolster the Japan-U.S. alliance even more than it has done up to now.

Chronology of Key Events

Year	Date	Event
1609		Satsuma's Iehisa Shimazu invaded the Kingdom of the Ryukyus and the Ryukyus came under Shimazu's control
1644		Ming Dynasty collapsed; Shunzhi Emperor (Qing) moved the capital to Beijing
1867	Dec.9	Imperial Rule restored, Shogunate eliminated
1872	Sep.14	Ryukyu Kingdom's Monarch designated as the Ryukyu Domain Head
1879	Apr.4	Ryukyu Domain eliminated and Okinawa Prefecture created
1884		Tatsushiro Koga (from Fukuoka Prefecture) explored the Senkaku Islands
1894	Aug.1	Sino-Japanese War started (declared war against the Qing Dynasty)
1895	Jan.14	Japan designated the Senkaku Islands as its territory
	Apr.17	Peace Treaty for the Sino-Japanese War (Treaty of Shimonoseki) concluded
1904	Feb.10	Russo-Japanese War started (declared war against Russia)
1909	Oct.26	Hirobumi Ito assassinated
1912	Jan.1	Republic of China established
	Feb.12	Qing Dynasty collapsed
	Jul.30	Death of the Meiji Emperor, Taisho Era started
1926	Dec.25	Death of the Taisho Emperor, Showa Era started
1937	Jul.7	Macro Polo Bridge Incident, Sino-Japanese War started
1939	Sep.1	Second World War started
1941	Dec.8	Pacific War started (declared war against the United States and United Kingdom)

Year	Date	Event
1943		War prospects eroded including the retreat by the Japanese military from Guadalcanal Island
	Dec.1	Cairo declaration announced
1945	Jul.26	Potsdam declaration announced
	Mar.26	US military landed on Kerama Island (Okinawa)
	Aug.15	War ended
1947	May.3	Japanese Constitution took force
1948	Dec.23	Seven people executed (including former Prime Minister Hideki Tojo) based on the findings of the International Military Tribunal for the Far East
1949	Oct.1	People's Republic of China established
1951	Sep.8	Concluded the San Francisco Peace Treaty
1952	Apr.28	San Francisco Peace Treaty and Japan-US Security Treaty took force
1956	Jun.9	Anti-base efforts became a nationwide battle in Okinawa
	Dec.8	Japan joined the United Nations
1964	Oct.16	China conducted its first nuclear weapon test
1969		UN Economic Commission for Asia and the Far East disclosed a report suggesting the possible existence of oil resource reserves around the Senkaku Islands
1970	Dec.20	Riot broke out in Koza City (Okinawa)
1971	Jun.11	Republic of China (Taiwan) claimed territorial rights to the Senkaku Islands
	Dec.30	China claimed territorial rights to the Senkaku Islands
1972	May 15	Okinawa returned
	Sep.29	Japan-China normalized diplomatic relations
1978	Apr.12	Many armed Chinese fishing boats entered waters around the Senkaku Islands
	Aug.12	Treaty of Peace and Friendship Between Japan and the People's Republic of China concluded
	Oct.25	China's Vice Prime Minister Deng Xiaoping called for putting the Senkaku Islands issue on hold at a press conference at the Japan National Press Club
1992	Feb.25	China's Territorial Waters Law claiming the Senkaku Islands as its own territory took effect
	Aug.24	China and South Korea established diplomatic ties
	Oct.23	Their Majesties the Emperor and Empress of Japan visited China

Year	Date	Event
1995	Sep.21	General rally by the Okinawa people protesting against the rape of a young girl
	Sep.28	Okinawa Prefecture Governor announced his intention to reject procedures for renewing use of US base land
	Oct.3	Japanese and US government reached a basic agreement to review contraction of US military bases in Okinawa
1996	Mar.23	Taiwan's first direct election; Taiwan Straits Crisis
	Apr.12	Japanese and US government agreed on a full return of US Air Station Futenma
	Dec.2	Special Action Committee on Okinawa (SACO) formed by the Japanese and US governments issued its final report; it stated that a replacement for Futenma will be built on the Eastern coast of the main Okinawa island
1997	Jan.16	Chief Cabinet Secretary declared the government's intent to build a replacement base for Air Station Futenma off the coast of Nago City (Okinawa)
1997	Aug.14	Asia currency crisis
2004	Mar.24	Okinawa Prefectural Police arrested Chinese nationals who went onto Uotsuri Island
2006	May 1	Japanese and US government disclosed a final report on reorganization of US forces in Japan that included the transfer of Air Station Futenma to the coast line of Camp Schwab (Nago City) by 2014
2008	Aug.8	Beijing Olympics held
2009	Aug.30	Democratic Party of Japan won control of the government in the 45th Lower House election
	Sep.16	Yukio Hatoyama Cabinet formed
2010	Jun.8	Naoto Kan Cabinet formed
	Sep.7	Chinese fishing boat rammed a Japan Coast Guard patrol boat off the Senkaku Islands
	Sep.23	Japan-US Foreign Ministers' Meeting confirmed application of Article 5 of the Japan-US Security Treaty to the Senkaku Islands
2011	Feb.14	China surpassed Japan in GDP in 2010 to become the world's No.2
	Mar.11	Great East Japan Earthquake
	Sep.2	Yoshihiko Noda government formed

Year	Date	Event
2012	Apr.16	Shintaro Ishihara called for having Tokyo City purchase the Senkaku Islands
	Aug.15	Hong Kong activists went onto Uotsuri Island
	Sep.11	Japan nationalized the Senkaku Islands
	Nov.15	Chinese Communist Party selected Xi Jinping as the General Secretary
	Dec.13	Chinese State Oceanic Administration plane violated Japan's territorial airspace by the Senkaku Islands
	Dec.16	LDP regained government control in the 46th Lower House election
	Dec.26	Second Shinzo Abe Cabinet formed
2013	Jan.19	Chinese military ship directed firearm control radar on a JMSDF helicopter in the East China Sea
	Jan.30	Chinese military ship directed firearm control radar on a JMSDF destroyer
	Mar.14	Xi Jinping became President of China
	Nov.23	China established an Air Defense Identification Zone in the East China Sea
	Dec.27	Okinawa Prefectural Governor announced approval of land reclamation on the coast of Henoko in Nago City, the target destination for Futenma Air Station
2014	Jan.7	Launch of the National Security Council (NSC Secretariat); Shotaro Yachi, a former Vice-Minister for Foreign Affairs, becomes the first Secretary General
	Jan.25	Prime Minister Abe meets with Indian Prime Minster Manmohan Singh in New Delhi; signs a joint statement on strengthening cooperation in national security and other areas
	Apr.1	Cabinet confirms the new "Three Principles on Transfer of Defense Equipment and Technology" to replace the Three Principles on Arms Exports
	Apr.24	Japan-US Summit Meeting held in Tokyo; President Obama clarified application of the Japan-US Security Treaty to the Senkaku Islands
	Apr.28	US and Philippine governments sign a new military agreement that permits joint use of Philippine military bases by the US military
	Jun.4	G7 Summit Meeting in Brussels, Belgium (through June 5)
	Jul.1	Cabinet confirms a new government opinion that allows limited approval of exercising collective self-defense rights
	Jul.8	Prime Minister Abe delivers a speech to the Australian Parliament; expressed gratitude for the "generous spirit" toward Japan
	Jul.17	Malaysian Airlines plane crashes in Donetsk (State) in Eastern Ukraine; Ukrainian President Petro Poroshenko concludes on July 18 that it was shot down by a pro-Russian militant group

Year	Date	Event
2014	Aug.10	Foreign Minister Kishida exchanges opinion with North Korean Foreign Minister Ri Suyong in Naypyidaw, Myanmar
	Sep.3	Launch of the revamped Second Abe Cabinet
	Nov.4	Midterm elections in the US; Republican Party secures majorities in the Senate and House of Representatives
	Nov.10	Prime Minister Abe meets with Chinese President Xi Jinping in Beijing; first Japan-China Summit Meeting in around three years and the first under the Second Abe Cabinet
	Nov.16	Takeshi Onaga, who stands against the move of US Air Station Futenma to Henoko, wins in Okinawa's Governor election as a newcomer
	Nov.16	Tripartite meeting of Japan (Prime Minister Abe), the United States (President Obama), and Australia (Prime Minister Abbott) in Brisbane (Australia); agreement on a policy of strengthening security cooperation
	Nov.21	Dissolution of the Lower House
	Dec.14	Lower House election; LDP and Komeito acquire 325 seats and exceed 2/3 of all seats
	Dec.17	President Obama announces a policy to normalize national ties with Cuba severed since 1961 and open a US Embassy in Havana
	Dec.18	UN General Assembly Main Session adopts a resolution criticizing North Korea's violation of human rights jointly proposed by Japan and the European Union (EU)
	Dec.24	Launch of the Third Abe Cabinet
2015	Jan.16	Prime Minister Abe visits Egypt, Jordan, Israel, and Palestine in the Middle East (through January 21)
	Jan.20	Islamic radical group ISIS kidnaps Japanese hostages
	Mar.9	Prime Minister Abe meets with Germany's Chancellor Merkel at the Prime Minister's resident
	Mar.12	UK Treasury announces its intent to participate in the Asia Infrastructure Investment Bank (AIIB); first from G7 nations
	Mar.18	Armed group attacks a science museum in Tunis, Tunisia; attack kills three Japanese nationals
	Mar.19	Japan-China Security Dialogue by Foreign Affairs and Defense officials from both governments takes place in Tokyo for the first time in around four years
	Mar.21	Tripartite Japan-China-RoK Foreign Ministers' Meeting in Seoul; agreement to make efforts to hold a tripartite Summit Meeting at the "earliest and most convenient timing"

Year	Date	Event
2015	Apr.11	President Obama meets Cuba's Head of the National Assembly of Popular Power Castro in Panama, the first Summit Meeting since severing ties; confirmation of the plan to normalize national ties
	Apr.14	First Japan-RoK Security Dialogue with Foreign Affairs and Defense officials from Japan and the RoK in around five years in Seoul
	Apr.15	Foreign Minister Kishida attends the G7 Foreign Ministers' Meeting in Germany; the meeting issues the first G7 Foreign Ministers' Declaration on Maritime Security
	Apr.15	China's Finance Ministry announces that the AIIB has 57 founding member countries
	Apr.22	Prime Minister Abe delivers a speech at the 60th Anniversary Summit Meeting of the Asian-African Conference (Bandung Conference) in Jakarta, Indonesia; Japan-China Summit Meeting
	Apr.27	Japan-United States Security Consultative Committee (2-plus-2) held in New York (US); agreement on new "Guidelines for Japan-US Defense Cooperation" for the first time in 18 years
	Apr.28	Japan-US Summit Meeting in the White House; criticism of China maritime initiatives and confirmation of strengthening the Japan-US alliance
	Apr.29	Prime Minister Abe delivers a speech to a joint session of US Congress (Senate and House of Representatives), the first-ever speech by a Japanese Primer Minister; expression of "deep repentance" for the Second World War
	May 14	Cabinet decision on security-related legislation; submission to the National Diet on May 15
	Jun.4	Prime Minister Abe meets with Philippines President Aquino in Tokyo; sharing of "serious concern" toward China's shoal reclamation activities in the South China Sea
	Jun.5	Prime Minister Abe announces Shima City (Mie Prefecture) as the location for the G7 Nations Summit being held in Japan in 2016
	Jun.6	Japanese and Chinese financial authorities meet for the Japan-China Financial Dialogue for the first time in about three years in Beijing; agreement on promotion of social infrastructure building in Asia
	Jun.7	G7 Summit Meeting in Elmau (Germany); announcement of a Leaders' Declaration expressing concern about tensions in the East China Sea and South China Sea mainly in light of China's activities (through June 8)
	Jun.22	Prime Minister Abe attends an event commemorating the 50th anniversary of normalization of Japan-RoK relations in Tokyo; RoK President Park Geun-hye attends a ceremony in Seoul
	Jun.29	US Congress passes a law giving Trade Promotion Authority (TPA) to President Obama for TPP negotiations
	Jun.29	AIIB holds a signing ceremony for the establishment agreement in Beijing

Year	Date	Event
2015	Jul.1	US President Obama restores diplomatic relations with Cuba for the first time in 54 years; announces an agreement for reopening embassies in respective capital cities
	Jul.2	North Korea notifies the Japanese government regarding a report on abductees that "it needs more time"
	Jul.4	Japan holds a Summit Meeting with leaders from the five Mekong River Area countries in Tokyo; Prime Minister Abe announces Official Development Assistance (ODA) worth 750 billion yen
	Jul.22	Japan discloses photographs and a map of gas field ocean platforms being developed by China in the East China Sea on the Ministry of Foreign Affairs web page
	Aug.14	Cabinet approval of Prime Minister Abe's statement marking the 70th year since the end of the war; Continues the expression of "deep repentance and apology" and also mentions invasion and colonial rule
	Sep.3	70th Anniversary of Victory over Japan Day commemorative events and parade in Beijing; attendance by Russian President Putin, RoK President Park, and others
	Sep.25	President Obama meets with Chinese President Xi Jinping in Washington DC (US); no agreement regarding China's shoal land reclamation activities in the South China Sea
	Sep.28	Japan-Russia Summit Meeting at the United Nations Headquarters in New York (US); agreement to move forward in negotiations targeting a solution to the Northern Territories issue
	Oct.5	Announcement of an overall agreement by the 12 countries participating in TPP negotiations (including Japan) in Atlanta (US)
	Oct.27	US Navy's Aegis destroyer conducts patrol activities within 12 nautical miles of a manmade island constructed by China in the Spratly Islands in the South China Sea
	Nov.1	First tripartite Japan-China-RoK Summit Meeting in three years in Seoul attended by Prime Minister Abe, China's Prime Minister Li Keqiang, and President Park; agreement to hold meetings regularly
	Nov.2	First Japan-RoK Summit Meeting by Prime Minister Abe and President Park in Seoul; agreement to continue government-level discussions on the comfort women issue and aim for an early solution
	Nov.13	Simultaneous terrorist attacks in Paris , France

(Local times; titles at the subject time)

About the Author

The Yomiuri Shimbun is a Japanese national newspaper with a 140-year history. Through the three headquarters and regional bureaus throughout Japan and major cities of the world, it reports on domestic and foreign issues on the morning and evening editions. Its morning newspaper alone exceeds 9,000,000 copies, giving the newspaper the largest circulation in the world.

（英文版）「日中」外交戦争
Perspectives on Sino-Japanese Diplomatic Relations

2017年3月27日　第1刷発行

著　者　読売新聞政治部
訳　者　ジョン・ロスマン
発行所　一般財団法人出版文化産業振興財団
　　　　〒101-0051 東京都千代田区神田神保町3-12-3
　　　　電話　03-5211-7282（代）
　　　　ホームページ　http://www.jpic.or.jp/

印刷・製本所　大日本印刷株式会社

本書は、新潮社より刊行された『「日中韓」外交戦争』（2014）、『安倍官邸vs.習近平』（2015）、『領土喪失の悪夢』（2014）より抜粋し英訳したものです。